Wingshooter's Guide to™

MINNESOTA

Upland Birds and Waterfowl

TITLES AVAILABLE IN THIS SERIES

Wingshooter's Guide to Arizona

Wingshooter's Guide to Idaho

Wingshooter's Guide to Iowa

Wingshooter's Guide to Montana

Wingshooter's Guide to North Dakota

Wingshooter's Guide to South Dakota

Wingshooter's Guide to Kansas

Wingshooter's Guide to Oregon

Wingshooter's Guide to™

MINNESOTA

Upland Birds and Waterfowl

Dr. Roland Kehr and Mickey Johnson

Wilderness
Adventures
Press™

Gallatin Gateway, Montana

This book was made with an easy opening, lay flat binding.

Published by Wilderness Adventures Press
P.O. Box 627
Gallatin Gateway, MT 59730
800-925-3339
Website: www.wildadv.com
email: books@wildadv.com

10 9 8 7 6 5 4 3 2 1

Printed in the United States of America

Library of Congress Cataloging-in-Publication Data:

Kehr, Roland, 1944–
     Wingshooter's guide to Minnesota : upland birds and waterfowl / Roland Kehr and Mickey Johnson.
          p.   cm.
     Includes bibliographical references (p.   ) and index
     ISBN 1-885106-62-9
     1. Upland game bird shooting--Minnesota Guidebooks.   2. Waterfowl shooting--Minnesota Guidebooks.   3. Minnesota Guidebooks.
     I. Johnson, Mickey, 1951–   .   II. Title.
SK323.K44   1999   99–15198
799.2'46'09776--dc21   CIP

Table of Contents

Introduction vii

Major Roads and Rivers of Minnesota (map) x

Minnesota Facts xi

Tips On Using This Book xii

Hunting Regulations 1

Upland Game Birds 19
    Ruffed Grouse 21
    Pheasant 29
    Woodcock 35
    Gray (Hungarian) Partridge 41
    Spruce Grouse 47
    Sharp-tailed Grouse 51
    Eastern Wild Turkey 57
    Common Snipe 61
    Sora Rail 63
    Virginia Rail 63

Waterfowl 65
    The Dabblers 65
    The Divers 72
    The Geese 78

Region 1 87
    Baudette / Roseau and Lake of the Woods Counties 95
    Hallock / Kittson and Marshall Counties 98
    Crookston / Pennington, Polk, and Red Lake Counties 100
    Bemidji / Beltrami and Clearwater Counties 102
    Ada / Norman and Mahnomen Counties 105
    Park Rapids / Hubbard and Northwestern Cass Counties 107
    Detroit Lakes / Clay and Becker Counties 110
    Fergus Falls / Wilken, Wadena, and Ottertail Counties. 112
    Alexandria / Grant, Douglas, Stevens, Pope, and Traverse Counties 115

Region 2 119
    International Falls / Koochiching and Northern Itasca Counties 124
    Ely / Northern St. Louis and Northern Lake Counties 127
    Grand Marais / Cook and Southern Lake Counties. 130
    Duluth / Southern St. Louis and Carlton Counties 133
    Grand Rapids / Southern Itasca and Northeastern Cass Counties 137

Region 3 141
    Brainerd / Southern Cass, Crow Wing, and Aitkin Counties 148
    Little Falls / Todd and Morrison Counties 152
    Hinckley / Mille Lacs, Kanabec, and Pine Counties 155
    St. Cloud / Stearns and Benton Counties 158
    Elk River / Sherburne and Wright Counties 160
    Mora / Isanti and Chisago Counties 162

Region 4 167
   Benson / Big Stone, Swift, and Chippewa Counties 172
   Willmar / Kandiyohi and Meeker Counties 174
   Montevideo / Lac qui Parle and Yellow Medicine Counties 177
   Hutchinson / Rennville, McLeod, and Sibley Counties 179
   Redwood Falls / Lincoln, Lyon, Redwood, and Brown Counties 182
   Worthington / Pipestone, Murray, Rock, and Nobles Counties 184
   Fairmont / Cottonwood, Watonwan, Jackson, and Martin Counties 186
   Mankato / Blue Earth, Waseca, Faribault, Nicollet, and Le Sueur Counties 189
Regions 5 and 6 193
   Owatonna / Rice, Steele, Dodge, and Goodhue Counties 199
   Albert Lea / Freeborn and Mower Counties 202
   Caledonia / Fillmore and Houston Counties 204
   Rochester / Wabasha, Olmstead, and Winona Counties 206
   Hastings / Caver, Scott, and Dakota Counties 209
   Forest Lake / Hennepin, Ramsey, Washington, and Anoka Counties 212
   Twin Cities Travel Hub 214
Finding Hunting Land in Minnesota 225
   State Wildlife Management Areas (WMAs) 226
   Minnesota Department of Natural Resources Area Wildlife Offices 241
   State Forests 243
   Minnesota National Forests 261
   Federal Wetland Management Districts (WMDs)
      and Waterfowl Production Areas (WPAs) 277
   National Wildlife Refuges (NWRs) 284
   Othe Public Land Opportunities 301
Appendix I: Traveling with Gun and Dog 303
Appendix II: Conditioning of Hunting Dogs 305
Appendix III: Hunter Conditioning and Clothing 307
Appendix IV: The Hunting Rig 308
Appendix V: Equipment Checklists 309
Appendix VI: Preserving Game Birds for Mounting 311
Appendix VII: Field Preparation of Game Birds for the Table 313
Appendix VIII: Game Bird Recipes for the Cook 314
Appendix IX: Recommended Product Sources 323
Appendix X: Minnesota Information Sources 325
Appendix XI: Organizations 328
Appendix XII: Guides, Outfitters, and Lodges 332
Recommended Reading 335
Index 337

Introduction

Over the years, my wife has come to the conclusion that planning an upcoming hunting or fishing trip has become as important to me, and in some cases as exciting, as the actual trip. The gathering of game or the taking of fish becomes almost anticlimactic. As an example, my collaborator on this book, Mickey Johnson, and I decided to hunt eastern Montana for the first time in the fall of 1995. We hadn't a clue as to what we were getting into. Fortunately, one of us noticed an ad for a book titled *Wingshooter's Guide to Montana* by Chuck Johnson and Ben O. Williams. Armed with the information and tips contained within the covers of that book, Mickey and I went on to have great hunting experiences right from the start.

Today, many of our hunting colleagues are envious of our successful upland hunting trips to Montana. Good planning is the key to our success. When I guide out-of-state hunters for ruffed grouse and woodcock here in Minnesota, I continually refer to concisely marked maps and notes that I have accumulated over the years. I actually prepare and print out checklists to be used prior to each hunt. With this book, Mickey and I want to provide hunters coming to Minnesota a chance to plan their own dream hunting trips.

This book was also inspired in part by an irate letter addressed to Ken Szabo's *Grouse Tales* newsletter. To paraphrase the letter, the grouse hunters (from the East Coast) had had a thoroughly unsuccessful hunt in Minnesota and were placing most of the blame on the state of Minnesota and, in particular, its Department of Natural Resources. The letter appeared shortly after the conclusion of the low point of the grouse cycle in Minnesota. Had these hunters reread the previous three years of Ken's newsletters or contacted the DNR before their hunt, this fact would have been apparent, and they may have chosen to reschedule their grouse hunting trip. Proper advance planning could have prevented this from happening.

We in Minnesota can get quite spoiled when our ruffed grouse are at the top of their 10-year cycle. When the birds are at or near the bottom of their cycle, we must adjust our tactics and expectations, just as we have to adjust our expectations. Proper advance planning can make a big difference. The following is an example of how trip planning will likely be done in the very near future.

It's spring, and the East Coast has finally recovered from the coldest, iciest winter in recent memory. You've just talked to a friend who spent a week hunting in Minnesota last fall. Wow! You can't believe how high his grouse flush rates were! How long has it been since you and your hunting buddies last hunted grouse in Minnesota—10 years—15 years? A few calls to your hunting buddies drums up the proper interest and you plan to gather the next night to o "cyberplan" your hunt.

Unlike previous planning sessions, this one takes place with you and your hunting partners seated in front of a computer screen. Since it has been quite awhile since your last trip to Minnesota, you'll need some current information. A look at the websites for Barnes and Noble (www.barnesandnoble.com) and Amazon.com (www.amazon.com) reveals the existence of a recently introduced hunting guide book for Minnesota: *Wingshooter's Guide to Minnesota*, published by Wilderness Adventures Press. It's the eighth book in a series designed for out-of-state and in-state hunters. Once you've determined where you want to hunt, you can use its prolific listings to set up local accommodations, contact information sources, and fulfill other needs as they arise. With a click of the mouse the book is ordered.

When it arrives, there are several good sources of information on current grouse numbers listed and a call to a Minnesota DNR game biologist confirms that grouse are near the top of their cycle. There is no better time to plan a hunt.

From your previous grouse hunting trips and the ruffed grouse habitat section you just read in the *Wingshooter's Guide*, you know you want to key in on areas holding lots of 10- to 16-year-old aspen trees. Since one of you has had hip surgery, perhaps there are some nonmotorized or hunter walking trails adjacent to the young aspen stands that would offer easier access. After perusing the area-specific information in the guidebook, you find that central or north central Minnesota would be a good potential hunting area because the terrain is rather flat.

A few clicks of the mouse later and you've entered the Minnesota Department of Natural Resources' home page listed in your guidebook and have gone to the forest view page, which has an extensive search engine. You want to find forest areas populated with 10- to 16-year-old aspen, and a click later a digitized map of Minnesota appears showing sites with aspen of the proper age. Zooming in, you center your search on Cass, Itasca, and Aitkin Counties. What a treasure trove of ideal aspen sites! By zooming down to the township level, you can find which sites have some road or trail access. Saving the best of these to your computer's hard drive, your group proceeds to the next search parameter.

Accessing a CD-ROM that contains digitized topographical maps, you download the appropriate topographical maps for the areas you're interested in hunting. The zoom features for these maps are great for enhancing detail. Next, you bring up a CD-ROM that provides enhanced background maps for your handheld GPS receiver. Its coverage of rural roads and forest trails is perfect for your needs. Switching the needed information to "transparent" mode, the background GPS-compatible information is overlaid on the appropriate topographical maps. Finally, you add the transparent version of the aspen site information overlay to the road/trail enhanced topographical map. Voila!

You print out copies of the enhanced maps for your hunting partners, and now it's time to make a decision. Each of you can review the copies and make a choice, and the area with the most votes becomes your destination. Each map has topographical features in the background, including altitude changes and water sources, such as streams and ponds for the dogs. Overlaying this are trails and roads as well as the aspen sites. What more could a cyberhunter want!

The following week, perched in front of the computer, a decision has been reached. *Wingshooter's Guide to Minnesota* is consulted as to nearby accommodations (dog friendly, of course). Reservations are made through the motel's website. Now that the date and place have been determined, it's time for you to access the

Minnesota Department of Natural Resource's electronic license site to obtain your hunting licenses online. A few minutes later, armed with hard copies of your electronic hunting licenses, you turn to a trip planning website, such as "www.mapquest.com," to determine the best travel route to your motel rooms in central Minnesota. Once finalized, the route map is printed and made available to all. Last, but not least, you generate packing and shopping lists on the computer and pass out copies to the rest of the hunting group. All information and maps pertaining to this grouse cyberhunt are downloaded to your laptop computer and GPS receiver. Now, the hard part, waiting until the start of the next bird hunting season in Minnesota! This fictionalized "cyberhunt" plan for ruffed grouse in Minnesota is not that far from reality. Many of the tools described above are in place and are waiting to be integrated with one another.

As you might have guessed, I am biased toward ruffed grouse hunting in Minnesota. The following pages of this book describe other upland birds and waterfowl that are hunted in Minnesota, but I would be willing to bet that most nonresident bird hunters are interested in pursuing the ruffed grouse.

The state of Minnesota, especially the northern half, is blessed with an abundance of accessible county, state, and federal public lands. To the nonresident or nonlocal hunter, the choice of a hunting destination can be overwhelming. It is our hope that the information in this book will make your species and destination choices much easier.

Residents of Minnesota consider themselves rather fortunate in regard to the abundance of upland birds and waterfowl within the state's borders: ruffed grouse and woodcock in the northern half of the state; sharp-tailed grouse in the northwest central region; wild turkeys spreading north and west from the bluffs of the southeast; pheasants maintaining their presence in the south central and southwest areas; Hungarian partridge residing in south central cover; Canada geese in all but the northeast corner; snow and blue geese along known migration corridors; and finally, ducks throughout the state.

We hope the information we have gathered and placed between the covers of this book will assist you in planning a successful hunt in Minnesota. Please take advantage of the information sources made available to you. Good luck and good hunting!

Dr. Roland Kehr

Major Roads and Rivers of Minnesota

Minnesota Facts

86,943 square miles
Ranks 12 in size in the nation

Population: 4,657,758 (1996 Census)
   Ranks 20 in nation in population
   55 people per square mile
Counties: 87
Time zone: Central

Attractions
   Mississippi Headwaters
   Pipestone National Monument
   Boundary Waters Canoe Area
   Lake Superior
   Iron Range
   Fort Snelling
   Mall of America
   Minnesota Zoo

Name Origin: Two Dakota Indian words (Minnay sotoa) meaning "clear water"
Nickname: Gopher State
Primary Industries: Agriculture, manufacturing, oil, natural gas, minerals, aircraft production
Capital: St. Paul
Bird: Loon
State Flower: Showy Lady's Slipper
Tree: Red Pine
Fish: Walleye
State Wildlife Management Areas: 1,034 (726,800 acres)
State Forests: 56 (3 million acres)

Tips on Using This Book

- Minnesota area codes are divided thus: 218 for the northern half of the state; 320 for the west central (excluding the metropolitan areas); 612 and 651 for the metropolitan Twin Cities area; and 507 for the southern third of the state.

- Always check with the Minnesota Department of Natural Resources for the most recent hunting regulations. Prices, season dates, and regulations can change from year to year.

- In any instance, if you are not certain whether or not the land you plan to hunt is private, ask first! Everyone's future hunting privileges depend on this. You may even get some valuable advice.

- Planning ahead is the key to a successful hunt and a more pleasurable experience.

- Minnesota has large amounts of public land administered under an equally large number of acronyms—which can lead to some confusion when looking for these lands. The following key should help you navigate:

  CRP — Conservation Reserve Program

  DNR — Department of Natural Resources

  NWR — National Wildlife Refuge

  PRIM — Public Recreation Information Maps

  SNA — Scientific and Natural Area

  WMA — Wildlife Management Area

  WMD — Wetland Managment District

  WPA — Wildfowl Production Area

Motel Cost Key
$ — less than $30 per night

$$ — between $30 and $50 per night

$$$ — $50 per night and up

Hunting Regulations Highlights

License Requirements

These are general license requirements. For license requirements to take other species, refer to the specific section in the handbook.

1998 Hunting and Trapping License Fees

Prices do not include the $1 issuing fee. There is no issuing fee for stamps, special goose permits, or turkey licenses.

Resident Licenses

Small Game $14.00**
Wild Turkey 16.00*
Senior Citizen Small Game 10.00**
State Migratory Waterfowl Stamp 5.00
State Pheasant Stamp 5.00
Special Canada goose permit 3.00
Individual Sports (small game hunting and individual angling) 21.50**
Combination Sports (small game hunting and husband/wife angling) 12.50**

Nonresident Licenses

Small Game $60.00**
Wild Turkey 55.00*

*Available through lottery drawings or the DNR License Bureau in St. Paul only.
**Includes a $4 surcharge used for wildlife land acquisition and management.

Possession

- All persons required to have a license (including stamps) must have it in their personal possession while hunting or trapping and while traveling from an area where they hunted or trapped.
- A person may not take, buy, sell, transport, or possess protected wild animals without a license, except as provided in the regulation handbook.

License Year

Licenses are valid during legal seasons between March 1 and the end of February. New licenses are required beginning March 1 each year.

Purchase

Minnesota Small Game and Deer Hunting licenses, Special Canada goose permits, state Migratory Waterfowl Stamps, and Pheasant Stamps can be purchased from county auditors' offices; sporting goods stores; and the DNR License Bureau in

Minnesota offers a mix of hunter training programs for everyone.

St. Paul. You must appear in person, except that a husband or wife may appear alone to purchase a Combination License. Wild turkey, moose, antlerless deer, and most bear licenses are awarded through a statewide lottery. Applications are available at DNR Wildlife offices, the DNR License Bureau, county auditors' offices, and license agents.

Border Waters

On all border waters with adjacent states or provinces, persons acting under a Minnesota hunting or trapping license may only take wild animals on the Minnesota side of the border.

Lost License

You may obtain a duplicate license at the DNR License Bureau in St. Paul, or pick up an application for a duplicate at any county auditor's office. The fee is $5.75 for a new Big Game License and $2.50 for all others.

Stamps

Most hunters must possess the appropriate stamps to hunt pheasants and waterfowl in Minnesota (see below). For a stamp to be valid, hunters must sign their name across its face. Federal stamps must be signed in ink.

Pheasant Stamp

Resident hunters age 18 or over and under age 65, and all nonresident hunters, must have a valid Minnesota Pheasant Stamp in their possession when hunting or taking pheasants, except: a) residents hunting on land they occupy as a principal residence, b) a person hunting on a licensed commercial shooting preserve, or c) residents on military leave.

State Migratory Waterfowl Stamp

Resident hunters age 18 or over and under age 65, and all nonresident hunters, must have a valid Minnesota Migratory Waterfowl Stamp (State Duck Stamp) in their possession while hunting or taking migratory waterfowl (see definition), except: a) residents who are hunting on their own property, b) persons taking only marked waterfowl released on a commercial shooting preserve, or c) residents on military leave.

Federal Migratory Waterfowl Stamp

Waterfowl hunters age 16 and over must have a valid Federal Migratory Bird Hunting and Conservation Stamp (Federal Duck Stamp) in their possession while hunting or taking migratory waterfowl. Federal Duck Stamps can be purchased at post offices or from many license agents.

Small Game Hunting

All residents age 16 and over, and all nonresidents, must have a valid Small Game License in their possession to take small game, except residents may hunt small game without a license on their own land if they occupy it as their principal residence.

All residents age 18 or over and under age 65, and all nonresident hunters, must have a valid Minnesota Pheasant Stamp in their possession to take pheasants.

Season Dates

These dates are as of 1998; check the current Regulations Handbook for up-to-date information. See table on following page.

Grouse Hunting Near Motor Vehicles

A person in the vicinity of a motor vehicle may not shoot a firearm or an arrow from a bow at a grouse, or at a decoy of a grouse placed by an enforcement officer, unless the person is at least 20 yards (60 feet) from the vehicle and the vehicle's engine is shut off. This provision does not apply to a person with a disability who has

1998 Small Game Hunting Seasons

Small Game	Open Season	Daily Limit	Possession Limit	Shooting Hours
Nonmigratory Birds				
Ruffed and spruce grouse	Sept 19–Dec 31	5 combined	10 combined	½ hour before sunrise to sunset
Sharp-tailed grouse (in open zone)	Sept 19–Nov 30	3	6	½ hour before sunrise to sunset
Hungarian partridge	Sept 19–Dec 31	5	10	½ hour before sunrise to sunset
Pheasant	Oct 10–Dec 13	2 cocks	6 cocks	9AM to sunset
Nonmigratory Small Game by Falconry				
	Sept 1–Feb 28	3 combined, not to include more than 1 hen pheasant	6 combined, not to more than 2 hen pheasants	½ hour before sunrise to sunset except pheasants may not be taken before 9AM

Migratory Birds (except waterfowl; waterfowl season regulations are distributed in September)

Small Game	Open Season	Daily Limit	Possession Limit	Shooting Hours
Crow*	July 1–Nov. 1	No limit	No limit	½ hour before sunrise to sunset
Woodcock**	Sept 19–Nov 2	3	6	½ hour before sunrise to sunset
Sora and Virginia rail	Sept 1–Nov 4	25 in aggregate	25 in aggregate	½ hour before sunrise to sunset
Common Snipe (Wilson's or jacksnipe)	Sept 1–Nov 4	8	16	½ hour before sunrise to sunset except same as waterfowl during waterfowl seasons

*Crows may also be taken at any time whenever committing or about to commit damage. Calls or decoys may not be used in closed season. Wildlife Management Areas are closed to crow hunting until September 1.
**Woodcock season dates and limits are tentative. Watch for announcement of final seasons in late summer.

a permit to shoot from a stationary motor vehicle. This restriction includes all motorized vehicles.

Party Hunting for Small Game

A "party" is defined as a group of two or more persons maintaining unaided visual and vocal contact with each other while hunting. A party may lawfully take small game in accordance with the following regulations:

- A member of the party may take more than an individual limit, but the total number of small game taken and possessed by the party may not exceed the combined limits of members of the party.
- Each party member may transport only an individual limit of small game.
- Party hunting is not allowed for wild turkeys or migratory game birds (ducks, geese, mergansers, coots, moorhens, woodcock, rail, and snipe).

Migratory Bird Harvest Information Program (HIP)

All hunters of migratory birds (ducks, geese, mergansers, woodcock, snipe, rails, coots, or gallinules) must identify themselves as migratory bird hunters at the time they purchase a small game or sports license. Anyone who has hunted or intends to hunt migratory birds should answer "yes" to the question on the license. Evidence of compliance must be carried while hunting migratory birds.

The answers to the screening questions about migratory bird hunting on the license will be used to survey hunters at a later date to more accurately estimate actual harvests. Improved harvest information will be used to better manage migratory bird populations and preserve hunting opportunities.

Use of Lead Shot

- No person may take ducks, geese, mergansers, coots, or moorhens with lead shot or while having lead shot in possession.
- Lead shot may be used statewide for hunting other small game in accordance with firearms restrictions in the handbook, except in federal Wildlife Refuges and Waterfowl Production Areas (see Federal Lands).

Closed Sharp-tailed Grouse Area

The area shown on the map on the next page is currently closed to sharp-tailed grouse hunting. Few sharptails live in the area, and the closure protects remnant populations of sharptails and prairie chickens (a similar-looking, protected species).

Woodcock, Rails, and Snipe

- Duck Stamps (state or federal Migratory Waterfowl Stamps) are not required to hunt woodcock, rails, or snipe.
- Shotguns used to hunt these birds must not be capable of holding more than three shells, unless plugged with a one-piece filler that cannot be removed without disassembling the gun, so its total capacity does not exceed three shells.

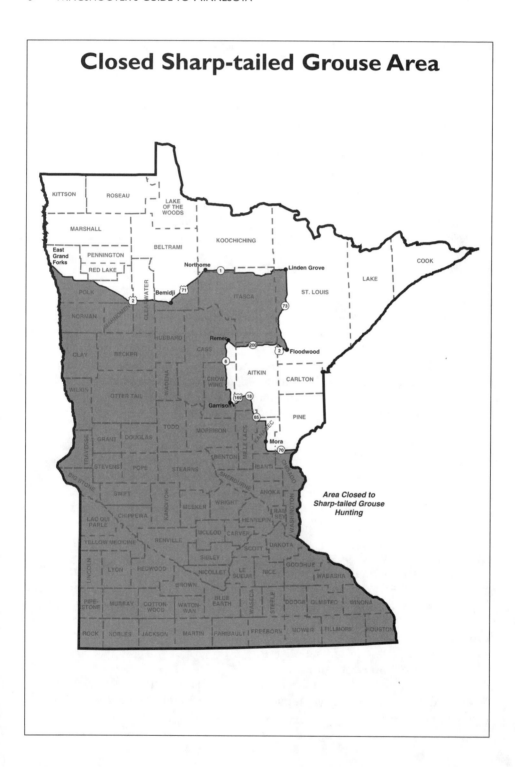

Closed Sharp-tailed Grouse Area

Area Closed to
Sharp-tailed Grouse
Hunting

Prohibited Methods

- A person may not take a grouse while within 20 yards of a motor vehicle (see above).
- A person may not take protected birds by the following methods: with a trap, net, or snare; using bird lime; with a swivel or set gun; by dragging a rope, wire, or other device across a field; or by using fire.
- A person may not shoot pheasants or Hungarian partridge with a rifle or handgun other than a .22 caliber rimfire using short, long, or long rifle ammunition.

Protected and Unprotected Animals

The following birds and mammals are protected in Minnesota by state or federal laws:

Protected Birds

- All birds for which seasons are established in these regulations are protected birds but may be taken as authorized.
- There is no open season on bobwhite quail, prairie chickens, cranes, swans, mourning doves, hawks, owls, eagles, herons, bitterns, cormorants, loons, grebes, or any other species of birds except unprotected birds (see below).
- Crows may be taken without a license in season or at any time when they are doing or are about to do damage. During closed season, calls or decoys may not be used.

Taking Protected Species

- No protected species may be taken in any manner in any area of the state except in accordance with these regulations.
- All protected species must be killed before being removed from the site where taken.

Unprotected Birds

House sparrows, starlings, common pigeons, chukar partridge, quail other than bobwhite quail, mute swans, and monk parakeets are unprotected and may be taken at any time.

Blaze Orange Requirements

A visible portion of at least one article of clothing above the waist must be blaze orange for anyone hunting or trapping small game, except for those hunting turkeys, migratory birds, raccoons or predators and anyone hunting with nontoxic shot. In addition, all hunters and trappers, except waterfowl hunters on the water or in a stationary shooting location, must wear blaze orange clothing in areas open under applicable laws and ordinances to firearms deer hunting, including the Muzzleloader Season. Red is not a legal color.

Although there is no prairie chicken hunting in Minnesota at present, this could change if efforts are undertaken now to develop habitat for the future. Hunter dollars, DNR programs, and landowner cooperation are the key for wildlife success.

Transportation of Game Birds
- Nonmigratory upland game birds (pheasants, grouse, Hungarian partridge) must have one leg and foot or the fully feathered head or a fully feathered wing intact.

Waterfowl

Definitions
- "Migratory game birds" means ducks, geese, mergansers, coots, moorhens (gallinules), woodcock, rails, and snipe.
- "Migratory waterfowl" means ducks, geese, and mergansers.
- "Undressed bird" means ducks and mergansers with one fully feathered wing and head attached or geese with one fully feathered wing attached.

License Requirements

Waterfowl hunters must have a Minnesota Small Game License in their possession while hunting unless they are exempt from a license requirement.

Stamp Requirements

- **Minnesota Migratory Waterfowl Stamp:** State Migratory Waterfowl Stamps (State Duck Stamp) cost $5 and are available from county auditors, the DNR License Bureau, and license agents. There is no issuing fee for stamps. The stamp is not valid unless the licensee signs it across the face.
- All resident hunters age 18 or over and under age 65, and all nonresident hunters, are required to have a Duck Stamp in their possession while hunting or taking migratory waterfowl. The exceptions are as follows:
  a) Residents who are hunting on their own property are not required to possess a State Duck Stamp, but must possess a Federal Duck Stamp.
  b) Residents who are in the U.S. Armed Forces and are stationed out of state may hunt waterfowl without a license and without a State Duck Stamp, if they have official military leave papers on their person. However, they must possess a Federal Duck Stamp.

Federal Migratory Waterfowl Stamp

- Waterfowl hunters aged 16 and older must carry on their person a valid Federal Migratory Bird Hunting and Conservation Stamp (Federal Duck Stamp) signed in ink across the face.
- Federal Duck Stamps cost $15 and are available at post offices and some license agents.

Stamp Requirements for Shooting Preserves

Persons hunting waterfowl on commercial shooting preserves are required to have both a Federal and a State Duck Stamp in addition to a Small Game License. The only exception is when taking only marked, pen-reared mallards.

Minnesota Waterfowl Hunting Regulations

Before hunting, you must consult the current Waterfowl Hunting Regulations (Supplement) available from most county auditor's offices, sporting goods stores, or the DNR License Bureau in St. Paul, to verify all rules and regulations.

This Minnesota Waterfowl Hunting Regulations Supplement includes information on special goose hunts and waterfowl limits and hunting dates, which are set in August and not available when the Hunting Handbook is printed.

All waterfowl hunters must also follow other state and federal regulations listed in the current Hunting Handbook, available from most county auditor's offices, sporting goods stores, or the DNR License Bureau in St. Paul. In that publication you will find all other necessary information to legally hunt waterfowl in Minnesota.

The Minnesota Department of Natural Resources works with landowners on harvest rotation and practices to improve wildlife habitat.

Blinds and Sinkboxes

- No person may erect a blind in public waters or on public land more than one hour before the open season for waterfowl.
- No person may take migratory waterfowl, coots, or rails using a sink box (a structure that allows a hunter to partially hide beneath the water surface) or in public waters from a permanent artificial blind.
- Any blind on public land or in public waters when not in use is considered public and not the property of the person who constructed it. Any use of threat or force against another person to gain possession of a blind is unlawful.

Decoys

- No person may place decoys on public lands or in public waters more than one hour before legal shooting hours for waterfowl.
- No person may leave decoys on public waters between sunset and one hour before legal shooting hours, except decoys may be left in waters:
  a) adjacent to private land under control of the hunter; and
  b) where there is not sufficient natural vegetation growing in the water to partially conceal a hunter. A person may not leave decoys in public waters between sun-

set and one hour before shooting hours if the decoys constitute a navigational hazard.

New for 1998

See new season dates and limits.

* Only one pintail is allowed in the daily bag.
* Goose zones and seasons have changed substantially since last year. Check the maps and tables carefully.

Goose Hunting

See the information below for general goose seasons and information on controlled goose hunting zones.

December Goose Hunts

* The Fergus Falls/Alexandria Goose Zone, Olmsted County, and the Twin Cities Metro Goose Zone will be open for Canada goose hunting Dec. 12-21. NO SPECIAL PERMIT IS REQUIRED.
* Shooting hours each day are one-half hour before sunrise to sunset. Limits are two Canada geese daily and four in possession. All other goose hunting regulations apply.
* In the Twin Cities Zone it is illegal to hunt geese from roads or rights-of-way or to hunt within 100 yards of permanent surface water (not including ice).

September Goose Hunt

A special permit is required to hunt Canada geese during the September season. All persons must have the permit to participate in these hunts, except residents under age 18 or over age 65 and persons hunting on their own property. There is a fee of $3 for the permit, which is available from license agents, county auditors, and the DNR License Bureau. There is no deadline for purchasing the permit. The small, self-adhesive permit can be affixed to your small-game license, and must be signed to be valid.

* The entire state, except the Northwest Zone (see Minnesota Hunting and Trapping Regulations Handbook), is open for Canada goose hunting September 5-15, 1998.
* Shooting hours are one-half hour before sunrise to sunset each day.
* Daily bag limits are shown on the maps in the current handbook by zone. Possession limits are double the daily bag limits.
* No one may take geese within 100 yards of any surface water, including but not limited to wetlands, lakes, rivers, and streams, except as specifically authorized.
* In the West Goose Zone (including the West-Central and Lac Qui Parle Zones) the restriction on taking geese within 100 yards of surface water is not in effect beginning the second Saturday of the season (Sept. 12, 1998).
* All other goose hunting regulations in the handbook apply during the September season.
* The controlled hunting zone at Lac Qui Parle WMA is closed to hunting.

Sharing a day's hunt with your children offers multiple rewards.

- These refuges are open to hunting during the September season: Goose refuges: Douglas County; Otter Tail County; and Sauk Rapids/Rice in Benton County; Waterfowl refuges: Harstad Slough in Stevens County.
- Taking Canada geese on public roads and rights-of-way is prohibited during the early season in the Metro Zone and in goose refuges open to goose hunting.

Special Falconry Season

Dates: Ducks, coots, and moorhens may be taken by falconry from October 3 to January 16, 1999. Geese may be taken by falconry from October 3 to January 1, 1999. Woodcock, rails, and snipe may be taken by falconry from September 1 to December 16, 1998.

Bag limits and hours: Three daily combined and six in possession combined. Falconry hours are one-half hour before sunrise to sunset, except after October 2, when they are the same as the waterfowl shooting hours.

*Although this sign warns hunters that these are tame duck,
a good hunter should know the difference.*

Nontoxic Shot Requirement

No person may use lead shot to take—or have lead shot in possession while taking—geese, duck (including captive-reared mallards), mergansers, coots, or moorhens. This restriction includes muzzleloading shotguns. Only steel shot, bismuth alloy shot, tungsten-polymer shot, tungsten-iron shot, or copper-, nickel-, or zinc-plated steel shot (or other nontoxic shot approved by the director of the U.S. Fish and Wildlife Service) may be used.

Bird Bands

Please report bird bands; call 1-800-327-BAND (2263). Biologists use information reported by hunters to manage waterfowl. If you shoot a banded bird, call the number above. The operator will want to know the band number and how, when, and where it was recovered. You will receive a certificate of appreciation with information about the bird. The band is yours to keep. Thank you for your help.

Waterfowl Migration & Hunting Report

For information on specific waterfowl hunts or public hunting areas, contact a regional DNR wildlife office, or call the DNR Information Center at 651-296-6157 (metro or outside Minnesota) or at 1-800-766-6000. Telecommunications for the Deaf (TDD): 651-296-5484 or 1-800-657-3929.

Waterfowl: General Information

Important! Because waterfowl seasons and limits aren't approved until mid-summer, final information on waterfowl are not included in the handbook.

Consult the Waterfowl Hunting Regulations Supplement available from county auditors' offices, sporting goods stores, some service stations and convenience stores, and the DNR License Bureau in mid-September for specific information on seasons and limits.

Migratory waterfowl are subject to both state and federal regulations.

Important Dates

The dates below are current as of 1998. Consult the current supplement for updated information.

Season Openers: The tentative opener for the regular waterfowl season is Oct. 3. Final dates will be announced in the Waterfowl Hunting Regulations Supplement, available in mid-September.

Early Goose Season: Early season goose permits can be purchased over-the-counter from license vendors any time after Aug. 10.

Blind Reservations-Lac Qui Parle: Hunters may apply to reserve hunting stations at Lac Qui Parle Wildlife Management Area (WMA). Applications with the earliest postmark between August 24 and September 16 will be accepted on a first-come, first-served basis. Additional details will be announced in early August.

Youth Waterfowl Hunt: Tentative date is September 19.

Transportation of Waterfowl

- Ducks and mergansers must have a fully feathered wing and the fully feathered head attached.
- Geese must have a fully feathered wing attached.
- Other migratory game birds (woodcock, rails, snipe, coots, and moorhens) must have feet and a fully feathered head attached.

Wild Turkeys

Important Dates

Check the Minnesota Department of Natural Resources Hunting and Trapping Regulations for season dates and application deadlines. You can also check online at www.dnr.state.mn.us to find this information.

Important! Applications must be postmarked or hand-delivered to the DNR License Bureau in St. Paul by the deadline date.

License Requirements

Licenses for the Fall and Spring Wild Turkey Hunts are awarded in separate computerized preference drawings. A small game license is not required to hunt wild turkeys.

Important! Hunters age 18 or over must possess a Wild Turkey Stamp to hunt wild turkeys in Minnesota. Created by the Legislature at the request of turkey hunters, the stamp proceeds are dedicated to wild turkey management and research.

Legal Weapons
Firearms
- A person may only use shotguns 20 gauge or larger, or muzzle-loading shotguns 12 gauge or larger.
- Only fine shot size No. 4 and smaller diameter may be used.

Bows and Arrows
- Bows must have a pull of no less than 40 pounds at or before full draw.
- Bows may not be drawn, held, or released by mechanical means, except by permit. A person may use a mechanical device attached to the bowstring if the person's own strength draws and holds the bowstring.
- Arrowheads must be broadheads that are sharp, have at least two metal cutting edges, are of barbless design, and are at least 7/8 inch in diameter; or must be of a blunthead design.
- "Retractable" broadheads that meet all other requirements of law are legal for wild turkeys if they: 1) are at least 7/8 inch in width at or after impact; and 2) are of a barbless design and function in a barbless manner.
- No person may use any arrow that is poisoned or has an explosive tip.

How to Apply for Wild Turkey Licenses
Eligibility
- Residents and nonresidents are eligible to apply.
- A Small Game License is not required to hunt wild turkeys.
- Applicants must not have had any small game hunting privileges revoked within one year before purchasing a Wild Turkey License.
- Applicants must be at least 16 years old, or possess a valid Firearms Safety Certificate, before the opening of the season.
- Preference is determined by the number of years that a person has submitted valid but unsuccessful applications since last receiving a license. The Fall and Spring Hunt preference systems are separate from one another. Success or failure in obtaining a license for one season has no effect on your preference in the other.

Applications
- Applications for the Spring Hunt and applications for the Fall Hunt are available from some license vendors, county auditors' offices, and the DNR License Bureau in St. Paul.
- There is a nonrefundable fee of $3 per applicant, payable by check or money order.
- Persons may apply individually or in a group of up to four persons.

Landowner/Tenant Special Drawing
- Up to 20 percent of the permits for each Wild Turkey Permit Area and time period will be issued to applicants who live as landowners or tenants on 40 or more acres of agricultural or grazing land within the Permit Area.

Party Hunting
- Party hunting for wild turkeys is prohibited.

General Restrictions
- Wild turkeys may not be taken with the aid of dogs. No person may be accompanied by a dog or dogs while hunting or assisting in hunting wild turkeys.
- Wild turkeys may not be taken with the aid of any electronic device.
- The use of live turkey decoys is prohibited.
- No persons who are afield hunting wild turkeys may have in their possession or in their control any firearm or bow and arrow except those defined as legal for taking wild turkeys.

Tagging
- The tag provided with the license must be punched with the date of the kill, signed, and attached to the wild turkey immediately after taking the bird.
- The tag must remain attached to the bird during transit.

Fall Wild Turkey Hunt
Fall Wild Turkey Hunting Permits are allocated by a computerized drawing for five-day hunting periods in October. Applications for 1999 Fall Wild Turkey Hunting Permits are available June 1, 1999.

Legal Shooting Hours
The legal shooting hours for the Fall Wild Turkey Hunt are one-half hour before sunrise until sunset.

Bag Limit
The bag limit for the Fall Hunt is one wild turkey of either sex.

Registration
Every person who takes a wild turkey must register the bird at a designated registration station no later than 24 hours after the time when taken.

The feathers, head and feet must remain on the wild turkey until it is registered.

No person may possess an unregistered wild turkey outside the zone where the bird was taken unless it is being transported in a direct route to a registration station.

Spring Wild Turkey Hunt (1999)
The following general regulations apply to Minnesota's Spring Wild Turkey Hunt. Complete information on spring wild turkey season dates, permit areas, and quotas are provided with application materials available in November.

Legal Shooting Hours
The legal shooting hours for the Spring Hunt are one-half hour before sunrise to 12 noon.

Turkeys like to travel in groups for safety, making it difficult to sneak up on them.

If you harvest a banded bird, be sure to get the information to the state DNR or the U.S. Fish and Wildlife Service. The information these agencies compile is important to the future of wildlife and hunting opportunities.

Bag Limit

The spring bag limit is one wild turkey with a visible beard. The beard is a feathered appendage protruding from the breast that is generally found only on males.

Registration

- Every person who takes a wild turkey must personally present the bird for registration at a designated registration station by 2 p.m. on the date taken.
- The feathers, head, and feet must remain on the wild turkey until it is registered.
- No person may possess an unregistered wild turkey outside the zone where it was taken unless it is being transported in a direct route to a registration station.

Upland Birds

Mention the words "upland bird" to a Minnesotan, and you will probably be regaled with tales revolving around ruffed grouse. During the peak of Minnesota's ruffed grouse cycle, one million-plus birds are harvested. Even at the cycle's low point, the number of ruffed grouse harvested will still exceed that of the second ranked upland bird in Minnesota—the ring-necked pheasant.

These two birds represent the extremes of upland bird hunting opportunities available in the state of Minnesota. Pheasants occupy agricultural areas that consist of private lands as well as state Wildlife Management Areas, while ruffed grouse inhabit the multifaceted edges of dense forests that consist of vast tracts of federal, state, and county public lands. One species lures groups of hunters to pursue it, while the other beckons to the solitary hunter.

In addition to ruffed grouse and ring-necked pheasant, upland hunters choosing Minnesota as a destination have many other choices: spruce grouse, sharp-tailed grouse, gray (Hungarian) partridge, woodcock, eastern wild turkey, common snipe, and rail. Each offers its own special challenge to the upland bird hunter.

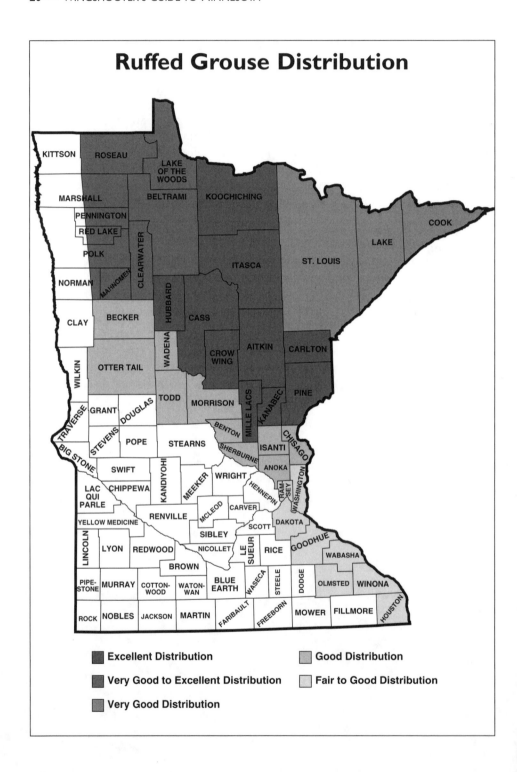

Ruffed Grouse

Bonasa umbellus

FIELD FACTS

Local Names
Partridge, pat, ruff

Size
Ruffed grouse average about 17 inches in length and have a 2-foot wingspan. Average weight is 1.5 to 2 pounds, with males a bit larger and weighing slightly more than females.

Identification in Flight
Ruffed grouse are nearly always heard before they are seen, exploding from the forest floor in a roar of wings. The squarish, fanned tail is easy to spot in flight.

Appearance

Ruffed grouse in Minnesota can vary greatly in color, from the so-called gray phase birds to the chestnut-colored red phase bird. About 30 different color variations are recognized in Minnesota. A dark band completes the tip of the large, fanned tail. If the band is uninterrupted, chances are the bird is male. Grouse legs are feathered and its feet have hairlike projections that allow it to walk on top of snow without sinking.

Sound and Flight Pattern

Ruffed grouse can flush with great commotion or move through the trees without a sound. Though they do not vocalize when flushed, some birds utter a soft "putt-putt-putt" just before flushing. In spring, male grouse sit on an object and begin a series of very rapid wing movements. As the wings move faster and faster, they mimic the sound of a balky gasoline engine. This "drumming" sound is part of the male grouse's courting ritual. Sometimes male grouse drum in the fall.

Similar Game Birds

Ruffed grouse spend most of their time in the woods, sometimes venturing to the edges between woods and fields to feed. Pheasants occupy the more open agricultural areas. Hen pheasants can be mistaken for ruffed grouse. Like pheasants, sharp-tailed grouse occupy more open brushy areas. The reclusive spruce grouse, while found in the forested areas of far northern Minnesota, has a different color scheme, no crest on the head, and prefers to sit when approached.

A ruffed grouse male strutting his stuff while crossing a forest service road.

Flock or Covey Habits

The ruffed grouse is not a covey bird. Even when a group of ruffed grouse is encountered, each bird flushes based on its own instincts. If groups of ruffed grouse are found together, it is likely to be a family unit that hasn't dispersed.

Reproduction and Life Span

Male ruffed grouse drum in the spring to attract females for mating purposes. Ruffed grouse are polygamous, and a dominant male can mate with numerous females. They nest in a shallow depression found close to the base of older trees, especially aspen. Hens lay from 9 to 12 eggs. Newborn chicks forage on insects for the first four to five weeks of their life. After that, they switch to a diet comprised of greens, buds, seeds, and fruits. By the time hunting season arrives, over 70 percent of the chicks have perished. Mortality continues unabated through the fall and winter seasons. If 1,000 ruffed grouse hatched in June, just 118 birds would be expected to survive through the following June. While ruffed grouse can survive four to five years, a bird making it to its second breeding season is a lucky bird indeed.

A ruffed grouse male drumming.

Feeding Habits and Patterns

As an aid to finding birds, veteran hunters routinely check a recently shot grouse's crop in order to determine the type of forage they have been utilizing. While interesting, the fact that ruffed grouse eat just about anything at any time means that this probably won't help you find birds. Studies show that grouse feed in the morning after the dew is off vegetation, and again in the late afternoon just before roosting time. Weather, impending weather changes, and hunting pressure can disrupt this feeding pattern.

Aspen trees provide the most important year-round sources of food for ruffed grouse in the form of green leaves, flower buds, and catkins. In most winters, aspen flower buds are the staple grouse diet. When grouse do not have access to this food, winter catkins of hazel, and to a lesser amount birch and willow, are consumed. Green leaves of clover and wild strawberry, as well as acorns also provide important seasonal food.

Preferred Habitat and Cover

Ruffed grouse are birds of young, disturbed forest lands. Today, logging accomplishes what wildfires did in the past—forest renewal. Ruffed grouse occupy about 60 percent of the land area of Minnesota. Not surprisingly, this represents most of

Aspens provide buds for a ruffed grouse meal.

Minnesota's forestland. The very best grouse habitat will be found where extensive 10- to 40-acre aspen clearcuts have taken place. The greater the number of these checkerboard cuts in an area the higher the ruffed grouse numbers.

Optimum ruffed grouse habitat should include: brushy areas and young aspen stands to provide cover and supply summer and fall foods; mature aspen stands with an understory of hazel or ironwood that provide food in the fall, winter, and spring; and dense sapling aspen stands to provide brood cover.

Areas with maximum ruffed grouse densities would have all of the above within 6 to 10 acres, providing all their annual habitat needs. Ruffed grouse do not prosper well in forests dominated by conifers because pines, spruce, and balsam fir provide effective screening for goshawks and great horned owls.

Locating Hunting Areas

In general, the north central area of Minnesota will hold the highest concentrations of ruffed grouse. How high is high? In 1998, I averaged 7.2 ruffed grouse flushes per hour hunting a small area in Cass County. During my guided trips, we averaged 4.4 ruffed grouse flushes per hour hunting a different area of Cass County as well as Wadena County. Keep in mind that the guided hunts utilized my dogs, the hunt operator's dogs, as well as the client's dogs. Because of the vast amount of public forest lands in Minnesota, here are my recommendations for locating good hunting sites:

- Look at the ruffed grouse density map contained within this book.

- Contact state wildlife managers in the areas you wish to hunt.

- After narrowing your search, procure the necessary maps (PRIM, national forest, county plat) to further define prime hunting areas.

- Contact the county land offices in the counties you've selected to get pertinent information on 6- to 10-year-old aspen clearcut sites and their recommendations as to where grouse might be found.

- Finally, focus on edge cover, whether it be along trails, forest roads, small streams, or forestland that has trees of varying ages.

Hunting Methods

Ruffed grouse are not early risers. This is especially true if a lot of moisture is on the ground or on the vegetation. Let moisture or frost burn off before heading into the woods. This is especially true if you're hunting with dogs. As birds feed again toward evening, the last hour before sunset can also be a very productive time. If hunting without dogs, move through good cover or habitat by employing a "stop and start" mode. Many ruffed grouse will sit tight and let a dogless hunter pass right by without flushing. By stopping every so often, you may cause a bird to get nervous and flush.

The state of Minnesota requires that a blaze orange clothing item be worn above the waist. In dense forest areas, it's much safer to wear "too much" blaze orange than not enough. Your life or the life of a hunting companion could depend on this.

A hunting method for ruffed grouse currently in vogue in many parts of Minnesota is road hunting for ruffed grouse with an ATV (all terrain vehicle). Last year, the state passed a law in which a person hunting ruffed grouse while in or on any kind of motorized vehicle must stop, turn off the ignition, and move at least 20 yards away from the vehicle before firing at a grouse. Be aware that there are hunter walking trails and other nonmotorized trails available to the walking hunter. Since most hunters utilizing a vehicle never leave a trail, you should have no problem finding birds if you head into the woods. The use of an ATV for hunting grouse is a definite plus for those who would not be able to enjoy ruffed grouse hunting without some motorized help.

This 10-year-old growth is a good place to find ruffed grouse.

Hunting Dogs

Many grouse hunters favor one of the pointing breeds to aid them in finding grouse. A dog that points birds allows a hunter to prepare for a shot, maneuver to have a more open shot, and get closer to the bird before shooting, thus reducing the likelihood of missing or wounding the bird. If hunting with a pointing breed that is accustomed to ranging out, you should allow the dog time to become accustomed to hunting grouse in dense woods. Always use a bell or beeper to keep track of your dog in dense woods.

Some hunters have had success hunting ruffed grouse with flushing dogs. Know your dog and its limitations, so that you won't expect too much of it during its first grouse hunt. A flushing dog, working well within range of the gun, might be a better choice than an inexperienced pointing dog prone to covering a lot of ground. A dog with a good nose to retrieve well-camouflaged, downed birds is a real asset to a grouse hunter.

Remember that Lyme disease is a problem for hunter and dogs. Vaccines are now available for both humans and dogs. Consult your physician and veterinarian.

Table Preparations

To many, the white and delicate meat of ruffed grouse is the filet mignon of the upland bird world. Since most grouse hunters skin their birds, care must be taken not to overcook and thus dry out or toughen this delicate meat (there are recipes beginning on page 314). The best overall advice: cook very quickly over high heat. This will seal and preserve the flavor and moisture of this grand bird.

Gun, Shot, and Choke Suggestions

Ruffed grouse can be hunted quite successfully with guns ranging from 28- to 12-gauge—keep in mind that as a walking hunter, you will be covering a lot of ground that is quite often strewn with many obstacles. Shot shell loads ranging from ¾ ounce to 1 ounce of lead will drop a grouse. Early in the season, when woodcock might be found with ruffed grouse, No. 8 and No. 9 shot could be recommended. Later in the season, as birds become prone to flush at greater distances, No. 8, No. 7½, and even No. 6 shot will meet a grouse hunter's needs. Cylinder or skeet chokes are good during the early part of the hunting season. Later, an improved cylinder choke can be used with good results.

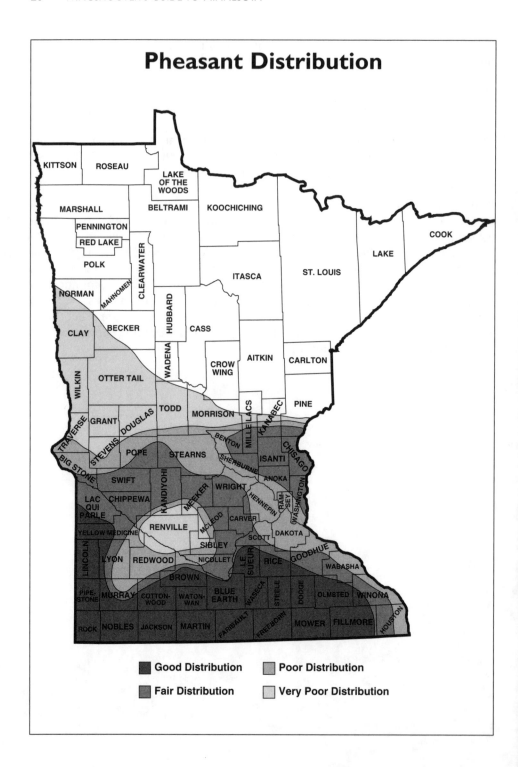

Pheasant Distribution

Pheasant

Phasianus colchicus

FIELD FACTS

Local Names

Ringneck, ring-necked pheasant

Size

An adult rooster pheasant weighs from 2.5 to 3 pounds. Its length from beak tip to tail tip can reach 3 feet, with more than half this length taken up by its long tail. Hens are smaller, weighing around 2 pounds, and have a much shorter tail.

Identification in Flight

As wild hen pheasants are not legal game, it is critical that hunters be able to distinguish a legal rooster from an illegal hen. This task gets complicated when dealing with young roosters or if bright sun renders certain identification impossible. If in doubt, just don't shoot. A mature rooster pheasant has a streaming tail, white neck ring, and cackles upon flushing to make identification easier.

Minnesota's pheasant fortunes are very dependent upon good habitat. This habitat base continues to decrease because of wetland drainage, changes in farming practices, and the loss of CRP-eligible land this past year. Winter weather conditions a couple of years ago just about wiped pheasants out in many western areas of Minnesota. Fortunately, the birds are getting needed help through the Pheasants Forever organization as well as state wildlife managers in the most affected areas.

Appearance

Minnesota's pheasants are a hybrid of many strains of pheasants that have been introduced into this country. Surprisingly, a mature rooster pheasant looks pretty uniform from one area to another.

Rooster pheasants have an iridescent blue-green head with a white spot on top, a white neck ring, and red patches around the eyes. Body feathers are mostly a burnished copper hue with black highlights. Its outer wing feathers are brown and barred with white, while the brown tail is barred with black. Legs vary from gray to yellow in color and always feature a characteristic spur.

The smaller hen is mostly light brown to tan in color, blending in very well with surrounding dead grasses. The hen's tail is significantly shorter than a rooster's, and its legs are spurless.

Sound and Flight Pattern

While on the ground, pheasants can be quite silent during hunting season. Roosters crow often during the spring mating season and occasionally in the fall. If flushed, roosters let loose with a series of short notes that are quite different from their mating crow. Hen pheasants are totally silent at all times. While pheasants appear to be slow in getting off the ground, once airborne, they quickly make up for lost time. They can maintain impressive flight speeds for a long distance.

Similar Game Birds

Where forest meets agricultural land or where open brushland meets agricultural land, ruffed grouse or sharp-tailed grouse might be confused with hen pheasants. Areas where this is likely to occur are usually devoid of pheasants or sharp-tailed grouse.

Flock or Covey Habits

Pheasants are not covey birds and even in those areas of Minnesota with the highest pheasant densities, birds are scattered rather than in flocks. Late in the season, during adverse weather conditions, pheasants may gather into flocks. These late-season flocks can be impossible to approach. It should be noted that some segregation by sex might occur late in the season.

Reproduction and Life Span

Pheasants are ground-nesting birds that nest in grassy cover, such as ditches, along streams, hay fields, or in CRP fields. Hens lay a dozen or so eggs from mid-May to mid-June. Roosters, having mated with several hens, play no part in tending the nest nor raising the young. Owing to unpredictable spring weather, hens are persistent renesters. Each time a hen renests, fewer eggs are laid. Thus, the best hatch years are those in which hens were successful in their first nesting attempts.

Most pheasants don't survive their first year. Hunters take 60 to 70 percent of the roosters with more being lost to weather and predators. Most hens never live to bring off a brood. They are victims of predators or farm machinery.

Feeding Habits and Patterns

Pheasant chicks, upon hatching and for a number of weeks thereafter, feed primarily on insects. As adults, they become mostly vegetarian. Adult pheasants do establish a feeding pattern that includes eating shortly after sunup and again in the late afternoon, followed by grit gathering before heading to roosting areas.

Once hunting season commences, pheasants alter their patterns and feed whenever they can without being disturbed.

Nutritionally, pheasants do quite well on waste grains such as corn and soybeans. Along with the need for winter cover, the importance of readily available nutritious food cannot be overemphasized. Minnesota's harsh winters can wreak havoc with food supplies for pheasants.

A rooster and hen pheasant tending to a nest in southwestern Minnesota.

Preferred Habitat and Cover

Other than roosting, Minnesota pheasants spend nearly all their time in crop fields from July until harvest. If grain and corn fields are interspersed with sloughs and marshes, they will move into these areas as grain is harvested, and fields are left bare of any bird-holding cover. Large, grassy CRP fields can hold a good number of birds if enough food is nearby. Changes in the CRP program in 1998 will lead to drastic cutbacks in lands eligible for CRP designation. As habitat decreases, so do bird numbers. Wetlands can be quite productive if food sources are nearby.

Locating Hunting Areas

Remember that food and cover are essential to finding pheasants. Likely spots to find pheasants include:

- Large blocks of cover, such as public hunting lands and CRP fields.
- Long, narrow "strip" cover areas, such as fencerows, ditches, meandering waterways, and small creeks.
- Standing corn, as long as you have permission to hunt and have enough hunters to hunt it properly.
- Shelter belts, farm groves, and other timbered areas where birds might seek protection and shelter from bitter cold and heavy snow cover.
- Stubble fields of corn or grain if there is enough stubble remaining in which birds can hide.

Looking for Sign

In snow or mud, pheasant leave telltale large, three-toed tracks. Pheasant roosting areas may be marked by olive-green and white pellet-sized droppings.

Hunting Methods

Pheasant hunting is probably one of the oldest upland hunting traditions in the country. As in any state where these birds are hunted, size and type of cover will dictate the hunting method. Large-sized plots of ground, such as CRP fields and some Wildlife Management Areas, may be best hunted by turning your dog loose and following its lead. Try to work the edges of large fields first as dogs may pick up the scent trail of birds moving back and forth from cover to food.

The block and drive method of hunting can be used on these large tracts of land as well as standing corn fields. A dogless hunter might have better luck hunting small, out-of-the-way cover using a combination of zigzagging and stop-and-start hunting methods.

On cold, dark days a hunter might find the most success hunting dense, thick roosting cover very early and very late in the day. On bright sunny days, the same time periods will find birds feeding in picked corn or grain fields.

Loud noises (slamming vehicle doors, talking loudly, etc.) put pheasants on the alert and prepared for escape. After securing permission to hunt private land or being the first hunter of the day to hunt a piece of public land, it can be extremely frustrating to see most, if not all, the legal roosters sail off the horizon due to hunt preparations that take on the commotion of a grade-school fire drill. Silence is golden!

Hunting With Dogs

Because pheasants can be very hard birds to kill cleanly, few pheasant hunters venture afield without a dog. Dogs help a pheasant hunter find birds, put them to wing, and bring them to the game bag. Opinion varies widely as to which dog breeds are best for hunting pheasants. Rather than making any recommendations, each hunter should know his or her dog's strengths and shortcomings in regard to pheasant hunting and proceed accordingly. Larry Brown, author of *Wingshooter's Guide to Iowa*, states: "The Iowa DNR states that dogless hunters lose 1 of every 3 birds that they knock down, while those with dogs lose 1 in 10. Experienced dogs can do even better."

Table Preparation

Pheasant are among the most succulent of all wild game. If it is a warm day, draw the birds in the field and get them on ice as soon as possible—the cleaning job can be finished at a later time. Soaking cleaned birds overnight in cold saltwater is a good idea, especially if you're dealing with badly shot birds.

As most pheasants are skinned rather than plucked, care must be taken not to dry out the meat during cooking. Cover with foil if roasting, cook them in liquid, or

Pheasants are known for crouching low and taking advantage of whatever cover is available.

lace bacon strips across the breast. It's best not to overcook this delicate white meat. Just as nothing can beat a "shore lunch" of freshly caught fish, the same can be said of "field grilling" a freshly shot bird. Try filleting the breast, marinate it in Italian dressing, top with pineapple slices, and grill quickly.

Gun and Shot Suggestions
- **Gauge:** 12 or 16.
- **Choke:** Improved and modified for doubles, modified for single barrels.
- **Shot:** A strong field load of 1⅛ to 1¼ oz. of No. 6 or No. 5 will be your best choice for pheasants. Late in the season, No. 4 is a good choice for heavily feathered birds. I've had great luck with my "pigeon load" reloads (3¼ dram to 1¼ oz.) nickel-plated lead No. 6 and No. 5 shot. If you plan to hunt pheasants on Federal Waterfowl Production Areas, be aware that you will have to use nontoxic shot (steel, bismuth, tungsten-iron, and tungsten-polymer). If your pheasant gun can't handle steel shot, look into bismuth or tungsten-polymer loads.

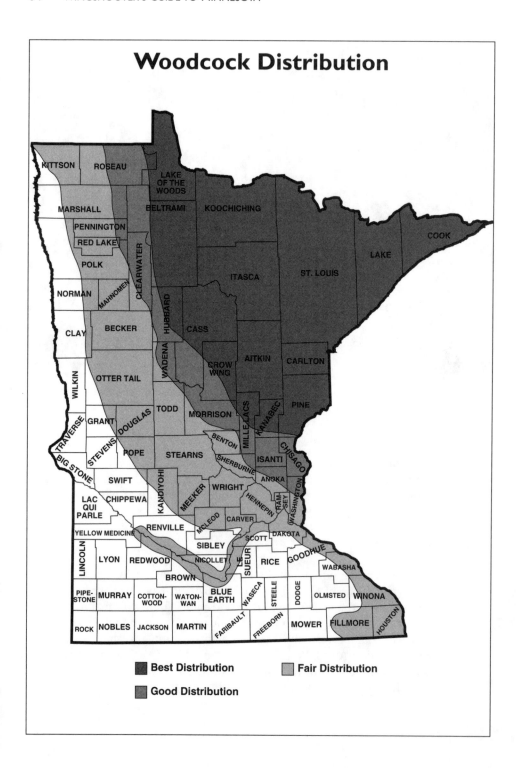

Woodcock Distribution

■ Best Distribution   □ Fair Distribution

■ Good Distribution

Woodcock

Scolopax minor

FIELD FACTS

Local Names
   Timberdoodle, bogsucker

Size
   Woodcock are stocky, migratory upland game birds. Females are larger than males, averaging 8 ounces and 6 ounces, respectively. They are between 10 and 11 inches in length with bills over 2 inches long.

Identification in Flight
   Woodcock appear small, chunky, and brownish-colored in flight, and the bill is usually visible. Woodcock have an initial erratic flight path before leveling off, and most flush from less than 100 yards. Many times, migrating birds flush from less than 30 yards. Flushed woodcock make a nonvocal twittering sound. This sound comes from air passing through the primary feathers as the bird takes off. Once heard, the twittering sound is good identification of the bird as it takes wing.

Appearance

The woodcock is a beautiful mix of browns and blacks, with bold black markings on the head, a long bill, and large black eyes. Its eyes are located on the side of the head, enabling the bird to see in all directions, including directly behind. Because the bird spends so much time with its bill in the mud, it needs a large field of vision to detect predators. The bill is extremely long (almost 3 inches) for such a small body, which stands only 8 inches high. The long, prehensile probing bill allows woodcock to probe moist soil and capture its primary food—earthworms. The larger female can be distinguished by the length of its bill, which is always longer than a dollar bill is wide. The male's smaller bill is always shorter than the width of a dollar bill. Other than the difference in size and bill length, males and females look virtually identical.

Seasonal Patterns

Woodcock are migratory upland game birds, passing through their range in what are called "flights." Woodcock begin arriving in Minnesota in mid-March, often well before winter snow is gone. Male woodcock begin courtship activity during the northward spring migration. They often return to the same breeding area year after year.

A breeding male establishes a "singing ground" that it defends from other males. Singing grounds are small openings, usually free of most woody vegetation, and are often near dense shrubs or young forest stands that provide nesting and brood-rearing habitat. Here, the male performs his unique courtship ritual to attract females.

The male woodcock's courtship performance lasts 30 to 60 minutes each day during the first and last hours of daylight. The male begins by giving a series of nasal sounds (*peents*). He then spirals upward to heights of 100 to 300 feet, producing a twittering sound as air rushes through the outer wing feathers. After reaching the peak of his flight, the male descends, emitting a series of vocal chirps until he glides to the ground near where the flight originated. Each flight lasts for about one minute and may be repeated a dozen or more times.

Female woodcock nest in or next to forest openings, often within 500 feet of a male's singing ground. Eggs are laid in a shallow depression covered with dead leaves are are light brown with darker brown blotches. They are incubated for 21 to 22 days, and upon hatching, chicks are ready to leave the nest, depending upon the female to help them find the insects that make up most of their diet. Within two weeks of hatching, chicks can fly, and two weeks later, their diet of earthworms is essentially the same as an adult's. By the Fourth of July, most chicks hatched in Minnesota are independent. They roost in grassy fields at night and seek dense cover (alder runs and young aspen stands) during the day.

Fall migration begins when enough snow cover or frozen ground makes feeding on earthworms difficult. In northern Minnesota, the fall woodcock migration usually begins the first week of October and peaks during the middle of the month. During this time, migrating birds can literally disappear from one day to the next. Migrants from further north may arrive in great numbers, or if the weather remains pleasant, trickle through in relatively small numbers on the way south. How long woodcock remain in Minnesota during fall migration depends on the weather. More often than not, most have left the state by early November.

Similar Game Birds

The woodcock bears some resemblance to its long-billed cousin, the common snipe. Both birds can be found in similar habitat: wetland fringes or woods adjacent to wet pastures or farm fields. Once in flight, the distinction is apparent. The snipe is much slimmer and more streamlined, with a whitish breast. Snipe fly faster and farther than woodcock and nearly always emit a shrill cry when flushed.

Preferred Habitat and Cover

Because woodcock are small birds that spend much of their time walking around on the ground in search of worms, their habitat requirements are quite specific. Woodcock need open cover at ground level so that they can feed and move unimpeded. They need dense overstory to protect them from predators. Regenerating forestland, especially with species such as aspen or alder that grow closely enough to shade ground vegetation, is the best woodcock habitat.

Locating Hunting Areas

Almost three-quarters of Minnesota's land area can hold woodcock. Suffice to say that the eastern half of the state has the best habitat—land dominated by aspen

An English setter locks up on point in dense cover. (Photo by Mickey Johnson)

and birch, mixed with old farm fields, and a few brushy lowland areas. Forests dominated by maples, oaks, pines, or spruce generally do not provide high-quality woodcock habitat.

Woodcock require a mix of small, scattered openings and dense stands of shrubs and young deciduous trees. Because this type of habitat does not remain a permanent fixture of the landscape, good woodcock habitat doesn't last on its own for very long.

Once you've chosen the areas in which you want to hunt woodcock, study topographical maps and contact a Minnesota DNR area wildlife manager in the area you've chosen to hunt woodcock to help narrow your choices.

Looking for Sign

Woodcock leave two telltale signs, and the presence of either is a sure indicator that birds have been in the area. Woodcock leave probe holes, made when they thrust their bills into the ground searching for worms. These show up best on moist, bare ground. The second sign is "whitewash," their characteristic white droppings about the size of a quarter or fifty-cent piece. There is a clear distinction between "old" and "fresh" whitewash, also. "Old" whitewash has the appearance of flat latex paint, while "fresh" whitewash is moist and has some slight body to it. Finding an area with a lot of probe holes and whitewash is proof that a flight is in residence or has just departed. Regardless, mark the spot down for future use.

Hunting Methods

Walking up woodcock is easier than ruffed grouse, since woodcock tend to sit much tighter than ruffed grouse. This can be a mixed blessing for a dogless hunter, as he or she may walk right by a tight-sitting, well-camouflaged woodcock. Hunting woodcock prior to the fall migratory flight can be quite frustrating—the habitat is wet, thick, and thorny; shooting conditions can border on the impossible; and the quarry is secretive and elusive. If hunting central Minnesota, as I do, the ideal woodcock hunting method would involve: a knowledge of the areas that migrating woodcock use year after year; woodcock hunting friends in northern Minnesota or southern Ontario who could alert me as to when the woodcock "flight" hits their area; and the ability to have time off from work when the "flight" hits my hunting areas.

Hunting with Dogs

While hunting woodcock with pointing dogs is considered by some as the classic method, many an owner of a close-working flushing or retrieving dog has enjoyed as much success as those who hunt pointers. Because of dense cover, a pointing dog should be equipped with a beeper collar or a bell. The advantage that a pointing dog gives to the hunter is that of placement—being able to utilize any small opening for shooting once the bird is flushed.

If a flushing dog is being used, a beeper collar or bell is still recommended. Be prepared for snap shots if hunting over a flushing or retrieving dog. Also, be aware that woodcock have a scent that some dogs find so objectionable they refuse to retrieve the downed bird.

Table Preparations

Unlike ruffed grouse and pheasant, woodcock have dark breast meat and white legs. The breast has a strong taste that can be compared to chicken liver. Many hunters don't care for the taste of woodcock. For those willing to eat this delicious game bird, dredge the deboned breasts in flour seasoned with your favorite spices and sauté in butter or olive oil. Don't overcook them—one minute on each side or to the point where the meat is slightly pink is enough. Another method is to wrap a deboned and seasoned woodcock breast around a water chestnut, wrap a strip of bacon around the breast/chestnut combo, secure with a wooden toothpick, and grill for a couple of minutes over hot coals or briquettes.

Gun and Shot Suggestions
- **Gauge:** 28, 20, 16, or 12.
- **Choke:** Cylinder and improved for doubles, or either choke for single barrels.
- **Shot:** A light field load of ⅞ oz. No. 8 or spreader loads of the same size are preferred. Many times, woodcock are found in conjunction with ruffed grouse hunting, and at such times, use the loads and chokes that are most advantageous for the more difficult species, in this case the ruffed grouse.

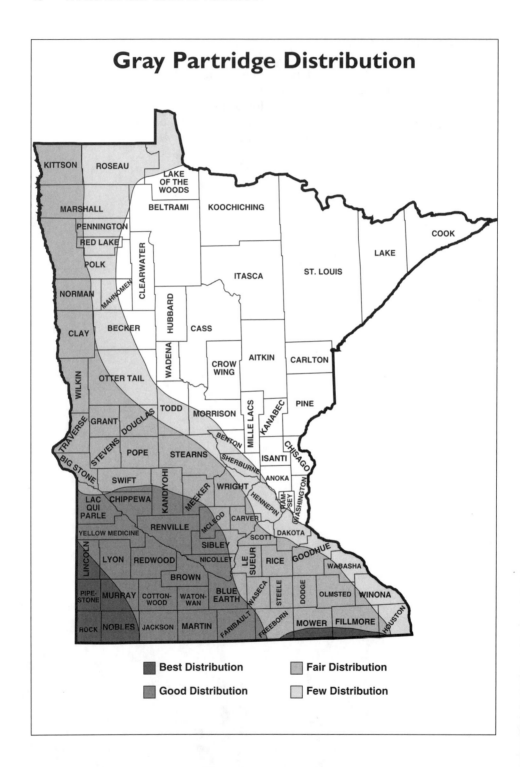

Gray Partridge

Perdix perdix

FIELD FACTS

Local Names

Hungarian partridge, Hun

Size

Huns weigh a little less than a pound, with males and females roughly the same size. They are about 12 to 13 inches long—bigger than a quail but smaller than a grouse.

Identification in Flight

A covey of Huns will flush in unison, with its small size, grayish body, and russet-colored tail as the key identifiers. The covey will usually fly together, rapidly beating their wings and turning together in flight. Upon flushing, they emit a call that sounds like squeaky door hinges.

Appearance

Huns are beautiful birds, with a brown face and throat, gray breast and flanks, and in males, a large chestnut patch on the belly. The chestnut patch may be either very small or absent in females, but other than that, both sexes are similar in appearance and size. The back is gray-brown leading down to a rust-colored tail. The legs and feet are almost black.

Sound and Flight Pattern

Gray partridge normally flush as a covey in one noisy rise, sounding like rusty door hinges. They fly up to a quarter-mile or more on the flush. Huns normally land as a covey after having been flushed. Wingbeats are rapid with periodic glides.

Flock or Covey Habits

Huns stick together more tenaciously than bobwhite quail, usually landing together after flushing. If scattered, a covey will reform quickly. Huns roost at night as a covey. One reason the covey formation is so important to Huns is that they spend more time in relatively open cover, and safety from predators is increased when 10 to 12 pairs of eyes and ears are on the alert for danger.

Reproduction and Life Span

Male gray partridge are monogamous. Early in the spring, males fight each other quite vigorously to establish breeding territories. The partridge nest is a grass-lined hollow containing 15 to 20 eggs. The male gray partridge remains in the vicinity during the egg incubation period to guard against predators. Once the chicks are hatched, the male plays an active role in raising them. Young partridge are able to fly at two weeks of age.

The brood remains together during the summer and usually make up a covey that a hunter will encounter in the fall. Coveys also contain adopted orphan chicks from other broods as well as unmated birds.

Partridge have a high mortality rate (up to 70 percent or more), with hunting not being a factor. Cold, wet weather during the spring, as well as effective predators, account for most of the gray partridge losses. A gray partridge over the age of two is a rare exception. Hunting gray partridge is usually incidental to pheasant hunting in south central Minnesota. DNR estimates that 24,000 to 28,000 gray partridge are shot by hunters annually.

Feeding Habits and Patterns

As with most game bird species, young gray partridge consume mostly insects in the first few weeks after hatching. As the year wears on, they switch to grains (mainly corn in Minnesota), seeds, and greens.

During hunting season, Huns feed primarily on corn. Before snow is on the ground, an unplowed field is a great place to look for birds. Huns are among the earliest to feed in the morning, usually well before first light. After eating, they can often be found along gravel roads gathering grit. They repeat this pattern in the evening before going to roost.

Preferred Habitat and Cover

Hungarian partridge prefer cover that is short enough to see over but tall enough to provide concealment. Most of the CRP land that is in gray partridge territory is too tall and too thick for their liking. Road ditches and cutover hay fields provide most of the necessary cover for these birds.

When hunting season opens in fall, these birds can be expected to spend most of their time in unharvested grain fields, especially corn. They can be quite difficult to hunt until most of the grain has been harvested.

Huns stay in or immediately around a picked corn field throughout winter. They do quite well at hiding under the stalk stubble. On windy days look for them on the downwind or lee side of a hill. Other areas providing cover for gray partridge are abandoned farmsteads (especially buildings) and large, discarded farm implement sites.

Locating Hunting Areas

Across the Hun's primary range in south central Minnesota, there are several key factors to look for when hunting partridge:

1. Early in the season, look for short grass near grain.

2. Hunt corn fields after they have been harvested but before they are plowed.

Young Hungarian partridge.

3. If there is snow cover, drive the back roads slowly as some coveys are easy to spot against the snow.

4. While pheasant hunting, look for Huns in areas of sparse cover when approaching areas of heavier cover preferred by pheasant. If you are looking only for pheasant, Huns can escape your gun due to the element of surprise.

5. Please check with the DNR's area wildlife office to get their information on areas to hunt.

Looking for Sign

Droppings are found in large bunches where a covey has roosted for the night. Huns can leave quite a collection of tracks in the snow and thus alert a hunter to the presence of birds in the area.

Hunting Methods

Very few Minnesotans can tell you much about hunting Huns. They usually blunder upon the birds while hunting pheasants. That fact, as well as the fact that the

A five-week-old Hungarian partridge chick.

best areas to hunt gray partridge are usually private farms, really reduces hunting pressure on these birds. If new to an area, contact the DNR's area wildlife office for the region.

Early in the season, Huns can be found in short grass areas adjacent to the corn fields in which they're feeding. After corn is harvested, walking the cutover fields is a good way to find birds. A dog is very useful since these birds hide under the stubble and are not prone to flush unless nearly stepped on.

Spotting and then trying to approach coveys outlined against snow cover can be an exercise in futility. Once flushed (usually out of shotgun range), watch where the covey resettles. The birds may drop into heavier cover that will allow you to approach them within shotgun range. While birds in the open are loath to let you approach too closely, once in heavier cover, they often sit very tight.

Hunting Dogs

Dogs can be a real help both in the early season as well as in the late season when there is stubble cover. When birds are in the open, it is better to hunt a dog that hunts well "at heel" until you are able to get close to the birds. Crippled Huns do not tend to run, and since they are usually downed in relatively open cover, they should be an easy retrieve for a dog.

Table Preparations

Huns are mostly dark meat and are very tasty. If taken on a warm day, they should be field dressed and put on ice in a cooler. Most hunters prefer to skin gray partridge.

One method for cooking these birds is to debone the breasts, place them in a marinade of your choice, and grill them quickly over hot coals, basting them with olive oil or the marinade. Another also involves deboning the breasts, then cutting them into narrow strips and placing them in a dish containing spice-laced olive oil. After 15 to 30 minutes of marinating, the strips are seared quickly on a griddle (one minute per side), and then placed on a platter of pasta.

Gun and Shot Suggestions

- **Gauge:** 20, 16, or 12.
- **Choke and Shot:** Early in the season, use at least an ounce of No. 7½ shot in an improved or modified choked barrel. Later in the season, use an ounce or more of No. 6 shot through a modified or full choke barrel.

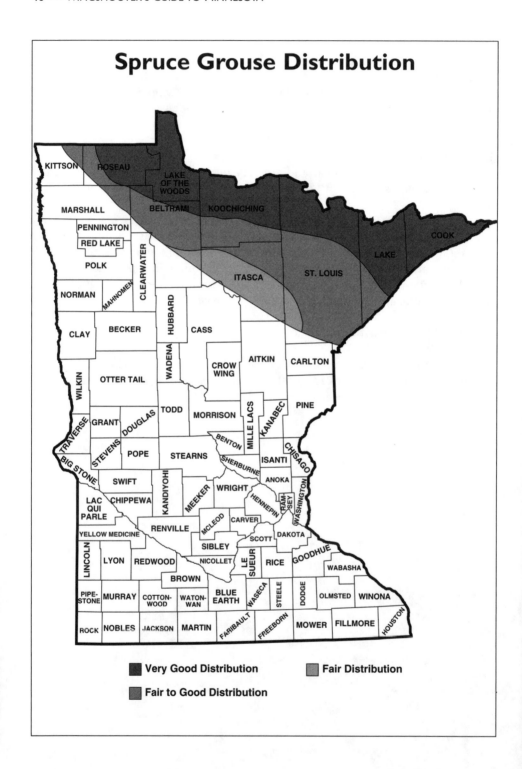

Spruce Grouse Distribution

Very Good Distribution

Fair Distribution

Fair to Good Distribution

Spruce Grouse

Dendragapus canadensis

FIELD FACTS

Local Names
Fool hen, spruce hen

Size
Spruce grouse average 15 to 17 inches in length and weigh between 1.5 to 2 pounds, with males a bit larger and weighing slightly more than females.

Identification in Flight
It is difficult to distinguish spruce grouse from ruffed grouse while in flight through their normal, dense forest cover.

Appearance

Spruce grouse resemble ruffed grouse but are slightly smaller. Male spruce grouse are much darker than male ruffed grouse, with a striking combination of a black throat and tail and contrasting grays and small areas of white. Spruce grouse of both sexes have black tails tipped with light brown to an orange-brown. During courtship displays and at some other times, male spruce grouse show a prominent comb of red skin above the eyes. On the ground, nervous ruffed grouse often walk with raised crests. Spruce grouse are more rounded, don't have crests, and prefer to sit. Few people can tell a flying spruce grouse hen from a ruffed grouse.

Sound and Flight Pattern

When flushed, spruce grouse tend to fly shorter distances than ruffed grouse. The spruce grouse's drumming is more muted and much shorter in duration than that of the ruffed grouse.

Reproduction and Life Span

Male spruce grouse establish a territory in which they will put on a rather elaborate and somewhat comical display to attract a female spruce grouse. Females lay from 4 to 9 eggs in a well-concealed location, often under low branches, in brush, or in deep moss in or near spruce thickets. Spruce grouse chicks initially feed on insects and then graduate to white spruce, larch, and jack pine needles as well as the leaves and fruits of blueberries. During winter, spruce grouse feed almost entirely on jack pine needles. Chicks are able to fly 6 to 7 days after being hatched. While spruce grouse might be expected to survive for 4 to 5 years due to the wildness of

This spruce grouse didn't want its picture taken.

their habitat, in reality, an adult spruce grouse making it to its second breeding season is a rarity.

Feeding Habits and Patterns

Spruce grouse feed early in the morning and again at sunset. Their dietary needs can be met by a good supply of conifer needles (particularly those of jack pine, white spruce, and black spruce), abundant plants such as blueberries and cranberries (including the leaves, fruits, and flowers), and insects for the chicks.

Preferred Habitat and Cover

Along with ready access to their food sources, spruce grouse preferences include primarily coniferous forest containing some trees having live branches that extend to the ground; sparse ground cover; and openings of a few hundred square feet scattered among the trees.

Locating Hunting Areas

Northern Minnesota counties bordering Ontario offer the best spruce grouse hunting. Area wildlife managers for those counties can offer the best advice on places to hunt spruce grouse. Because spruce grouse do not fear humans, many hunters choose not to hunt the "fool hen."

Table Preparation

The meat of younger spruce grouse can be as light in color as that of the ruffed grouse, while older birds have darker meat. Owing to their primary diet of needles, one might be advised to marinate deboned spruce grouse breasts prior to grilling them over hot coals.

Gun, Shot, and Choke Suggestions

- **Gauge:** 28, 20, 16, or 12.
- **Choke:** Improved and modified for doubles, modified for single barrels.
- **Shot:** Lead loads in ¾ to 1 ounce employing No. 9 or No. 8 shot.

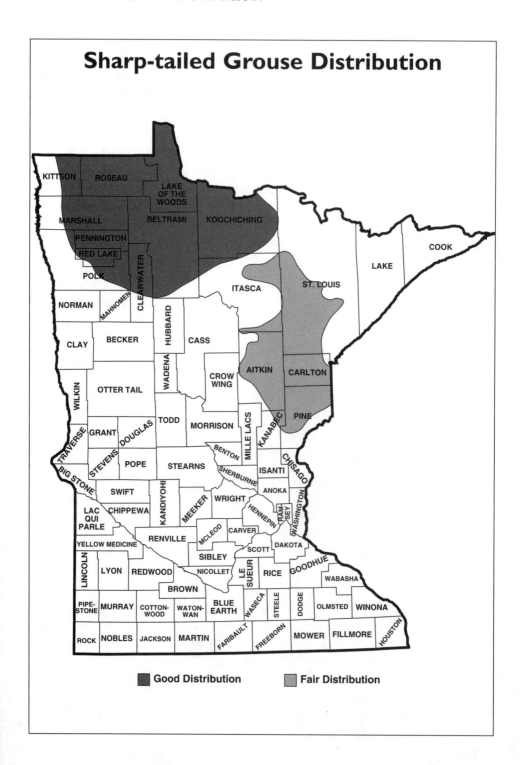

Sharp-tailed Grouse Distribution

Sharp-tailed Grouse

Tympanuchus phasianellus

FIELD FACTS

Local Names

Sharptail, prairie grouse

Size

The sharp-tailed grouse closely resembles its woodland cousin, the ruffed grouse, in size, being close to 17 inches long and around 2 pounds.

Identification in Flight

The repeated kuk-kuk-kuk-kuk call of a flushing sharp-tailed grouse is almost a taunt. Sharp-tailed grouse also show large amounts of white from their wings. In profile, the pointed tail is evident and its flight is a series of rapid wing-beats and glides.

Appearance

The two long, central tailfeathers give this bird its name, and during the male's gaudy courtship dance, the sharp tail is very evident. Like most birds of open prairie and brushland, sharptails display a pattern of brown, tan, white, and black that helps them blend well with their grass and brushland habitat. Sharptail wings have white dots along the primary feathers.

Although sharptails could be confused with prairie chickens or hen pheasants, they have much more white on the wings and belly than either the prairie chicken or pheasant. Also, opposed to the horizontal brown barring pattern on the prairie chicken, the sharptail has a pattern of brown Vs on the breast.

Even in fall, the male's yellow eye comb and purple air sac along the neck are noticeable as you brush back the feathers. During the courtship dance, the air sac inflates and is very prominent, and the yellow eye comb becomes engorged.

Sound and Flight Pattern

Although sharptails stay in coveys during hunting season, they flush in staggered ones and twos with a rush of wings and loud kuk-kuk-kuk-kuk calls. Its flight is composed of a series of rapid wingbeats and glides that takes the departing sharptail well out of gun range. Sharptails have been known to fly up to a couple of miles before alighting on the ground. They are as quick when flying into the wind as they are on calm days.

Sharp-tailed grouse dance in the spring to attract females.

Daily Habits and Food

Sharptails feed before sunrise and at sunset and often travel 1 to 3 miles a day. The various shrubs that comprise brushland provide both cover and food resources. In summer, both adults and young sharptails eat insects and fruit. In autumn, they forage on seeds and small grains and fruits, such as cherries, blueberries, and cranberries. In agricultural areas, fall offerings include small grains, such as oats, flax, wheat, and barley. During winter, sharptails feed on buds of aspen and paper birch and on catkin-bearing shrubs. Unharvested corn and sunflowers also provide an important winter food.

Preferred Habitat and Cover

Sharp-tailed grouse were once one of Minnesota's most abundant and popular game birds. Unfortunately, due to changes in sharptail habitat, their numbers have declined dramatically. The sharptail has narrow habitat requirements that include

Quite commonly, a lone sharptail can be seen keeping watch in the brush above its flock.

a complex mixture of expansive, open grass and brushlands at least 2 square miles in size.

Habitat for sharp-tailed grouse is open grass and brushland, such as natural meadows, open bogs, abandoned farm clearings, and inactive commercial rice paddies. Sharptails do not tolerate tall trees, especially evergreens. If trees grow over 25-feet tall within one-half mile of a dancing ground (lek), the habitat likely will be abandoned because the tree cover inhibits the bird's ability to see and escape hawks and owls. Brushlands around the lek satisfy the sharptail's needs for shelter, nesting cover, and food.

Reproduction and Life Span

Each spring, male sharptails perform a courtship display on a dancing ground or lek to attract hens for mating. Leks are open areas under an acre in size and may be located on a small rise. Leks are seldom located closer than 200 yards to brush or trees that are over 4 feet tall.

After breeding, hens select a nest site within one-half mile of the lek in an elevated site of dense grass or low brush. They lay about a dozen eggs. Chicks are able to fly after 10 days and become increasingly independent of their mother. During their first weeks, chicks feed on insects before switching to a bud, berry, and seed diet in the fall. Typically, about one-half of the brood survives until fall.

Good sharptail cover is sometimes found near the edges of brush, such as that found near Thief Lake Wildlife Management Area.

Locating Hunting Areas

As stated previously, sharptail habitat has decreased markedly in Minnesota. In response, the DNR has closed most of the state to sharp-tailed grouse hunting. The state's open hunting areas offer the best opportunity to add these birds to a hunter's bag.

Find the primary sharptail range on the bird distribution map and compare that to the state's open hunting areas. Then contact the DNR's wildlife offices in the areas you decide to hunt to get help in locating public or private lands that meet your needs.

You can also contact the Minnesota Sharp-tailed Grouse Society for help in locating suitable hunting sites. Their address is listed in Appendix XI, Organizations section of this book.

Hunting Methods

Owing to the open brushlands that sharptails occupy, it is preferable to hunt with a dog. Personally, I prefer one of the pointing breeds because of the expanse of ground to be covered in order to locate these birds. A hunter should be aware that sharp-tailed grouse stagger their flush into ones, twos, and threes—remain on the alert after the initial flush of one or two birds.

Table Preparations

Sharp-tailed grouse meat is dark, and some find it strong to the taste. I find it best to field dress the birds as soon as possible and place them on ice. Most hunters skin the birds and debone the breasts. Soaking the breasts overnight in milk is a method used by some hunters to soften the taste of the meat. Others use a marinade prior to grilling.

Gun, Shot, and choke Suggestions

- **Gauge:** 20, 16, or 12.
- **Shot:** 1⅛ to 1¼ ounce of No. 7½ or No. 6 lead shot.
- **Choke:** Improved and modified for doubles, modified for single barrels.
- Considering the distances at which sharp-tailed grouse might be taken, one might even shy away from the 20-gauge. These can be tough birds to drop cleanly, and considering the effort to locate them, it's not worth taking a chance on slightly wounding a bird.

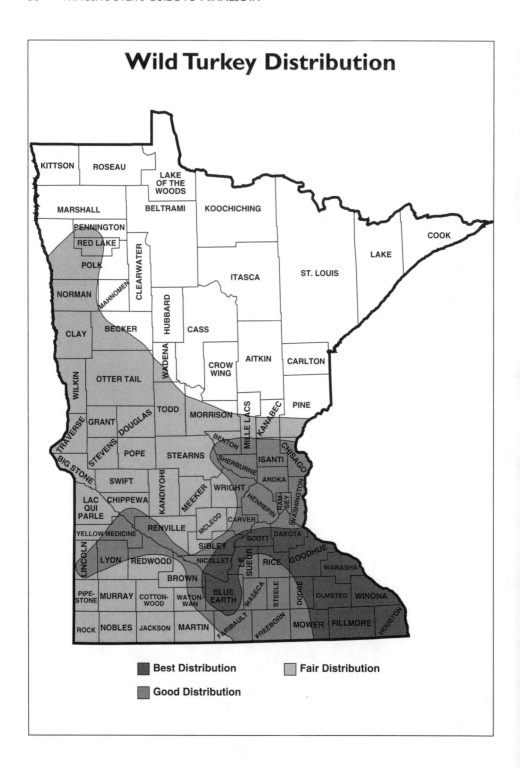

Eastern Wild Turkey

Meleagris gallopavo silvestris

FIELD FACTS

Local Names
   Gobbler, wild turkey, tom

Size
   An adult male (gobbler) in Minnesota averages nearly 18 pounds; an immature male (jake) about 14 pounds; and a hen 10 to 12 pounds.

Identification in Flight
   Turkeys spend much more time on the ground than in the air. However, when they do take to the air, they are very impressive birds—hard to mistake for anything else because of their size and body profile.

Appearance

Although a male turkey's body feathers are bronzelike in color, the tips are black. This gives the male a shiny, almost jet-black appearance when seen on the ground. The head varies in color between red and white during the breeding season, but a gobbler almost always has a distinctive white cap on the very top of his head. Especially when seen from the side, a male's beard, composed of long threadlike feathers, is a distinguishing feature. The male also has prominent spurs on his legs, which on an adult may be over an inch long.

Hens are darker brown in color and have a duller appearance than males. A hen's head appears blue or brown. Unlike gobblers, hens do not have spurs.

Turkeys are perhaps the most vocal of all our upland game birds and certainly have the widest vocabulary. The ability to imitate as many of these sounds as possible and know when and where to do so is one of the keys to successful turkey hunting.

Flock or Covey Habits

Other than springtime, when males separate to establish breeding territories, turkeys spend most of their time in flocks. After hatching her young, the hen and poults stay together throughout the summer. Jakes begin striking out on their own in the fall. In winter, turkeys once again flock, establishing themselves near food and the best cover available.

Reproduction and Life Span

Depending on the arrival of true spring weather, mating season can start as early as the beginning of April and can last through most of May. Turkeys are polygamous,

Turkeys can often be found roosting in trees.

and a dominant gobbler attracts numerous hens to his harem, fighting to keep all other male rivals away.

The hen makes her nest in the woods, a depression in the ground lined with leaves and well concealed by bushes, branches, or logs. An average clutch is about 12 eggs, although a hen may lay up to 20 eggs, and the incubation period is about four weeks.

Poults are able to fend for themselves almost immediately, although they cannot fly until they are about two weeks old. Like most ground-nesting game birds, turkey hatchlings are extremely vulnerable to predators and inclement weather. Long periods of cold and rain are particularly lethal to poults right after hatching. Although turkeys can live for up to 10 years or more, a bird that survives half that long in the wild is quite rare.

Feeding Habits and Patterns

Throughout much of its range, the turkey's major source of food is mast, such as acorns and nuts gathered from the timberlands in which the turkey spends most of its time. Turkeys are extremely adaptable when it comes to food, and in Minnesota, they have readily adapted to grain fields, especially corn fields, which are almost always located quite close to wooded habitat. Even in the heavy snowbelt in and

Diligent spring turkey hunting can bring rewards such as this.

around St. Cloud, Minnesota, turkeys have done very well as long as standing corn is available to them.

Turkeys tend to feed shortly after sunup, loaf and dust during the middle of the day, and feed again an hour or two before roosting.

Preferred Habitat and Cover

Minnesota's mature southeast timber tracts were home to the first introduction of turkeys. Since then, the birds have spread west and as far north as Little Falls, Minnesota, near the center of the state. Minnesota DNR officials feel that as long as the birds have access to lots of standing corn during periods of deep snow, they'll do well. Eastern wild turkeys prefer relatively open, mature timber as opposed to newer regrowth.

Locating Hunting Areas

Minnesota's fall and spring turkey seasons are governed by a license lottery, specific permit areas, and quotas. Because of these restrictions, we recommend that those entering the lottery attend the DNR's turkey hunting workshops. Once you know your permit area, get in contact with the wildlife office for that area—their representatives are quite enthusiastic about the turkey program's success and have helpful information to offer. Since you may need permission to hunt on private land, the advice you get from area offices can be very beneficial.

Looking for Sign

Since turkeys move around a great deal, their presence is usually easy to find. Turkey droppings are much larger than other birds, and male droppings are hooked on one end. Turkeys do a lot of ground scratching, similar to squirrels, but covering a larger area. Turkey tracks are much larger than other birds and are rather easy to find in damp, wet conditions or during periods in which snow covers the ground.

Hunting Methods

Prospective wild turkey hunters must send license applications to the DNR License Bureau in St. Paul, Minnesota. There is a nonrefundable fee of $3 per applicant. Licenses for the fall and spring turkey hunts are awarded in separate, computerized preference drawings. A small game license is not required to hunt turkeys. Preferences are separate for each drawing, that is, your success in a fall drawing will have no effect on your preference standing in a spring drawing. All successful applicants must purchase a turkey hunting license as well as a wild turkey stamp to hunt wild turkeys in Minnesota. The proceeds of the stamp, requested by turkey hunters, are dedicated to wild turkey management and research.

The spring hunt bag limit is one wild turkey with a visible beard (the feathered appendage protruding from the breast that is generally found only on males). The fall hunt bag limit is one wild turkey of either sex.

In spring, a well-camouflaged hunter tries to attract a courting male by imitating a hen turkey. In the fall, when all turkeys are legal game, the object is to scatter a flock and then sit down, waiting for them to reassemble. Calling is often unnecessary.

Table Preparations

Wild turkey meat is delicious and far superior to its domestic kin. For something different, filet the deboned breast into strips, marinate, and grill quickly. If you're dealing with a big old tom, you may want to put the wings and legs into a crock pot and let it cook all day.

Gun, Shot, and Choke Suggestions

Turkey hunting is best done with a 12-gauge shotgun choked full or extra full, using 1½ ounces of copper-plated No. 5 shot. In Minnesota, one cannot use shot larger than No. 4.

Common Snipe

Gallinago gallinago

Appearance

Snipe are closely related to woodcock and are often confused with the latter. However, snipe are not as stocky, and the bird has more gray than a woodcock, which is tan. The head is boldly striped over the crown, and the small rusty tail contrasts with the rest of the gray-brown-white body. Its bill and legs are long, and like the woodcock, females are slightly larger.

Daily Habits and Food

Snipe are crepuscular, flying near dawn and dusk to feed, and are associated with wetland habitat, making them a nice addition to a day spent waterfowling. Snipe eat marsh insects and invertebrates almost exclusively, using their long, pointed bills to probe through the soft earth and mud near potholes and marshlands. Snipe begin their migration when the weather turns cold.

Seasonal Patterns

Snipe usually arrive in Minnesota after the ground is soft enough for them to feed. Males precede females by 10 to 15 days and quickly establish territories. Upon the female's arrival at the breeding grounds, males perform an aerial courtship display that is quite dazzling. Although these flights may occur at any time of the day, they usually take place at dusk and on moonlit nights.

The snipe nest begins as a simple scrape, but layers are added as egglaying progresses. The clutch consists of 4 heavily blotched, buff eggs. Young common snipe develop and grow rapidly. At three weeks, chicks can be as heavy as molting adults.

Snipe probe moist soil or mud for earthworms, insect larvae, snails, and other animal foods.

Young-of-the-year common snipe begin gathering in flocks in late July, building to large numbers by mid-August. Snipe start their southward migration when the ground becomes too hard for them to probe for food.

Habitat
Common snipe use a wide variety of shallow wetlands, including those that lack standing water or are temporary. Shallow wetlands are the primary habitat during breeding, wintering, and migration. If your feet are wet, you will more than likely be in good snipe habitat.

Locating Hunting Areas
Though common snipe can be found in most wetland areas, conversations with wildlife managers indicate that the far north central or far northwest parts of Minnesota hold the most birds. Minnesota is one of the leading northern states in number of common snipe bagged, but there is very little other information available about these birds. Again, contact area wildlife offices for up-to-date information.

Hunting Methods
A great way to start off the hunting season in Minnesota is to walk after snipe through marshes, around the edges of potholes, or through a damp field that has collected some water. Minnesota's snipe and rail season opens in September, the earliest of the fall hunting seasons. While pointing dogs are not much use, flushing dogs are the ticket when snipe hunting. Snipe hunting will get a flushing dog in shape for the season. The cover will be damp and moist, the dog will stay cooler, and you can get some fine shooting.

Remember—you can't use lead shot when hunting snipe. Only nontoxic loads can be used, such as steel, bismuth, tungsten-iron, or tungsten-polymer.

Table Preparations
Even though there is not a lot of meat on them, if you like woodcock, you'll like snipe—there is almost exactly the same amount of breast meat, and the taste is almost identical. Follow any recipe for woodcock or dark meat, and snipe will be delicious.

Gun, Shot and Choke Suggestions
- **Gauge:** 28, 20 16, or 12
- **Shot:** A light field load of 1 to 1⅛ oz. of No. 7 steel or bismuth is the ideal load. Tungsten is also legal, though it may be hard to find in light loads and small shot.
- **Choke:** Improved and modified for doubles, or modified for single barrels.

Sora Rail
Porzana carolina

Appearance
Soras are the most abundant and widely distributed of North American rail. They are small, plump, grayish-brown rails with a stubby yellow bill, black mask on the face and throat, and greenish legs. Sora vocalizations include a high-pitched, descending "whinny," a whistled "kerwee," and a variety of short, sharp, "keek" calls when startled.

Virginia Rail
Rallus limicola

Appearance
Virginia rails are small, reddish-colored birds with gray cheeks and a long, slightly decurved bill. Its wings are rich chestnut, the legs and bill are reddish, and its flanks are banded black and white.

General Observations
The Sora and Virginia rails, the two rail species common to Minnesota, are small, secretive birds that live along the shoreline of wetlands. They are most common in cattail marshes and emerging vegetation in shallow water. Although these solitary birds do not concentrate in large number in any one area, the southwestern part of Minnesota is the best region to look for them. Prairie potholes with shallow areas are the best, followed by river bottoms.

Rail season opens September 1, and the best time to hunt them is early in the season as they are early migrators. Although shooting a rail in flight is not all that difficult, finding them can be. It's best to put on hip boots and walk in shallow water to flush them out as you would a pheasant. Rails fly like bees and are not much of a challenge to shoot. Use light loads, a small gauge, and a wide-open choke, because these birds will be close when you shoot them. Nontoxic shot must be used when hunting rails. While there isn't much meat on a rail, the meat is tasty.

Waterfowl

THE DABBLERS

General Characteristics

Dabblers or puddle ducks are a common sight in many areas of Minnesota. They are found in roadside ditches, small farm ponds, flooded fields, rivers and streams, as well as the large refuge marshes. They utilize shallow water, usually no deeper than 5 to 6 feet deep, and feed by tipping up and harvesting aquatic plants and insects. Because of their well-centered legs they are able to walk well and are efficient at feeding in picked-over grain fields. Males are brilliantly colored and their wing color patterns are a major identification tool. Hens, on the other hand, are drab and inconspicuous in comparison. They are strong fliers.

Species and Identification

Mallard *(Anas platyrhynchos platyrhynchos)*
- **Other Common Names:** Greenhead (drake); susie (hen)
- **Males:** Metallic green neck and head and a bright yellow bill with a black nail. Males show a conspicuous white neck-ring that transforms into a solid chestnut-brown breast. The sides and belly are pearl gray, while the back and rump coverts are metallic black, and tailfeathers are white. These birds are large with orange legs and feet.
- **Females:** Mottled brown head and neck, dark cap and accent line across eye, and a mottled orange bill with a dark nail. Hens are mottled brown overall.

A pair of mallards.

Pair of black ducks.

Black Duck *(Anas rubripes)*
- **Other Common Names:** Black mallard, red leg
- **Males:** Medium-brown neck and head, dark cap and accent line across eye, and bright yellow bill with a dark nail. Male black ducks are a mottled, burnt-cork brown overall. Their brown base color is a rich chocolate hue. These birds are large and have coral-colored legs. They are frequently found in flocks of mallards.
- **Females:** Medium-brown neck and head, dark cap and accent line across eye, and mottled olive-green bill with a dark nail. Hens are similar to males.

Wood Duck *(Aix sponsa)*
- **Other Common Names:** Woodie, squealer
- **Males:** Metallic blue and green neck, crested head, white throat with two white, curved bars that run behind the eye and at the back of the head crest. The bill is bright yellow, red, white, and black with a black nail. The breast is chestnut brown and decorated with tiny white triangles, and its belly is white. A metallic, plum-colored zone separates the side coverts from the tail. The rump coverts and tail are metallic black. Birds are medium-sized with yellow legs and feet and red eyes.
- **Females:** Gray neck and crested head, dark cap, white throat, pronounced white eye patch, and dark bill with dark nail. Bodies are mottled brown overall, belly feathers are white, legs and feet are yellow, and eyes are brown.

Pair of wood ducks.

Northern Pintail *(Anas acuta acuta)*
- **Other Common Names:** Sprig, sprigtail
- **Males:** Solid brown head with long white neck. When viewed from the right angle, an iridescent purple sheen is visible on the side of the head behind the eye. The bill is solid black with a powder blue accent running the length of the sides. Male pintails are medium-gray overall with an intricate black vermiculation that covers the side coverts and scapular feathers. The breast and belly are white, which contrasts with the velvety-black back and rump coverts. The long, pin-shaped tailfeathers are black. These are large birds with gray legs and feet. Their eyes are brown.
- **Females:** Mottled brown head and neck, bill is mottled blue-gray with a dark nail. Hens are mottled brown overall with dark back coverts fading to white belly feathers. They have gray legs and feet.

Blue-winged Teal *(Anas discors)*
- **Other Common Names:** Bluewing, summer teal
- **Males:** Solid blue head and neck with a pronounced white crescent on the side of the face in front of the eye. Its crown blends to black, and its bill is solid black. Male blue-winged teal are buff-colored overall, with an intricate field of black polka dots that cover the breast, side coverts, and belly feathers. The back and rump coverts are black with slightly visible mustard chevrons. The dark tailfeathers are also highlighted with mustard. These birds are small and have yellow legs and feet. In flight, one of the male's most distinguishing features is the large gray-blue patch on the wing.
- **Females:** Mottled brown neck and head, dark cap and accent line across eye, white throat, and mottled blue-gray bill with a dark nail. Hens are mottled brown overall with yellow legs and feet.

A beautiful collection of pintail ducks.

Green-winged Teal *(Anas crecca carolinensis)*
- **Other Common Names:** Greenwing, common teal
- **Males:** Brown neck and head, head crests in a brown crown, a solid metallic green zone extends from around the eyes to blend into a well-developed black mane on the back of the neck, and black bill. The breast is cream-colored and accented with small black polka dots. A white chevron comes off the shoulder and separates the breast and side coverts. The tail feathers are medium-gray and separated from the side coverts by a triangular zone of mustard-tinged, buff-colored feathers. The belly is white. These birds are very small with gray legs and feet.
- **Females:** Mottled brown head and neck, dark cap and accent line across eye, and a mottled blue-gray bill with black speckles and a dark nail. Hens are mottled brown with darker back coverts fading to white belly feathers. They have gray legs and feet.

American Wigeon *(Anas americana)*
- **Other Common Names:** Baldpate, gray duck
- **Males:** Light cream neck and head heavily flecked with black; crown of head is solid white; an extensive metallic green zone extends from the back of the eye to blend at the base of the neck; and a powder blue bill with a black nail and highlights. The breast and side coverts are light plum and etched with fine black vermiculation. The back and upper rump coverts are patterned in gray and white. The pin-shaped tailfeathers and its surrounding coverts are black, and the belly is white. These birds are medium-sized and have gray legs and feet.
- **Females:** Light cream neck and head lightly flecked with black, and a powder blue bill with a black nail and highlights. The breast and side coverts are light

Blue-winged teal stretching a wing.

plum. Scapular feathers, and back and upper rump coverts are mottled in plum and olive-gray, and the belly is white. These birds have gray legs and feet.

Northern Shoveler *(Anas clypeata)*
- **Other Common Names:** Shoveler, spoonbill
- **Males:** Metallic green neck and head with a solid black bill that is spoon-shaped. Male shoveler has white breast and scapular feathers. Side coverts and belly are chestnut-brown. Back and rump coverts are metallic black, and tailfeathers are white. These birds are medium-sized and have orange legs and feet.
- **Females:** Mottled brown neck and head, dark cap and accent line across eye, mottled olive green and orange bill with a dark nail. Hens are mottled brown overall with darker back coverts and lighter belly feathers. They have orange legs and feet.

Gadwall *(Anas strepera)*
- **Other Common Names:** Gray duck, gray mallard
- **Males:** Mottled gray neck and crested head with light gray cheeks, dark highlight across the eye, and solid black bill. Male gadwall are a medium-gray overall with an intricate black vermiculation that covers the breast, side coverts, and scapular feathers. Scapulars are pointed and highlighted with a muted orange, and the belly is white. Back and rump coverts are a deep velvety black, and tailfeathers are gray. These birds are large with orange legs and feet.

Female shoveler.

- **Females:** Mottled brown neck and head, dark cap and accent line across eye, and mottled orange bill with a dark nail. Hens are mottled brown with darker back coverts fading to a white belly. They have orange legs and feet.

Habits and Habitat

At first light, puddle ducks leave their nighttime roosting areas to seek food. These feeding flights can last until midmorning, depending on flock size and weather. During midday, birds return to marshes and other bodies of water to loaf and rest. They fly out again during the late afternoon or at dusk to feed, returning at dark to their roosting areas.

In Minnesota, dabblers can be found tucked into small beaver ponds and streams in the heart of the state's forest region or their more conventional habitats—potholes and prairie marshes. Because of the significant topographical changes that occur across the state, it is advisable to contact the Department of Natural Resources' area wildlife manager for the region in which you hope to hunt ducks. In addition, owing to Minnesota's geographical location and waterfowl hunting season timetables, early migrating dabblers (teal and wood ducks) may have already left the state.

Hunting the Dabblers

Hunting waterfowl is an American tradition, and the various methods that have evolved are as broad and diverse as the continent is big. Pass shooting, decoying, floating, and jump shooting are some of the ways to hunt dabblers in Minnesota.

Pass shooting is the simplest type of duck shooting and requires the least amount of equipment. A shotgun, nontoxic shells, camouflage clothing that is adequate for the weather, and something to carry the downed birds would meet a pass shooter's needs.

Birds follow certain watercourses and familiar flight lanes year after year. Weather is a key factor in when and how high the ducks will be flying. Once a prime hunting spot has been located, a well-hidden hunter can return repeatedly to the same place and take birds.

A more traditional form of waterfowl hunting involves decoying ducks into shotgun range. Today's modern plastic decoys are a wonder of species mimicry. Decoy spreads can range from a few decoys tossed onto a small beaver pond to an elaborate field spread of 50 to 100 decoys. Again, hunter concealment is of utmost importance. After placing decoys in the ducks' preferred area, make sure that you're concealed well enough that wary ducks won't flair from your decoy spread.

Minnesota's extensive number of rivers and streams makes floating for ducks a viable choice. Floating a small stream in a canoe or small johnboat can make for some exciting moments when rounding a bend and coming upon a flock of unsuspecting ducks.

Last, but not least, there's jump shooting. Whether walking a small stream or stalking a beaver pond tucked deep in the woods, there is a real adrenaline rush as ducks climb for altitude as you make your presence known.

If you take the time and make an effort to practice, using a duck call can mean the difference between success and failure. Being able to flush a flock of unsuspecting ducks without shooting, wait in hiding, and then successfully call the returning ducks back within shotgun range makes all the practice worthwhile.

Table Preparation

Dabblers primarily eat plant matter and make excellent table fare. Whether skinned, breasted out, or plucked, take care not to overcook this dark meat. If you are concerned about *Salmonella*, remember—these are wild, not domestic, birds.

Gun and Shot Suggestions
- **Gauge:** 12, 10.
- **Choke:** Improved cylinder/modified for double guns, modified for single barrels.
- **Shot:** Nontoxic loads must be used when hunting waterfowl. BB, No. 2 or No. 4 shot will handle all conditions. Nontoxic shot includes: steel and tungsten-iron for guns built for steel shot, as well as bismuth and tungsten-polymer for older guns that cannot shoot steel shot.

THE DIVERS

General Characteristics

Because diving ducks have evolved for life on open water, their bodies are shorter and more streamlined than those of puddle ducks. Their legs are set back to facilitate swimming, but this makes walking more difficult for diving ducks. As their name indicates, these duck dive, sometimes to great depths, to get their food. They feed on aquatic plants and animals, small fish, and insects. Diving ducks have to run on the water surface to get up speed for flight.

Male diving ducks are colored in solid patterns of gray and black or white and black. Unlike the dabblers, wings of divers hold no color. Depending on the species, the head color can be red, purple, or green. A diving duck's profile on the water shows a low tail at or near the waterline, contrasting to the high tail of dabblers, making them easily recognizable even from great distances.

Species and Identification

Ring-necked Duck *(Aythya collaris)*
- **Other Common Names:** Ring-billed duck, ringbill
- **Males:** Solid dark neck and crested head appearing black at a distance and metallic purple in hand. Bill is medium blue-gray with a white band and black tip and nail. The male ringneck's breast, back, and rump are black. Its side coverts are white at the shoulders, fading to a silver gray. These birds are medium-sized and have large paddle feet. Their eyes are orange-yellow.
- **Females:** Solid brown neck and crested head with a slight white crescent behind the bill and a white ring around the eye. Bill is mottled in medium blue-gray with a white band and a dark nail. Hens are mottled brown overall, with light brown side coverts and bellies. They have large gray paddle feet and brown eyes.

Lesser Scaup *(Aythya affinis)*
- **Other Common Names:** Bluebill
- **Males:** Solid dark neck and crested head appearing black at a distance and metallic purple in hand. Bill is blue-gray with a black nail. Its breast and upper rump coverts are black, while the side coverts are white. The bird's scapulars are also white but etched with unbroken black vermiculation. These birds are medium-sized with large gray paddle feet and yellow eyes.
- **Females:** Solid brown neck and crested head with a white crescent in front of the eye. Bill is mottled in medium blue-gray with a black nail. The hens are mottled brown overall, with some white showing on the side coverts and belly. The birds have large gray paddle feet and yellow eyes.

Redhead *(Aythya americana)*
- **Other Common Names:** Pochard
- **Males:** Solid red neck and head with a blue-gray bill that has a black tip and nail. Male redheads are a silver-gray color overall, with some dark feathers highlighting

Lesser scaup drake.

their rump coverts. These birds are large and have large gray paddle feet. Their eyes are orange-yellow.

- **Females:** Soft brown neck and head darkening to a medium-brown crown. The bill is blue-gray with a black bill tip and nail. The hen's side coverts are the same brown as her neck and head. The back and upper rump coverts are a darker olive hue. These are large birds with large gray paddle feet and brown eyes.

Bufflehead *(Bucephala albeola)*
- **Other Common Names:** Butterball
- **Males:** Solid-colored dark neck and large crested head appearing black at a distance and metallic blue-green in hand. These birds have a white zone that quarters in a pie-shaped wedge, with the point originating at the eye and expanding to the back of the head. Bill is blue-gray with a dark tip and nail. The male bufflehead has a white breast and side coverts. Delicate black lines etch the outer edges of the bird's side coverts. Its belly consists of shades from white to gray. They are small, have large pink paddle feet, and dark brown eyes.
- **Females:** Gray neck and crested head with a white crescent behind the eye. Bill is mottled in light to medium blue-gray. Hens are mottled gray overall, with a light colored breast and light gray side coverts and belly. These birds are small, have gray paddle feet, and brown eyes.

Bufflehead drake.

Goldeneye *(Bucephala clangula americana)*
- **Other Common Names:** Whistler
- **Males:** Solid metallic green neck and crested head with a white spot in front of the eye and a solid black bill. Goldeneyes have a triangular head shape and a short, thick neck. The bird's breast, belly, and side coverts are a brilliant white with delicate black striping showing at the top of the side coverts. The back, rump, and tail coverts are black. These birds are large and have orange legs and feet. Their eyes are yellow.
- **Females:** Medium brown neck and crested head. Bill is dark blue-gray with a black nail. The hen's side coverts are mottled gray and white, with the belly turning to solid white. The back and upper rump coverts are mottled gray with light gray highlights. These are large birds, having orange legs and feet and yellow eyes.

Canvasback *(Aythya valisineria)*
- **Other Common Names:** Can
- **Males:** Solid red neck and head with a black bill. Canvasbacks have a triangular head shape and thick long neck. This bird's back and side coverts are pearl white in a mature male and light gray in an immature bird of the year. Rump coverts are black and the short tailfeathers are colored silver-gray. Canvasbacks are large and have large gray paddle feet. Their eyes are red.
- **Females:** Soft brown neck and head fading to light brown on the cheeks, with a black bill. A female canvasback is a soft mottled brown overall, with highlights of

Goldeneye drake.

pearl gray on the bird's back and side coverts. These birds are large and have large gray paddle feet. Their eyes are brown.

Hooded Merganser *(Mergus cucullatus)*
- **Other Common Names:** Sawbill, fish duck
- **Males:** Solid black neck and crested head with a white crescent radiating from the eye to the back of the crest, and a solid black merganser sawbill. Hooded mergansers have a pronounced triangular head shape and a short, thick neck. The bird's belly and breast are a brilliant white. Heavy black striping accents the transition to the bird's light sienna side coverts. The back, rump, and tail coverts are black. These birds are small and have yellow legs and feet. Their eyes are yellow.
- **Females:** Rather drab with russet-brown heads and crests that are considerably smaller than those of the males. The back is a dusky brown and the breasts and side coverts are gray. They have yellow legs and feet as well as yellow eyes.

Greater Scaup *(Aythya marila mariloides)*
- **Other Common Names:** Broadbill, bluebill
- **Males:** Solid dark neck and crested head appearing black at a distance and metallic green in hand. Bill is blue-gray with a black nail that is broader than that of the lesser scaup. The male has a black breast and upper rump coverts. Its side coverts are whiter than those of the lesser scaup. These are large birds with large gray paddle feet and yellow eyes.

Canvasback drake.

- **Females:** Solid brown neck and crested head with a white crescent in front of the eye. The hens are mottled brown overall, with some white showing on the side coverts and belly. These are large birds with large gray feet and legs. Their eyes are yellow.

Ruddy Duck *(Oxyura jamaicensis rubida)*
- **Other Common Names:** Butterball
- **Males:** Mottled gray neck, crested head with black crown and white cheeks. Bill is blue-gray with a dark nail. The male has a mottled olive-brown breast, back, and rump. The belly and underside of the rump is light olive-gray. Ruddys are classified as stiff-tailed ducks because of their straight, erect, feathered tails. These birds are small-sized and have large gray paddle feet. Their eyes are brown.
- **Females:** Mottled olive-brown neck and crested head with dark crown and slight white feather highlights on the cheek. Bill is mottled olive-brown with a dark nail. The female has a mottled olive-brown breast, back, and rump. The birds are small-sized with large gray paddle feet and brown eyes.

Habits and Habitat

Diving ducks are birds of open, deep-water impoundments. They raft on open water for the protection it offers and to dive for food. Divers tend to congregate in large flocks, and the groups of ducks observed loafing midday in big rafts on big water are generally made up of diving duck species.

Hunting the Divers

In the big waters of Minnesota—large lakes, rivers, and impoundments—divers can be hunted in the traditional ways developed in the East—from layout boats or over large, diving duck decoy setups. Many times, divers can be taken while hunting puddle ducks. If you find diving ducks buzzing your puddle duck decoy setup, try adding a half dozen to dozen diver decoys (canvasback, redhead, or scaup) to your puddle duck spread. Pass shooting diving ducks is another exciting method to take these fast flying bullets. If you decide to try hunting specifically for diving ducks, find out what method the "locals" are using to save time and perhaps increase your success.

Table Preparations

Of all the diving ducks, canvasbacks, followed by redheads and ringnecks, make for the best table fare. That's because these ducks feed primarily on aquatic plants. Goldeneyes, ruddy ducks, buffleheads, and mergansers eat a high percentage of animal matter that can adversely affect the flavor of the meat. When cleaning diving ducks take notice of the degree of fish odor the meat carries. If the odor is strong, it's best to marinate the meat before preparing it. As with puddle ducks, you are dealing with wild birds, so don't overcook them.

Gun and Shot Suggestions

- **Gauge:** 12, 10
- **Choke:** Improved cylinder/ modified for double guns, modified for single barrels.
- **Shot:** Nontoxic waterfowl loads of BB, No. 2 or No. 4 shot. Nontoxic shot now includes steel and tungsten-iron for guns that can shoot steel as well as bismuth, and tungsten-polymer for older guns that cannot handle steel shot. Try to pattern your gun with the waterfowl loads you plan to use to get the best gun/choke/load combination.

The Geese

General Characteristics

All goose species are very gregarious and concentrate on their staging and wintering areas in large numbers. Geese are voracious eaters in agricultural fields and seldom eat alone. They are often drawn to fields where birds are already on the ground and feeding. These birds are very vocal and are often heard before they are seen. While feeding on the ground or loafing on the water, there will always be a few birds (sentinels), with their heads erect, on the lookout for danger. Geese feed into the wind so that they can take off quickly if danger approaches.

Flocks are made up of family groups that are more distinct early in the season, with one bird in the flock, the oldest and wisest, ever alert to danger. This is usually the bird seen at the head or front of their flying "V" formations. Unlike ducks, which require ever-diminishing wetlands to provide for their nutritional needs, geese have adapted to using cultivated fields and urban green space (especially golf courses) for a practically unlimited food source.

Geese do not require water to feed, however, they do need undisturbed areas in which to loaf at midday and roost at night. A critical habitat requirement is either a refuge area that geese can retire to and remain unmolested or large pieces of open water where they can raft in the middle, away from repeated disturbance.

Species and Identification

Lesser Snow Goose *(Anser c. caerulescens)*
- **Other Common Names:** Blue goose, brant
- **Males and Females (white phase):** Completely white except for black wingtips. The feet and legs are rosy red, and the bill is pink with a black "grinning patch." Immature birds are a little grayer with grayish brown bill, legs, and feet.
- **Males and Females (blue phase):** Birds have white heads and white upper necks with slate-gray bodies. They have whitish tail coverts and varying amounts of white on their bellies. The bills are pink with black "grinning patches." The feet and legs are rose-red.

Ross' Goose *(Anser rossii)*
- **Other Common Names:** Little wavie
- **Males and Females:** Small white goose with black wingtips. They are much smaller than a snow goose and have a shorter neck. The bill is pink with a white nail, and its legs and feet are pink. Their call is pitched more highly than that of the snow goose, and their wingbeat is more rapid.

White-Fronted Goose *(Anser albifrons frontalis)*
- **Other Common Names:** Specklebelly, specklebelly brant, speck
- **Males and Females:** Neck and head are solid olive-brown, with the exception of a white highlight on the front of the bird's cheek and forehead; the bill is reddish-

Snow geese aren't abundant in Minnesota, but there are some to be found along the flyways in the western part of the state.

pink with a white nail. The body is primarily olive-brown with the breast a lighter hue. The belly blends to white with black accent bars interspersed across the breasts. The legs and feet are orange.

Canada Goose *(Branta canadensis)*
- **Other Common Names:** Honker, Canada
- **Males and Females:** Black bill, legs, and feet; black head and neck with a white cheek patch that usually covers the throat; gray-brown to dark brown back and wings; sides and breast a mouse gray to brown; white belly, flank, and under tail coverts; and black tail and rump separated by a white V-bar. There are 11 subspecies of the Canada goose. In 1962, the giant Canada goose (Branta canadensis maxima), which was believed to be extinct, was rediscovered during a goose banding operation in Rochester, Minnesota. Since that time, state wildlife biologists and conservation groups have succeeded in reintroducing this subspecies to its former habitats.

Habits and Habitat

While the loss of wetlands has not boded well for duck populations, the ability of geese to feed on cultivated grains has led to such significant increases in some of

These Canada geese are using the skiing method for landing.

their numbers that some species have reached a nuisance level in many areas, municipalities, and even some states. Because geese use a mixture of habitats, their numbers grow at unbelievable rates.

Geese do require water in the form of large open water as well as marshy roosting and loafing sites. Geese leave these roosting sites to feed in nearby fields. Later in the morning, they head back to these water refuges to rest and loaf. Again in late afternoon, they head out to feed, returning to their roosting areas after dark. In the past decade, more and more Canada geese are cutting their southward migration short and remaining further and further north from their traditional wintering grounds.

Hunting Geese

Until recently, goose hunting was strictly a cold climate endeavor, requiring an inordinate amount of gear and decoys. Now, Minnesota has an early goose season in September. In fact it can be too hot for a successful outing! Minnesota now leads the nation in the number of Canada geese harvested each year. In fact, the number of Canada geese taken by goose hunters in Minnesota is second only to the number of mallard ducks taken by duck hunters in Minnesota.

Canada goose numbers have grown significantly, even in and around metropolitan areas such as the Twin Cities. These geese are at home on this river backwater just a few miles north of St. Paul.

Other than refuges, federal waterfowl production areas (WPA), and state wildlife management areas (WMA), most of Minnesota's goose hunting takes place on private land. Areas with nuisance goose problems are increasing at such a rate that wildlife managers can't keep up with them, given the constraints of the U.S. Fish and Wildlife Service.

A nonresident or nonlocal goose hunter has several options for finding a private place to hunt geese. After determining an area to hunt, contact the Minnesota DNR area wildlife manager who oversees that area. He or she may be able to put you in touch with farmers who have nuisance geese. Contacting area grain elevators can be another source of pertinent information. Finally, visit restaurants frequented by local farmers to secure hunting site information.

A considerable investment in time and gear is a reality of goose hunting. Yet, year after year, goose hunters refuse to try out the new waterfowl loads that have been developed. They are expensive, but if they allow you to cleanly kill your birds and reduce cripples, that should be sufficient incentive. Today's waterfowler has a choice of premium steel, tungsten-iron, bismuth, and tungsten-polymer shot shells.

Take the time (and money) to pattern some of these loads in your gun to arrive at the best gun/choke/ load combination to kill waterfowl cleanly.

This past fall I had a chance to use tungsten-iron shot on Canada geese. I was shooting in close proximity to two hunting companions who were using steel shot. Of the three of us, I would consider myself the poorest shooter. Yet, time and again, the tungsten-iron shot dropped geese that a combination of the other two hunters hit but couldn't kill! Based on that day's shooting, I have become a tungsten-iron shot believer. Patterning your shotgun to arrive at the best load / gun/ choke combination should be a part of your trip planning process.

Canada goose at 75 yards— too far

Canada goose at 45 yards— barely within range

Canada goose at 30 yards— within range

Reduce Crippling

Use the chart showing the size of geese at certain ranges to estimate the effective shooting range for geese. Make a copy of the chart, tape it to a wall, and then place your shotgun muzzle against the goose drawings as shown below. The goose will appear about the same size as would a real goose at the distances indicated.

If more than half the goose is hidden by the barrel muzzle, then the goose is beyond 50 yards and is too far away for a clean shot.

Table Preparations

Geese have dark meat and a large, flat breast. If you shoot a fair number of geese and freezer space is a concern, filet the breast meat and freeze in compact packages. Deboned, these breast fillets are delicious when barbecued on a hot grill with olive oil and your favorite spice mix. Just don't overcook the meat. You can smoke the breasts and enjoy at your leisure.

If taking home just a few birds, you might choose to pluck the birds while they are still warm and then cook them whole with the skin on. Because of their low fat, be sure to baste a goose regularly while roasting.

While Canada geese are legal to hunt, be careful to distinguish them from swans, which are not legal.

Gun and Shot Selections
- **Gauge:** 10, 12
- **Choke:** Modified and improved modified for doubles, modified for single barrels.
- **Shot:** For small geese, nontoxic shot sizes in BB and BBB will suffice. For large geese or extended range, step up to BBB and T shot. If using some of the newer nontoxic loads, you will want to pattern your gun / choke combinations to arrive at the most lethal load.

GET YOUR GOOSE: TIPS AND TACTICS FOR BAGGING A HONKER

(courtesy of Minnesota Department of Natural Resources)

To bring down a Canada goose, a hunter needs to fire the right load, with the correct lead, at a bird that is within range. To improve your odds, follow these simple guidelines at home and in the field:

At Home

The right load: Although it's a big bird, a goose has a relatively small vital zone. The total area in which pellets will kill a goose is just one-tenth the bird's total size. To ensure that you hit the vital zone with enough pellets and "oomph," you need to pattern your gun and find the correct load.

To test loads, place a 40- by 40-inch-square sheet of paper at the distance you will be firing at flying geese (for most hunters and situations, that's about 30-50 yards). Fire at a point you mark on the paper. Do this at least five times, each on a new sheet. Draw a 30-inch-diameter circle around the densest pattern area on each sheet and count the pellets that hit inside the circle. This is the pattern density. Try different loads and chokes until you find one that puts enough pellets (35-55 depending on the load) into the circle, which ensures that enough will hit the goose's vital zone for a clean kill.

Most experts say the best loads for geese are sizes 1, BB, BBB, or T steel shot. For most hunting situations, BB shot is the most effective load. It has plenty of pellets and enough firepower to bring down a goose. Guns are usually 10- or 12-gauge. Because steel shoots "tighter" than lead, the best chokes for geese are modified and improved modified. However, different guns fire differently, which is why you should pattern your particular gun.

Distance: One of the biggest mistakes goose hunters make is to shoot geese that are flying out of range ("sky busting"). This can cripple birds, flare off approaching geese, and may cause approaching flocks to fly even higher.

To get a sense of how geese appear at various distances, tape a copy of the chart on page 82 to a wall and put your gun barrel up to each drawing. Do this until you can judge whether a real flying goose is 30, 45, or 75 yards away.

➤ A good rule of thumb used by goose guides is this: If the end of the barrel covers more than half the bird (more than 50 yards), it is too far away for a clean kill.

Practice: Many goose hunting experts say the best way for hunters to improve their success is to practice on clay birds before the day of the hunt. When you consider the time and money that goes into goose hunting, the cost of a few rounds of sporting clays or skeet beforehand to learn the right amount of lead is a wise investment. (Editor's note: use loads that have the same velocity as that of your waterfowl load).

➤ If the weather is cool at the range, try shooting in the clothes you'll wear in the goose blind. You might not hit as many clay targets as you would in shirt sleeves, but it's a good way to practice firing in a bulky raincoat or overalls.

In the Field

Distance: When you shoot at an approaching goose, make sure it is close enough for a clean kill. At least half the bird should show from behind the muzzle. Some hunters have the skill to occasionally drop a bird "from the stratosphere," but for most hunters, making a kill at over 60 yards is just luck.

Lead: It takes practice to find the correct lead for geese. The big birds have slow wingbeats that make them appear to be lumbering along, but actually, they're moving as fast as a mallard. Lead accordingly.

Concealment: Geese can see you more easily than you think. Any movement or the reflection off shiny objects, such as metal sunglasses and bright gun barrels, can flare a flock from 200 yards or more. Use as much camo as possible and move only when the birds aren't flying nearby.

Decoys and Calls: For pass shooting, hunters set up where geese are known to fly. The trick is to keep from moving or shooting too early and scaring off birds.

To increase your odds of bringing geese within range, learn to use a call and how to place decoys. A few well-timed calls or a properly placed decoy spread can draw geese from hundreds of yards away. Videos are especially helpful at showing hunters how to use decoys and calls.

A flock of Canadas coming in for a landing.

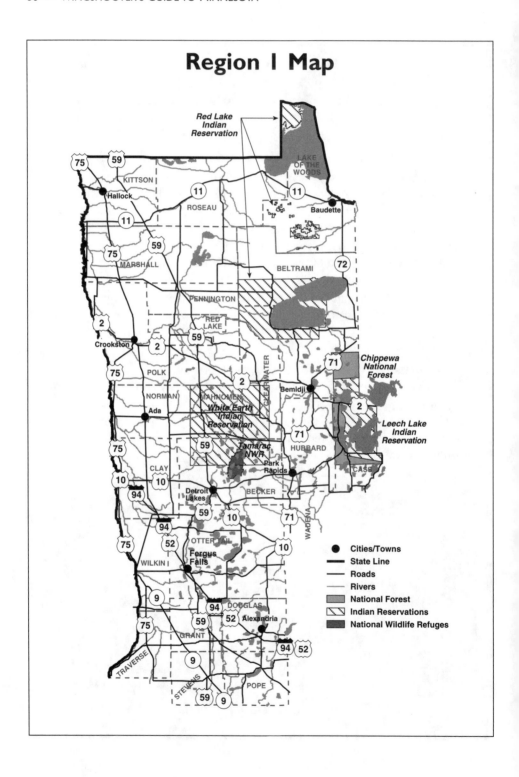

Region I Map

Red Lake Indian Reservation

LAKE OF THE WOODS

KITTSON
Hallock
ROSEAU
Baudette

MARSHALL
BELTRAMI

PENNINGTON

RED LAKE

Crookston
POLK
NORMAN
Ada

MAHNOMEN
White Earth Indian Reservation
Tamarac NWR
Park Rapids

CLEARWATER
Bemidji

Chippewa National Forest

Leech Lake Indian Reservation

HUBBARD
CASS

CLAY
Detroit Lakes
BECKER

OTTER TAIL
Fergus Falls
WILKIN

WADENA

DOUGLAS
Alexandria

GRANT

TRAVERSE

STEVENS
POPE

● Cities/Towns
— State Line
— Roads
— Rivers
National Forest
Indian Reservations
National Wildlife Refuges

Region I

This is the Red River Valley country, with grain, sugar beet, and livestock farms as far as the eye can see. The formation of Lake Agassiz during the glacial period and its eventual recession created this area's features, now consisting of the Red River and its tributaries.

The borders of this region include Canada to the north, North Dakota to the west, US 12 to the south and State Highways 71 and 72 north to Baudette. One of Minnesota's largest Indian reservations, Red Lake, straddles the counties of Beltrami, Koochiching, Lake of the Woods, and Roseau. Hunting the reservation is closed to nontribal members except by special authorization of the tribal council, which is usually not difficult to obtain.

While there is no hunting allowed within the Agassiz National Wildlife Refuge, located in Marshall County, there are areas to the south and east that are set aside for hunting. To obtain more information, call the Minnesota Department of Natural Resources' Region I office at 218-755-3958.

The region's variety of habitat makes it an ideal location to hunt migratory waterfowl, sharptail, ruffed grouse, spruce grouse, and to a lesser degree, woodcock and Huns. Because many of the state's wildlife management areas are in and around bodies of water, they are ideal spots to find a variety of game birds.

Look for ruffed grouse in wooded areas featuring aspen, alders, and poplar, and having a variety of berries that are abundant early in the season. Spruce grouse are more likely to be found in the eastern edges of this region, where there are conifer trees that provide the needles that make up their diet. Woodcock are also found to the east, where the worms they prefer live in the soft, moist soil. During dry years, they will be found closer to streams and other bodies of water. Look for them where there is little grass and where the shade from overhead cover prevents the growth of other vegetation.

Three areas that stand out for waterfowl production and hunting opportunities are Thief Lake, Red Lake, and Roseau River Wildlife Management Areas. Both waterfowl production and hunting opportunities are of great importance to the state in terms of quality habitat and usage by hunters and others who enjoy the outdoors.

Hunting and fishing licenses and fees have helped establish and maintain state and federal departments of natural resources in both the United States and Canada. In return, the monies collected find their way back to local communities. Wildlife management areas, such as Red Lake, Roseau, and Thief Lake, are prime public locations that draw hunters, fishers, and outdoor recreation enthusiasts.

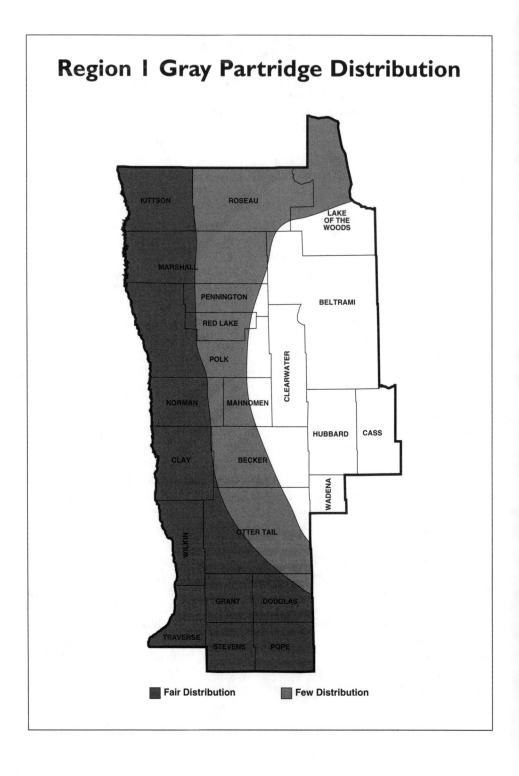

Region 1 Gray Partridge Distribution

KITTSON

ROSEAU

LAKE OF THE WOODS

MARSHALL

PENNINGTON

RED LAKE

BELTRAMI

POLK

CLEARWATER

NORMAN

MAHNOMEN

HUBBARD

CASS

CLAY

BECKER

WADENA

WILKIN

OTTER TAIL

GRANT

DOUGLAS

TRAVERSE

STEVENS

POPE

■ Fair Distribution   ▥ Few Distribution

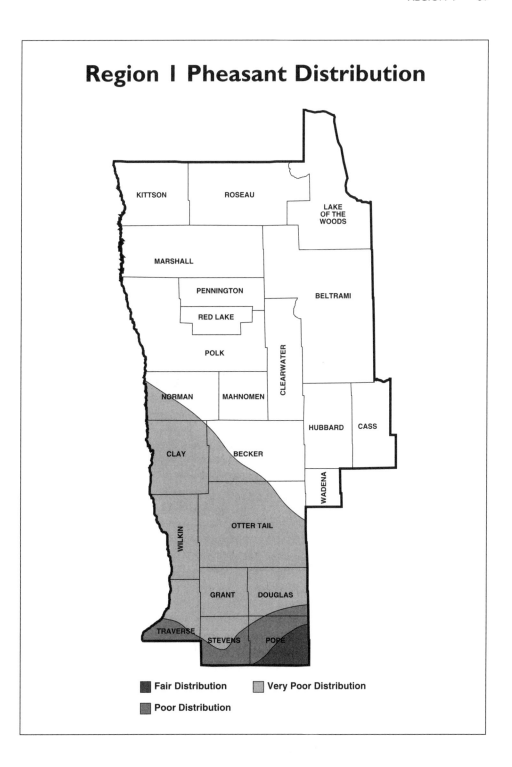

Region 1 Pheasant Distribution

KITTSON

ROSEAU

LAKE OF THE WOODS

MARSHALL

PENNINGTON

RED LAKE

BELTRAMI

POLK

CLEARWATER

NORMAN

MAHNOMEN

HUBBARD

CASS

CLAY

BECKER

WADENA

WILKIN

OTTER TAIL

GRANT

DOUGLAS

TRAVERSE

STEVENS

POPE

■ Fair Distribution ▨ Very Poor Distribution

▨ Poor Distribution

Region I Ruffed Grouse Distribution

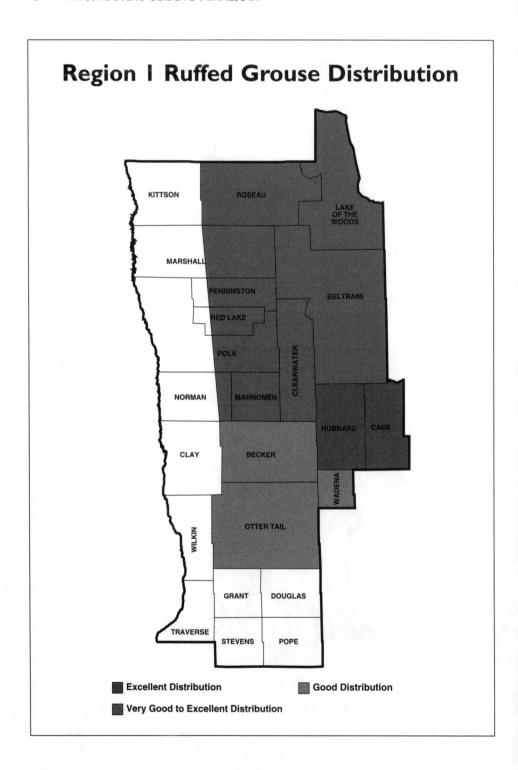

KITTSON
ROSEAU
LAKE OF THE WOODS
MARSHALL
PENNINGTON
RED LAKE
BELTRAMI
POLK
CLEARWATER
NORMAN
MAHNOMEN
HUBBARD
CASS
CLAY
BECKER
WADENA
WILKIN
OTTER TAIL
GRANT
DOUGLAS
TRAVERSE
STEVENS
POPE

Excellent Distribution   **Good Distribution**
Very Good to Excellent Distribution

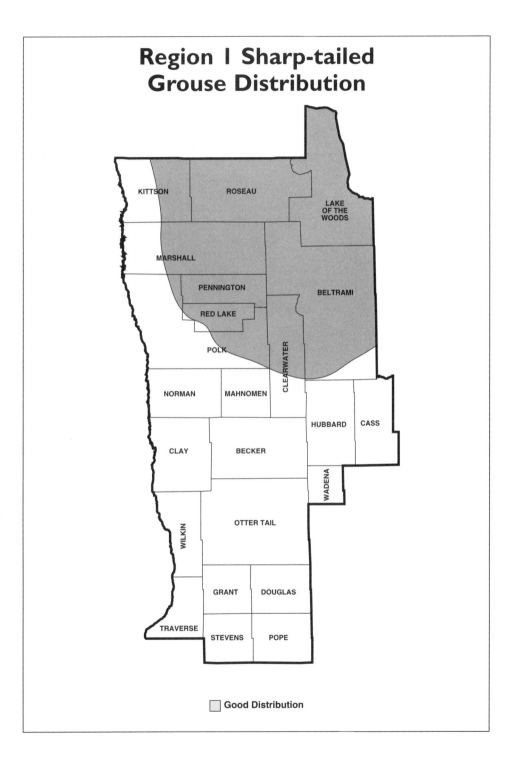

Region 1 Sharp-tailed Grouse Distribution

KITTSON

ROSEAU

LAKE OF THE WOODS

MARSHALL

PENNINGTON

RED LAKE

BELTRAMI

POLK

CLEARWATER

NORMAN

MAHNOMEN

HUBBARD

CASS

CLAY

BECKER

WADENA

WILKIN

OTTER TAIL

GRANT

DOUGLAS

TRAVERSE

STEVENS

POPE

Good Distribution

Region 1 Spruce Grouse Distribution

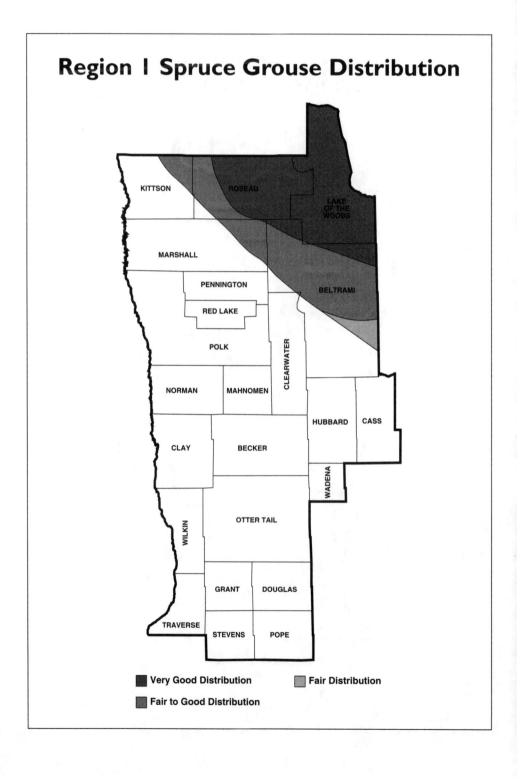

Region I Wild Turkey Distribution

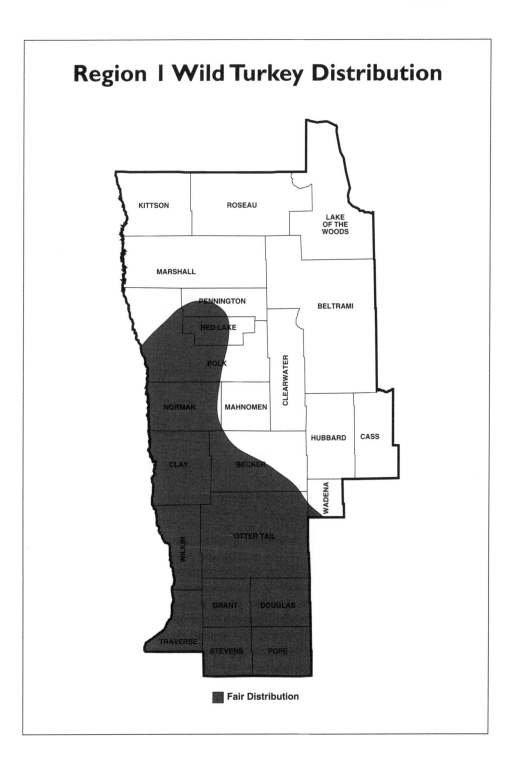

KITTSON

ROSEAU

LAKE OF THE WOODS

MARSHALL

PENNINGTON

RED LAKE

BELTRAMI

POLK

CLEARWATER

NORMAN

MAHNOMEN

HUBBARD

CASS

CLAY

BECKER

WADENA

OTTER TAIL

WILKIN

GRANT

DOUGLAS

TRAVERSE

STEVENS

POPE

■ Fair Distribution

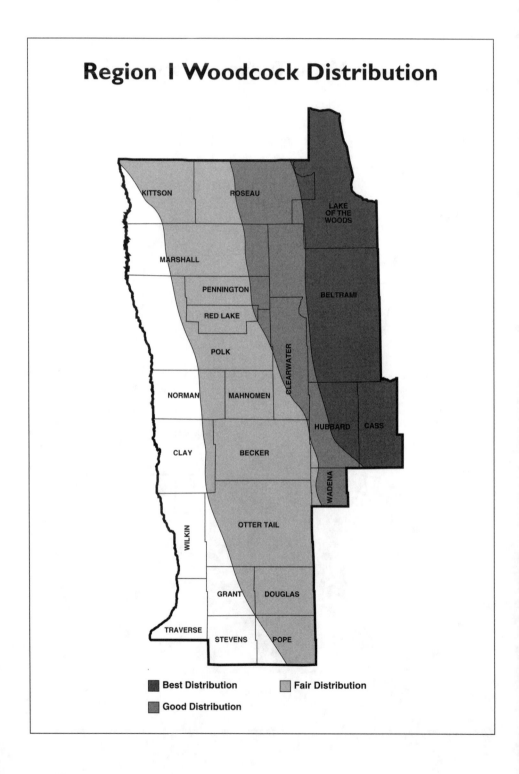

Region I Woodcock Distribution

Baudette
Roseau and Lake of the Woods Counties

County Population:	Baudette Population–1,150
Roseau–16,323	October Temperature–48°
Lake of the Woods–4,495	County Acres in CRP:
County Area:	Roseau–136,886
Roseau–1,663 sq. mi.	Lake of the Woods–4,813
Lake of the Woods–1,297 sq. mi.	WMAs–13 (15,229 acres)

Located in northwestern Minnesota on State Highway 11 just south of Lake of the Woods, Baudette is a small resort town that grew out of the fur trade of the 1800s. Today, it is host to fishermen from around the world who seek walleye, large northern pike, and muskies.

Logging and commercial fishing are the two primary industries in the area other than tourism. The rotation of forest cutting, which creates forests of varied age, aids greatly in the quality of habitat for upland game birds found in the area.

Ruffed and spruce grouse numbers are good and can be generally found in the aspen wood lots and conifer trees that grow in the area. Sharptail numbers are down, and consequently, sharptail hunter numbers have also dropped. Good woodcock numbers are found in low-lying areas, but again, there are not that many hunters seeking them. Areas similar to the Roseau River WMA are good for both rail and snipe before their migration and are hunted very little, if at all. Very little Hun activity is found in this area.

Currently, there are low numbers of mallards and blue-winged teal. Jump shooting over potholes is the best bet early in the season. Late season is the time to hunt diving ducks in shallow water. Overall, Canada geese are the area's bread and butter.

UPLAND BIRDS
Sharptail, Ruffed Grouse, Spruce Grouse, Woodcock, Hungarian Partridge, Rail, and Snipe

WATERFOWL
Ducks and Geese

ACCOMMODATIONS
Royal Dutchman Motel, Hwy 11 East / 9 units with a scenic view of the Rainy River / Color cable TV / Free in-room coffee, picnic area and kitchenettes / Close to town and good restaurants / Pets are welcome / 218-634-1024 or 800-908-1024 / $-$$

Rainy River Resort, Route 1, Box 91 / 5 cottages, 9 bedrooms / Color TV and kitchens / Golf and snowmobile trails nearby / Grouse and duck hunting guide available / Pets are welcome / 218-634-3117 / $

Northern tip of Lake of the Woods County, an aerial view showing the southern end of the great lake, patches of woods, and the flatness of that terrain.

CAMPGROUNDS AND RV PARKS

Zippel Bay Resort, HC 2, Box 51, Williams 56686 / Water, electrical hookups, showers, flush toilets, firepits, store, firewood, game room and dump station / Lodge, dining, cocktail lounge, floating deck and gazebo / Grouse and waterfowl hunting guides are available / Pets are welcome / 218-783-6235 or 800-222-2537 / $-$$

RESTAURANTS

Ranch House, Hwy 11 / Breakfast, lunch, and dinner / Open Mon–Sat, 5:30AM–10PM; Sunday at 6AM / 218-634-2420

Sheree K's Buffet and Grill, P.O. Box 977 / Lunch buffet, dinner, authentic Mexican, and burgers / 218-634-2181

VETERINARIANS

Rainy River Vet Hospital, 101 West Main / Tuesday and Thursday, call 218-634-2060 / Other times, call 218-285-7044

SPORTING GOODS STORES

Holiday Station, Hwy 11 / 218-634-2210

AUTO REPAIR
Johnson's Auto, Hwy 11 / 218-634-1636
Cenex, Hwy 11 / 218-634-1313

AIR SERVICE
Baudette International Airport / Northwest Airlink (Northwest Airlines) / 800-225-2525

MEDICAL
Baudette Clinic, Southwest 5th Street / 218-634-1655
LakeWood Health Center, 600 South Main Street / 218-634-2120

TAXIDERMIST
Lakeshore Taxidermy, HC 02 Box 109A, Warroad 56763 / 218-386-3400

FOR MORE INFORMATION
Lake of the Woods Area Tourism Bureau
P.O. Box 518
Baudette, MN 56623
218-634-1174 / 800-382-FISH
Fax 218-634-2915

Jeff Dittrich
Minnesota Department of Natural Resources Wildlife Sections
Route 1, Box 1023
Baudette, MN 56623
218-634-1705

Gretchen Mehmel
Red Lake Wildlife Management Area
218-783-6861

Hallock
Kittson and Marshall Counties

County Population:	Hallock Population–1,267
Kittson–5,510	October Temperature–48°
Marshall–10,676	County Acres in CRP:
County Area:	Kittson–95,837
Kittson–1,097 sq. mi.	Marshall–201,322
Marshall–1,772 sq. mi.	WMAs–29 (117,696 acres)

Located in far northwestern Minnesota, these two counties are filled with grain fields as far as the eye can see. Evening travelers in this area should be on the lookout for the occasional moose crossing the road. The town of Hallock sits at the crossing of US 75 and County Road 175 and is a farming community at the separation point of the Two Rivers.

Waterfowl and upland game birds are to be found in and around the wildlife management areas in these counties. Some private land is accessible, but it is very important to ask first.

Some of the best habitat in the state for sharptail can be found here, but numbers are down due to poor reproduction. Woodcock and grouse numbers are good in the area. In wet years, access can be difficult due to high water tables.

Thief Lake Wildlife Management Area has special regulations. Presently, there is a limit on the number of geese that can be taken. Good mallard hunting is found near potholes and waterways.

UPLAND BIRDS
Sharptail, Hungarian Partridge, Ruffed Grouse, Spruce Grouse

WATERFOWL
Ducks and Geese

ACCOMMODATIONS
Gateway Motel, 702 South Atlantic / 9 units / Pets allowed / 218-843-2032 / $
Valley Motel, 808 South Atlantic / 12 units and 4 trailer houses available, cable TV and phone / Pets allowed / 218-843-2828 or 218-843-3647 / $-$$

CAMPGROUNDS AND RV PARKS
Lake Bronson State Park, Lake Bronson 56734 / 2 miles east of Lake Bronson on Hwy 59 / 194 tent and RV sites, flush toilets, showers and dump station / Pets allowed / 218-754-2200 / $

RESTAURANTS
Margie's Cafe, 146 South Second / Family diner / Breakfast, lunch, and dinner / Mon–Sat, 5:30AM–5PM / 218-843-2008
Judy's Cafe, Atlantic Avenue South / Family diner / Breakfast, lunch, and dinner / Mon–Sat, 5:30AM–9PM

A straight overview shot of the farm country to be found near Hallock with its woodlots and open fields on a flat horizon.

VETERINARIANS
Greenbush Veterinary Clinic, 1 Animal Lane, Greenbush 56726 / 218-782-2310

SPORTING GOOD STORES
Coast to Coast Store, 326 South Atlantic Avenue / 218-843-2442
Agri Sports, Hwy 75 and County Road 62 / 218-843-2591

AUTO REPAIR
C and M Ford, Hwy 75 North / 218-843-2652

AIR SERVICE
City of Hallock Airport, Route 1, Box 118 / 218-843-2076 / Small aircraft only /
Northwest Airlines (Mesaba) into Thief River Falls / 800-225-2525

MEDICAL
Kittson Memorial Clinic, 1010 South Birch / 218-843-2165

TAXIDERMIST
Wilderness Taxidermy, R6 Box 335, Thief River Falls 56701 / 218-681-5636

FOR MORE INFORMATION
Hallock Chamber of Commerce
City Hall
Hallock, MN 56728
218-843-2737

Paul Telander
Thief Lake Wildlife Management Area
218-222-3747

George Davis
Minnesota Department of Natural
    Resources Wildlife Section
P.O. Box 154
Karlstad, MN 56732
218-436-2427

Crookston
Pennington, Polk, and Red Lake Counties

County Population:	Crookston Population–8,116
Pennington–13,647	October Temperature–50°
Polk–32,808	County Acres in CRP:
Red Lake–4,456	Pennington–75,750
County Area:	Polk–124,913
Pennington–617 sq. mi.	Red Lake–43,394
Polk–1,971 sq. mi.	WMAs–42 (24,646 acres)
Red Lake–432 sq. mi.	

Located in northwestern Minnesota at the convergence of US 75 and US 2, Crookston is a small college town at the fork of the Red Lake River. This is a town built on the blood and sweat of pioneer farmers trying to make a living in this tallgrass prairie area and on the mills that ground the farmers' wheat. It was also the area's railway hub.

Sharptail numbers are on the rise, but a lack of consistently good habitat is a problem. Eastern Red Lake County is the best bet for finding better sharptail numbers. Hun numbers are way down, and local people would just as soon not have you hunt them. Ruffed grouse and woodcock are marginal because of the limited number of aspen woodlots to be found.

Many state and federal areas are open to waterfowl hunters and are very good for puddle ducks, such as mallards, gadwalls, and pintails. Early wood duck and pintail hunting is very good in and around lakes, potholes, and waterways.

Canada geese are once again at the top of everyone's list around here. Field hunting is good, and area farmers may be eager for hunters to thin out the goose population. Some fee hunting is available in the area as well, but check local grain elevators and restaurants for information to find the areas where geese are a nuisance.

UPLAND BIRDS
Sharp-tailed Grouse, Hungarian Partridge, Ruffed Grouse, and Woodcock

WATERFOWL
Ducks and Geese

ACCOMMODATIONS
Country Club Motel, Hwy 2 and 75 Northwest / 20 units, nonsmoking rooms, Cable TV and in-room coffee / Pets allowed / 218-281-1607 / $-$$

Golf Terrace Motel, 1731 University Avenue / 17 units, cable TV, restaurant, laundry, and convenience store next door / Pets allowed / 218-281-2626 / $-$$

CAMPGROUNDS AND RV PARKS
Crookston Central Park, Ash Street and Mitchell Lane / Bath house with showers and flush toilets / 218-281-1242

RESTAURANTS
Irishman's Shanty, 1501 South Main / Mon–Sat, 6AM–10PM; Sun, 4–10PM / Breakfast, lunch, and dinner / Bar / Hamburgers, ribs, steaks, and seafood / Off-sale liquor / 218-281-9912

RBJ's Restaurant, 1601 University Avenue, Crookston, MN 56716 / Open daily 6AM–10PM / Take-out and family dining / 218-281-3636

VETERINARIANS
Dr. Bruce Pierce, Valley Animal Hospital, 214 South Main / 218-281-4231

SPORTING GOODS STORES
Grove Motor Sports, 1001 Bruce Street / 218-281-5617
Pamida, 635 Marin Avenue (Hwy 75 South) / 218-281-2241
Sports Etc., 121 West Robert Street / 218-281-2240

AUTO REPAIR
Brost Chevrolet/Cadillac, 1600 University Avenue / 218-281-1930
Nelson Motors, Hwy 75 South and Marin / 218-281-1925

AIR SERVICE
Crookston Municipal Airport, Hwy 75 North / 218-281-2625 / Northwest Airlines (Mesaba) into Thief River Falls / 800-225-2525

MEDICAL
Altru Clinic, 400 South Minnesota Street / 218-281-9100
Riverview Healthcare Association, 323 South Minnesota Street / 218-281-9200

TAXIDERMIST
Wildlife Taxidermy, RR2, Box 46 / 218-281-1027

FOR MORE INFORMATION
Crookston Chamber of Commerce
1915 University Avenue, Suite 2
Crookston, MN 56716
218-281-4320 or 800-809-5997

Terry Wolf
203 West Fletcher Street
Crookston, MN 56716
218-281-6063

John Williams
Minnesota Department of Natural Resources Wildlife Section
123 Main Avenue North
Thief River Falls, MN 56701
218-681-0946

Bemidji
Beltrami and Clearwater Counties

County Population:
    Beltrami–37,615
    Clearwater–8,467
County Area:
    Beltrami–2,505 sq. mi.
    Clearwater–995 sq. mi.
	Bemidji Population–11,682
	October Temperature–50°
	County Acres in CRP:
	    Beltrami–14,316
	    Clearwater–8,937
	WMAs–54 (79,707 acres)

The town of Bemidji is located on the shores of Lake Bemidji at the intersection of US 71 and 2. It is considered the "first city on the Mississippi," and is surrounded by resorts, lakes, forests, and year-round experiences for everyone. Lumber brought white settlers to this part of Minnesota. Today, the area's forests and lakes offer many opportunities for both hunter and fisherman to enjoy their passions to the fullest here.

Look to the aspen woodlots and alder brush lowlands for some excellent ruffed grouse and woodcock opportunities. Hunting for wood ducks, mallards, blue-winged teal, and ring-necked ducks is very good early in the season. Look for water with wild rice and plenty of submerged vegetation. Some hunting opportunities exist for local geese, but migrating flocks are few and far between.

UPLAND BIRDS
Ruffed Grouse and Woodcock

WATERFOWL
Ducks and Geese

ACCOMMODATIONS
Bel Air Motel, State Hwy 197, 1350 Paul Bunyan Drive Northwest / 23 units, Cable TV, in-room coffee / Pets allowed / 218-751-3222 or 800-798-3222 / $-$$

Best Western Bemidji, 2420 Paul Bunyan Drive / 60 units, indoor pool, whirlpool, sauna, continental breakfast, cable TV, 24-hour restaurant adjacent, supper club and lounge adjacent / Pets allowed / 218-751-0390 or 800-528-1234 / $$-$$$

CAMPGROUNDS AND RV PARKS
Paradise Resort, HC 3, Box 204, Pennington 56663 / 11 lakeside cabins, 10 campsites and 5 RV hookups, laundry, lodge, groceries and hunting guides / Pets allowed after September 6 / 218-835-6514 or 800-845-9124 / $-$$

Hamilton's Fox Lake Campground, 2555 Island View Drive Northeast / 15–30 amp electric, water and sewer sites, 11 - 20 amp electric and water sites, tent sites, dump station, fire pits, wood, lodge, RV supplies, propane tank and vehicle refill station, laundry, bathrooms and shower rooms / 218-586-2231 / $-$$

A beaver pond and house are often good areas for water-fowl, such as this one near Bemidji.

RESTAURANTS

Union Station, America Avenue South / Microbrewery / Open for lunch and dinner 7 days a week / hamburgers to lobster tail / 218-751-9261

Dave's Pizza, 422 West 15th Street / Open 5PM daily / Pizza and pasta / Beer and wines / 218-751-3225

Gangelhoff's Restaurant at the Northern Inn, 3600 Moberg Drive Northwest / Breakfast, lunch, and dinner / Open weekdays, 6AM–10PM; Weekends, 7AM–10PM / 218-751-9500

Perkins Family Restaurant and Bakery, 1120 Paul Bunyan Drive / Open 24 hours, 7 days a week / Breakfast, lunch, and dinner / 218-751-7850

VETERINARIANS

Bemidji Veterinarian Hospital, 2919 Bemidji North / 218-751-2753

SPORTING GOODS STORES

K-Mart, Paul Bunyan Drive Northwest / 218-751-5630

Holiday Gas Station, 408 Midway Drive /218-751-3116

Pamida, 200 Paul Bunyan Drive Southwest / 218-751-4521

AUTO REPAIR

R&D Auto Repair, 402 Paul Bunyan Drive Southeast / 218-751-3361

Pine Ridge Auto Repair, 950 Paul Bunyan Drive Northwest / 218-751-2355

AIR SERVICE
Mesaba Airlines, 4015 Moberg Drive Northwest / 218-751-3726 / Northwest Airlines (Mesaba) 800-225-2525

MEDICAL
North Country Regional Hospital, 1100 West 38th Street / 218-751-5430

TAXIDERMIST
Nature's Image Taxidermy, Hwy 2 West / 218-751-8117

FOR MORE INFORMATION
Bemidji Chamber of Commerce
300 Bemidji Avenue
P.O. Box 850
Bemidji, MN 56601
218-751-3541 or 800-458-2223

Steve Caron
Minnesota Department of Natural Resources Wildlife Sections
2114 Bemidji Avenue
Bemidji, MN 56601
218-755-2964

Ada
Norman and Mahnomen Counties

County Population:
  Norman–7,832
  Mahnomen–5,222
County Area:
  Norman–876 sq. mi.
  Mahnomen–556 sq. mi.
	Ada Population–1,723
	October Temperature–50°
	County Acres in CRP:
	  Norman–43,707
	  Mahnomen–16,817
	WMAs–27 (15,532)

Located at the crossroad of State Highways 9 and 200, Ada is truly in the heart of sunflower, wheat, sugar beet, and all-around farm country. The eastern part of this area is at the edge of forest and lake country.

Wooded areas provide ruffed grouse opportunities, and this is also the north-ernmost end of the ever-expanding turkey range in Minnesota. Few ruffed grouse or woodcock are to be found in the limited areas of aspen stands. Turkeys can be found at the southern edge of these counties and are surviving where hazelnut brush is found, however, there are not huntable numbers yet.

Waterfowl are found on the area's few rivers and western potholes, but numbers are greater on the eastern lakes. As in other parts of Region I, the duck population is good early in the season on potholes, lakes, and other waterways. Goose hunting can be good, but access can be hard to find. Local restaurants and grain elevators are the best bet to find goose hunting opportunities.

UPLAND BIRDS
Ruffed Grouse and Woodcock

WATERFOWL
Ducks and Geese

ACCOMMODATIONS
Norman Motel, West Hwy 200 / 14 Units, air-conditioning, phone, color TV, indoor pool, and restaurant / RV hookups / Pets allowed / 218-784-3781 / $-$$

CAMPGROUNDS AND RV PARKS
Elk Horn Resort and Campground, Waubun 56589 / 80 RV and tent sites / Pets allowed / 218-935-5437 or 800-279-4830 / $

Shooting Star Lodge Campgrounds, Casino Drive 777, Mahnomen 56557 / 47 paved parking sites and tent sites / Laundromat and shower facilities / 218-935-2701 or 800-453-7827 / $

RESTAURANTS
Lana Jo's, 106 East Fourth Avenue / Mon–Fri, 7AM–4PM; Sat, 7AM–11PM / Breakfast, lunch, and dinner / 218-784-2665

VFW, 415 West Main Street / Mon–Sat, 5PM–10PM / Bar and lounge / Steaks and hamburgers / 218-784-7557

VETERINARIANS
Mahnomen Veterinary Service, 210 North Main Street, Mahnomen 56557 / 218-935-5124

SPORTING GOODS STORES
Sjoidal Hardware, 402 Main Street / 218-784-3581
Durheim's, 106 Third Avenue West / 218-784-3744

AUTO REPAIR
Cenex, 202 West Main Street / 218-784-2481
Anderson Oil, Hwy 200 East / 218-784-2878

AIR SERVICE
Norman County Airport / 218-784-725 / Small aircraft only
Northwest Airlines, Fargo, North Dakota / 800-225-2525

MEDICAL
Bridges Medical Services, Fourth Avenue East / 218-784-5000

TAXIDERMIST
D J Taxidermy, Box 475 / Mahnomen, MN / 218-935-2176

FOR MORE INFORMATION
Ada Chamber of Commerce
P.O. Box 1
Ada, MN 56510
218-784-3540

Steve Caron
Minnesota Department of Natural Resources Wildlife Section
2114 Bemidji Avenue
Bemidji, MN 56601
218-755-2964

Terry Wolfe
203 West Fletcher Street
Crookston, MN 56716
218-281-6063

Park Rapids
Hubbard and Northwestern Cass Counties

County Population:	Park Rapids Population–3,020
Hubbard–16,717	October Temperature–50°
Cass–24,531	County Acres in CRP:
County Area:	Hubbard–2,347
Hubbard–923 sq. mi.	Cass–891
Cass–357 sq. mi.	WMAs–20 (15,091 acres)

Itasca State Park, located in the heart of this area, is home to the Mississippi River's headwaters. You can still see stands of over 200-year-old white pines that make you feel you are now on the western edge of the great north woods that make up Minnesota's upper portions. Park Rapids is at the park's southern gateway, located at the intersection of US 71 and State Highway 34. Lakes are abundant, with the rivers and streams that connect them beginning their journey toward the Gulf of Mexico.

Ruffed grouse are in abundance in this area and are most commonly found in the aspen woodlots and alder swamp lowlands. Better-than-average woodcock hunting is to be found around the Tamarac National Wildlife Refuge. Woodcock will be found in low and wet areas.

Early in the season, wood duck and mallard hunting is good wherever there is any water to be found. Diving duck hunting is very good around Leech Lake.

UPLAND BIRDS
Ruffed Grouse and Woodcock

WATERFOWL
Ducks and Geese

ACCOMMODATIONS
Lee's Riverside Resort-Motel, 700 North Park / 9 Units housekeeping style / color cable TV /Close to town and restaurants / Pets allowed / 218-732-9711 or 800-733-9711 / $$-$$$

Terrace View Motor Lodge, North Hwy 71, 716 North Park / 20 units and 4 cabins / Color TV / Close to town / Pets allowed / 218-732-1213 or 800-731-1213 / $-$$

CAMPGROUNDS AND RV PARKS
Spruce Hill Campground, Rt.4, Box 449 / 57 sites on Long Lake / Sanitation station / Game room, fire pits, ice, and other convenience items / 218-732-3292 / $

Calm waters offer a peaceful refuge for waterfowl northeast of Park Rapids.

RESTAURANTS

Rocky's Pizza House, Intersection Hwy 34 and 71 / Great pizza, many different sandwiches, appetizers and beer / Mon–Thurs, 11AM–9PM; Sat, until 11PM; Sun, 4PM–9PM / 218-732-322

Vacationaire Supper Club, HC 05, Box 291 / Very good steaks and seafood with breakfast on the weekends 8:30am–10am / Cocktail bar and lounge / Wed–Sat, 5PM–10PM; Sun, Noon–4PM / 218-732-527

Antler's Restaurant, 211 South Main / Serving breakfast all day and specializing in caramel rolls, general cafe fare with good portions / Mon–Sat, 6:30AM–4PM; Sun, 6:30AM–2PM / 218-732-4583

Magoo's Sportsman's Hideaway, Hwy 35 East / Four TVs, bar and variety of 14 different sandwiches / Mon–Sat, 11AM–1AM

Great Northern Inn, 218 East 1st / Breakfast all day long, dinner and lunch specials / Big meals at small prices / Mon–Sat, 6AM–7PM; Sun, 7AM–2PM

VETERINARIANS
The Ark Animal Hospital, 1.5 miles north of Hwy 34 on County Road 4 /
218-732-3119

SPORTING GOODS STORES
Fuller's Sporting Goods, 112 South Main / 218-732-5227
L&M Supply, RR1 / 218-732-7337
Holiday Station Store, 719 East 1st / 218-732-7136
Pamida, East Hwy 34 / 218-732-9715

AUTO REPAIR
Thielen Motors, Hwy 34 East / 218-732-3347
Orton's Park Rapids 76, 100 South Park / 218-732-8010

AIR SERVICE
Park Rapids Municipal Airport, Hwy 71 South / 218-732-8528 / Small and
personal jet aircraft only
Northwest Airlines (Mesaba) / Bemidji, MN / 800-225-2525

MEDICAL
St. Joseph's Area Health Services, 2 blocks west and 6 blocks south of the Hwy 71
and 34 junction / 218-732-3311

TAXIDERMIST
Bear Creek Bait and Taxidermy Inc., HC 06, Box 432 / 218-732-7337

FOR MORE INFORMATION
Park Rapids Chamber of Commerce
Hwy 71 South
Park Rapids, MN 56470
800-247-0054

Rob Naplin
Minnesota Department of Natural
Resources Wildlife Section
301 South Grove
Park Rapids, MN 56470
218-732-8452

Detroit Lakes
Clay and Becker Counties

County Population:	Detroit Lakes Population–7,316
Clay–52,994	October Temperature–50°
Becker–29,394	County Acres in CRP:
County Area:	Clay–38,411
Clay–1,045 sq. mi.	Becker–27,701
Becker–1,311 sq. mi.	WMAs–35 (12,529 acres)

Detroit Lakes is located at the intersection of US 10 and US 59. Surrounded by over 400 lakes, all within 25 miles, this town draws large tourist numbers. It is considered a four-season area and is enjoyed by many throughout the year. While there is a lot of water in the area, there are plenty of farms, as well. Northwest of Detroit Lakes is the Tamarac National Wildlife Refuge that consists of 43,000 acres of prime habitat for many different species of wildlife.

Limited numbers of pheasants can be found in and around the wildlife management areas and on farmland where access can be difficult to obtain. Ruffed grouse are found in the area's few aspen groves. Tamarac National Wildlife Refuge offers some good woodcock hunting.

Good early-season jump shooting for wood ducks and mallards can be found on any of the area's shallow waters. Geese numbers are good and are best found by asking the Department of Natural Resources' wildlife biologists and at local granaries.

UPLAND BIRDS
Pheasant, Ruffed Grouse, and Woodcock

WATERFOWL
Ducks and Geese

ACCOMMODATIONS
Super 8 Motel, 400 Morrow Avenue / 39 units / Continental breakfast and color cable TV / Pets allowed / 218-847-1651 or 800-800-8000 / $$-$$$
Castaway Inn and Resort, Hwy 10 East / 24 units (9 cottages and 15 motel units) / Hot tub, beach, color TV, and laundromat / Pets allowed / 218-847-4449 or 800-640-3395 / $-$$$

CAMPGROUND AND RV PARKS
American Legion Campground, 810 West Lake Drive / Within the city limits on Detroit Lake / Full hookups, complete bathroom facilities, laundry, store, meals, beverages, and freezer / Open until October 1 / 218-847-3759
Birchmere Family Resort and Campground, Rt.1, Box 159, Frazee 56544 / Located on Toad Lake / 30 wooded sites and full hookups / Lakeside

cottages / Showers, laundry, and firewood / Pets allowed / 218-334-5741 or 800-642-9554 / $-$$$

RESTAURANTS

Grover-Lindberg Truck Stop Restaurant, Hwy 10 West / Open 24 hours a day, 7 days a week / Great homestyle cooking—"Where you'll always get more food than you're used to" / 218-847-1624

Zorbaz Pizza and Mexican Restaurant, 402 West Lake Drive / Open Mon–Sun, 11AM–1AM / Very casual dining and bar / Excellent Mexican foods and pizza / 218-847-5305

Fireside Restaurant and Bar, 1462 East Shore Drive / Closed Mondays, open Wed –Sat, 5:30PM–10:30PM / Nationally famous BBQ ribs, steaks, and seafood cooked over an open charcoal fire / 2 bars / 218-847-8192

VETERINARIANS

Detroit Lakes Animal Hospital, 701 Hwy 10 East / 218-847-5674

SPORTING GOODS

Holiday Station Store, 233 East Frazee Street / 218-847-4883
Lakes Sport Shop, 930 Washington Avenue / 218-847-2645
Pamida, Hwy 10 East / 218-847-3107

AUTO REPAIR

A-1 Automotive Service, 204 NP Road / 218-847-2483
Brend Repair, Hwy 34 East / 218-847-6882

AIR SERVICE

City of Detroit Lakes Airport, Hwy 10 West / 218-847-9937 / Small aircraft
Northwest Airlines (Mesaba) / Fargo, North Dakota / 800-225-2525

MEDICAL

St. Mary's Regional Health Center, 1027 Washington Avenue / 218-847-5611

TAXIDERMIST

Richwood Taxidermy, RR2 Box 175a / 218-847-4830

FOR MORE INFORMATION

Detroit Lakes Regional Chamber of Commerce
700 Washington Avenue
P.O. Box 348
Detroit Lakes, MN 56502
218-847-9202 or 800-542-3992

Earl Johnson
Minnesota Department of Natural Resources Wildlife Section
P.O. Box 823
Detroit Lakes, MN 56501
218-847-1578

Fergus Falls
Wilken, Wadena, and Otter Tail Counties

County Population:
  Wilken–7,376
  Wadena–13,404
  Otter Tail–54,160
County Area:
  Wilken–752 sq. mi.
  Wadena–536 sq. mi.
  Otter Tail–1,980 sq. mi.

Fergus Falls Population–13,217
October Temperature–50°
County Acres in CRP:
  Wilken–11,566
  Wadena–2,834
  Otter Tail–57,263
WMAs–44 (20,172 acres)

Located just off Interstate 94 and State Highway 210, Fergus Falls is split by the Otter Tail River. Power was originally generated by the river and provided an electrical supply for this community. At one time, the railroad transported grain from the area's farms to mills in the Twin Cities. Today, this still-bustling community is home to a college and small businesses that keep its economy strong.

While there are few pheasants in the area, turkey numbers are climbing as flocks become more established. Farmland provides good habitat for both pheasant and turkey. Look for fair numbers of both birds in the lowland areas north and west of Parkers Prairie. Ruffed grouse numbers are good in aspen groves, while woodcock migrate through the areas where there is ample wet lowland.

Good duck hunting opportunities are found anywhere there is water, and geese are abundant. Wildlife management areas found here are generally located around bodies of water, attracting all kinds of waterfowl.

UPLAND BIRDS
Pheasant, Ruffed Grouse, Turkey, and Woodcock

WATERFOWL
Ducks and Geese

ACCOMMODATIONS
American Motel, 526 Western Avenue North / 60 rooms / Indoor pool, sauna, whirlpool suites, breakfast bar, and color cable TV / Pets allowed / 218-739-3900 or 800-634-3444 / $$$
Jewel Motel, 1602 Pebble Lake Road / 14 rooms / TV / Pets allowed / 218-739-5430 / $$

CAMPGROUNDS AND RV PARKS
Swan Lake Resort, Rt.6, Box 426 / 30 sites and cabins / Located on Swan Lake / Groceries, firewood, and hot showers / Pets allowed on a leash / 218-736-4626 / $-$$

Canada geese seem to love foraging in the harvested fields near Fergus Falls.

RESTAURANTS

Viking Cafe, Lincoln Avenue / Open 7 days: Mon–Sat, 5:30AM–9PM; Sun, 7AM–5PM / Specializing in breakfast and fresh baked pies and pastries / 218-736-6660

Mabel Murphy's, 3401 Hwy 210 West / Mon–Fri, 11AM–2PM and 5PM–10PM; Sat, 5PM–10PM; Sun, 5PM–9PM / Lounge open Mon–Thurs, 11AM–10PM; Fri–Sat, 11AM–11PM; Sun, Noon–9PM / Great steaks, prime rib, seafood, and pasta / Cocktail lounge / 218-739-4406

VETERINARIANS

Fergus Falls Animal Care Clinic, 112 North Cascade / 218-736-6916

SPORTING GOODS

Holiday Station Store, 305 Union Street / 218-739-3803

Pamida, 226 Lincoln Avenue Southeast / 218-736-5448

AUTO REPAIR

Fergus Tire Center Inc., City Center Mall, 222 West Cavour Avenue / 218-739-2261

Minnesota Motor Co., 1108 Pebble Lake Road / 218-739-3331 or 800-332-7142

AIR SERVICE
Northwest Airlines (Mesaba) / Fargo, North Dakota / 800-225-2525

MEDICAL
Fergus Falls Medical Group, 615 South Mill / 218-739-2221 or 800-247-1066

TAXIDERMIST
Ottertail Taxidermy, RR3, Box 26 / 218-739-2009

FOR MORE INFORMATION
Fergus Falls Area Chamber of Commerce
202 South Court Street
Fergus Falls, MN 56537
218-739-6951 or 800-726-8959

Doug Wells
Minnesota Department of Natural Resources Wildlife Section
1221 Fir Avenue North
Fergus Falls, MN 56537
218-739-7576

Alexandria
Grant, Douglas, Stevens, Pope, and Traverse Counties

County Population:	Alexandria Population–8,405
Grant–6,185	October Temperature–50°
Douglas–31,274	County Acres in CRP:
Stevens–10,694	Grant–16,112
Pope–10,969	Douglas–29,445
Traverse–4,331	Stevens–11,120
County Area:	Pope–27,854
Grant–547 sq. mi.	Traverse–5,362
Douglas–634 sq. mi.	WMAs–102 (14,568 acres)
Stevens–562 sq. mi.	
Pope–670 sq. mi.	
Traverse–574 sq. mi.	

Sitting in Alexandria's Runestone Museum is the Kensington Runestone, believed by some to be proof that the Vikings made it this far inland while exploring North America. It is more likely that the Scandinavian farmers who settled the area were the first of their people to venture here. Located off of Interstate 94 north of the Twin Cities, Alexandria today still has its farms, but also a great number of resorts on the area's lakes that provide vacation opportunities for many a traveler.

Pheasant hunting ranges from poor to fair, although when mild winters provide better nesting opportunities, it's possible to have better bird numbers. In and around the Browns Valley area, turkey numbers are good, and if habitat remains favorable, there should be good numbers in the future as well. Very few aspen groves mean very few ruffed grouse hunting opportunities.

While geese numbers are very high here, the problem is access. Once again, checking with the local grain elevators and restaurants can be helpful in finding landowners willing to grant access.

Mallards can be found in and around water to the west. The eastern portion of this area holds good numbers of diving ducks and wood ducks. Standing wild rice and aquatic vegetation are good indicators for finding ducks.

UPLAND BIRDS
Pheasant, Turkey and Ruffed Grouse

WATERFOWL
Duck and Geese

ACCOMMODATIONS
Skyline Motel, 605 30th Avenue West / 12 units / In-room coffee, refrigerators, color cable TV, and microwaves / Pets welcome/ 320-763-3175 or 800-467-4096 / $-$$$

These snow geese are coming in to join the flock for a late evening meal.

Super 8 Motel, 4620 Hwy 29 South / 57 units / Continental breakfast and color cable TV / 320-763-6552 or 800-800-8000 / $$-$$$

CAMPGROUNDS AND RV PARKS
Viking Motel and Campgrounds, 1903 AGA Drive and Airport Road / 34 units and RV sites / Continental breakfasts, color cable TV, and game room / Pets allowed / 320-762-0512 or 800-827-1611

RESTAURANTS
Flagship Restaurant and Fuel Stop, I-94 and Hwy 29 (Exit 103) / Open 24 hours a day / Home style cooking, salad bar, Sunday buffet, and bakery / 320-762-1944

D Michael B, Viking Plaza Mall (3015 Hwy 29 South) / Open daily 11AM–1AM / "Fall off the bone ribs," hot specialty sandwiches, and bar / 320-762-2697

Becky's Coffee House, 1501 Broadway Street / Mon–Fri, 6AM–6PM; Sat, 8AM–5PM; Sun, 9AM–4PM Sun / Excellent coffee, homemade soups, sandwiches, and desserts / 320-762-8535

VETERINARIANS
Alexandria Veterinary Clinic, 710 3rd Avenue West / 320-762-8112 or 800-642-6263

SPORTING GOOD STORES
Holiday Station Store, 320 3rd Avenue East / 320-762-0447
Wal-Mart Store, 515 50th Avenue West / 320-762-8945

AUTO REPAIRS
Champion Auto Stores, 3109 Hwy 29 South / 888-763-3197
B and J's Auto Service, 823 6th Avenue East / 320-763-5335

AIR SERVICE
Chandler Field Airport, Aga Drive / Smaller aircraft
Northwest Airlines (Mesaba) / St. Cloud, 800-225-2525

MEDICAL
Douglas County Hospital, 111 17th Avenue East / 320-762-1511 / Emergency
   room: 320-762-6000

TAXIDERMIST
Craig's Taxidermy, 211 4th Avenue East / 320-763-7806

FOR MORE INFORMATION
Alexandria Lake Area Chamber of Commerce
206 Broadway
Alexandria, MN 56308
320-763-3161 or 800-235-9441

Kevin Kotts
Minnesota Department of Natural Resources Wildlife Section
Rt.1, Box 1A
Glenwood, MN 56334
320-634-4573

Region 2 Map

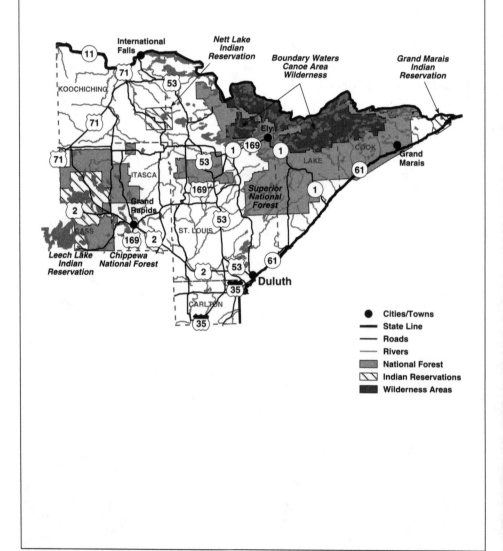

International Falls

11

71

KOOCHICHING

71

71

Nett Lake Indian Reservation

53

53

Boundary Waters Canoe Area Wilderness

Ely

1 169

1

LAKE

53

ITASCA

169

Grand Rapids

53

Superior National Forest

COOK

Grand Marais

61

Grand Marais Indian Reservation

1

2

CASS

169 2

ST. LOUIS

Leech Lake Indian Reservation

Chippewa National Forest

2

53

61

2

35

Duluth

CARLTON

35

● Cities/Towns
— State Line
— Roads
— Rivers
▨ National Forest
▨ Indian Reservations
▨ Wilderness Areas

Region 2

This region, more than any other, resembles the picture that many people have of Minnesota. Tourists visit during all four seasons to enjoy the woods, lakes, and wildlife found here. This area's boundaries extend from Duluth up to Grand Portage along Lake Superior's north shore, west toward International Falls, and south to Grand Rapids along US 71 and State Highway 6.

Canadian fur traders ventured south to this area hunting the abundant beaver and other furbearing animals found here. Giant white pines drew loggers from the East, where forests had been depleted. In 1865 people came in search of the gold that was thought to exist in the rocky areas north and west of Duluth. But it was iron ore, not gold, that propelled the region's economy.

The Mesabi Iron Range runs through the middle of this region and remains an integral part of its economy. A few of the lakes created by the mining industry are now used by both locals and tourists for boating and fishing.

Logging continues to fuel the paper mills and other wood products industries of this region. While many find logging objectionable, where it has been done properly, it has had a very positive impact on the quality and abundance of wildlife found here.

From the late 1800s to the present, the growth industry in this region has been tourism. Many state and federal parks cover this region, and much of it is dedicated to the many waterways to be found here. From Voyageurs National Park just east of International Falls to the Boundary Waters Canoe Area ending at the Gunflint Trail and Grand Marais to the east, there are the many rivers and streams that flow into Lake Superior providing fishing opportunities and scenic beauty for all to enjoy. Many interior lakes offer fishing, boating, and swimming in the summer and hunting, ice fishing, and snowmobiling in the winter. Both the Chippewa and Superior National Forests have many hiking, skiing, and hunting trails, making it accessible to all who wish to enjoy Minnesota's truly bountiful outdoors.

Region 2 Ruffed Grouse Distribution

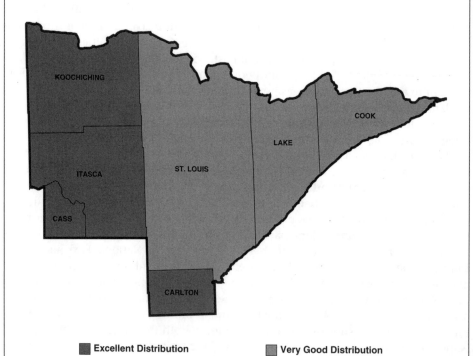

KOOCHICHING

ITASCA

CASS

ST. LOUIS

LAKE

COOK

CARLTON

■ Excellent Distribution   ■ Very Good Distribution

Region 2 Sharp-tailed Grouse Distribution

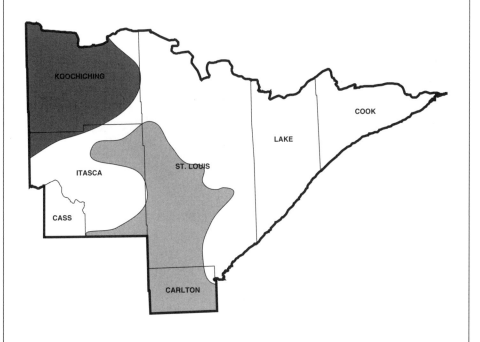

Good Distribution   Fair Distribution

Region 2 Spruce Grouse Distribution

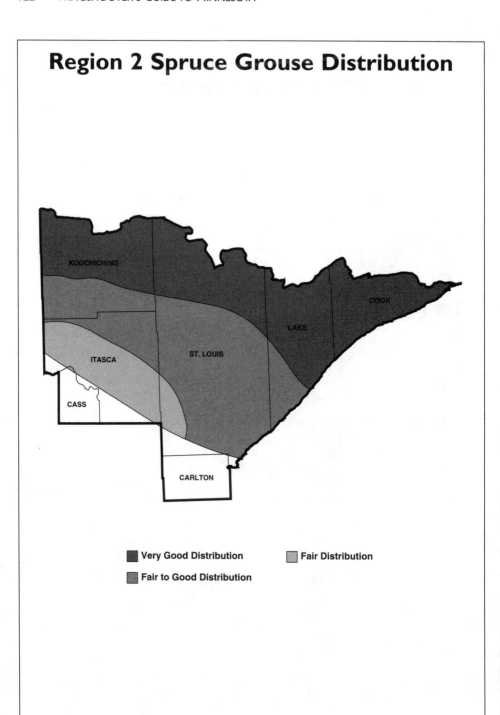

Region 2 Woodcock Distribution

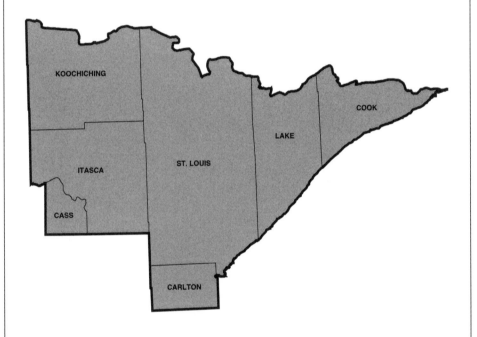

KOOCHICHING

COOK

LAKE

ITASCA

ST. LOUIS

CASS

CARLTON

▨ Best Distribution

International Falls
Koochiching and Northern Itasca Counties

County Population:
  Koochiching–15,868
  Itasca–16,409
County Area:
  Koochiching–3,102 sq. mi.
  Itasca–2,665 sq. mi.
	International Falls Population–7,751
	October Temperature–50°
	County Acres in CRP:
	  Koochiching–13
	  Itasca–154
	WMAs–9 (4,636 acres)

International Falls is located where US 71 and US 53 convene before entering Canada. This border town has a rich history, from the prehistoric burial site known as Grand Mound to the Bronko Nagurski Football Museum. The two main industries today are timber, with its mills and logging, and the tourism generated by the many lakes and natural wonders to be found in the area. Voyageurs National Park and the Rainy River area draw visitors year-round.

Plenty of spruce grouse can be found in the evergreen forests and cedar swamps found in the region's southwest. Ruffed grouse are common everywhere there are aspen groves. Woodcock are in either of these areas where there is low, moist ground. There are still fair numbers of sharp-tailed grouse to be found in the west and south; however, there is limited hunting because access is not readily available on the private lands where the birds are found.

Waterfowl hunting in this area is somewhat limited and good only early in the season. Local birds migrate quickly, and birds moving down from the north do not stay around for very long.

UPLAND BIRDS
Ruffed Grouse, Spruce Grouse, Sharp-tailed Grouse, and Woodcock

WATERFOWL
Ducks and Geese

ACCOMMODATIONS

Days Inn, 2331 Hwy 53 South / 58 rooms / continental breakfast, color cable TV, whirlpool, and sauna / Pets allowed / 218-283-9441 or 1-800-DAYS INN / $$

Thunderbird Lodge, 2170 County Road 139 / 15 motel rooms and 10 modern cabins / Fantastic restaurant and lounge / Pets allowed on leash and in carrying kennels / 218-286-3151 or 1-800-351-5133 / Room rates $$-$$$ / Daily cabin rates $$$

Holiday Inn, Hwy 71 West / 127 units / Color TV, bar, restaurant, indoor pools, whirlpool, and sauna / Pets allowed in smoking rooms / 218-283-4451 or 1-800-331-4443 / $$-$$$

Another well used forest service road just south of International Falls that allows hunters to get farther into the woods to use trails in search of spruce and ruffed grouse.

CAMPGROUNDS AND RV PARKS

Arnold's Campground and RV Park, Hwy 53 and 21st Street / 24 sites / Flush toilets, hot showers, tent sites, full hookups, dump station, and drive-thru sites / 3 blocks to town / 218-285-9100 / $

RESTAURANTS

International Skillet, Hwy 53 and Memorial Drive / Open 24 hours, 7 days / Family style complete menu served all hours

The Spot Supper Club/Firehouse Restaurant and Lounge, Hwy 53 and 18th Street / Open 5PM–1AM / Casual dining with steaks and seafood / 218-283-2440

VETERINARIANS

Rainy River Veterinary Hospital, 900 Third Avenue / 218-285-7044

SPORTING GOODS

The Outdoorsman's Headquarters, 11th Street and Hwy 53 / 218-283-9337
Holiday Station Store, 713 Third Avenue and Hwy 53 / 218-283-9843

AUTO REPAIR

Borderland Auto Repair Etc. Inc., 2201 Second Avenue West / 218-283-9366
Forestland Sales and Service, 11th Avenue and 5th Street / 218-283-3400

AIR SERVICE

International Falls Airport / 218-283-4630 or Northwest Airlink 1-800-225-2525

MEDICAL

Falls Memorial Hospital, 1400 Hwy 71 / 218-283-4481

TAXIDERMIST

American Taxidermy, 200 Second Avenue / 218-283-4414 OR 1-800-TEAMFISH

FOR MORE INFORMATION

International Falls Area Chamber of Commerce
301 Second Avenue
International Falls, MN 56649
218-283-9400 or 1-800-325-5766

Frank Swendsen
Minnesota Department of Natural Resources Wildlife Section
392 East Hwy 11
International Falls, MN 56649
218-286-5434

Ely
Northern St. Louis and Northern Lake Counties

County Population:	Ely Population–3,891
St. Louis–199,454	October Temperature–50°
Lake–10,695	County Acres in CRP:
County Area:	St. Louis–448
St. Louis–6,226 sq. mi.	Lake–None
Lake–2,099 sq. mi.	WMAs-6 (3,946)

State Highway 169 north leads to what some consider the end of the road and the small town of Ely. Both mining and logging are practiced here, but Ely is probably best known as a destination for entering the Boundary Waters Canoe Area Wilderness. Every year, thousands of hikers and canoeists take off from Ely into the wilderness. And winter is just as busy as Ely hosts the hearty souls who enjoy dogsledding, winter camping, cross-country skiing, snowmobiling, and ice fishing.

A fair population of spruce grouse can be found in the area's evergreen forests and cedar swamps. Ruffed grouse populations are very good in and around aspen groves. Woodcock numbers are just fair in this area.

Puddle duck hunting is good early in the season before migration starts. Jump shooting is very popular around area potholes. Local birds migrate early, and a few opportunities exist for flights of bluebills coming out of Canada.

UPLAND BIRDS
Ruffed Grouse, Spruce Grouse, and Woodcock

WATERFOWL
Ducks and Geese

ACCOMMODATIONS
Budget Host Motel, 1047 East Sheridan / 17 units / cable TV and in room coffee / Pets allowed / 218-365-3237 / $$-$$$

Shagawa Inn Resort and Motel, P.O. Box 148, Dept. MA / 9 units / Knotty pine cabins, 4 with kitchenettes, cable TV, housekeeping cabins, and a small campground / Pets allowed / 218-365-5154 / $$-$$$

West Gate Motel, 110 North Second Avenue West / 15 units / Color TV, nonsmoking rooms, and continental breakfast / Pets allowed / 218-365-4513 or 1-800-806-4979 / $-$$$

CAMPGROUNDS AND RESORTS
Silver Rapids Lodge and Campground, HC 1, Box 2992 / Lakeside camping, full hookups, excellent restaurant, lounge, modern showers, flush toilets, cabins, and motel units / Pets allowed in campers or in a limited number of cabins / 1-800-950-9425 / $-$$$

Typical overview of the area around Ely and the Boundary Waters Canoe Area Wilderness dotted with lakes and diverse forests.

RESTAURANTS
Northern Grounds Cafe, 117 North Central / Open 7 days, 6:30PM–10PM / Specialize in Panini sandwiches, homemade soups and desserts / 218-365-2560
Ely Steak House, 216 East Sheridan / Open Mon–Sat, 11:30AM–1AM / Great steaks and a lounge / 218-365-7412
Vertin's Cafe, Pub and Supper Club, 145 East Sheridan Street / Open 7 days, 6AM–10PM / "Comfort food at a comfortable price," 3 dining areas and a bar with a fireplace / 218-365-4041

VETERINARIANS
Ely Veterinarian Clinic, 318 East Miners Drive / 218-365-5911

SPORTING GOODS

Holiday Station Stores, 1037 Sheridan Street East / 218-365-6003

Pamida, 115 East Chapman Street / 218-365-4700

AUTO REPAIR

Ely Auto Services, 1614 East Harvey Street / 218-365-5994

AIR SERVICE

Ely International Airport / 218-365-3444 / Mesaba Airlines—seasonal service in and out of Ely / International Falls is the next closest airport and is served by Northwest Airlines, which is linked to Mesaba / 1-800-225-25255

MEDICAL

Ely–Bloomenson Community Hospital and Ely Area Ambulance Service, 328 West Conan Street / 218-365-3271

TAXIDERMIST

Champa Louie Taxidermy, 1237 Sheridan Street East / 218-365-6310

FOR MORE INFORMATION

Ely Chamber of Commerce
1600 East Sheridan Street
Ely, MN 55731
218-365-6123 or 1-800-777-7281

Fred Thunhorst
Minnesota Department of Natural Resources Wildlife Section
1429 Grant-McMahan Boulevard
Ely, MN 55731
218-365-7280

Grand Marais
Cook and Southern Lake Counties

County Population:	Grand Marais Population–1,239
Cook–4,437	October Temperature–53°
Lake–10,695	County Acres in CRP:
County Area:	Cook–None
Cook–1,451 sq. mi.	Lake–None
Lake–2,099 sq. mi.	WMAs-3 (680 acres)

Near the top of what is known as the Arrowhead, along US 61, sits the small town of Grand Marais. Grand Marais started as a trading post on the shores of Lake Superior and has the feel of a snug Maine harbor town. It is at the eastern end of the Boundary Waters Canoe Area and is located near the trailhead of Gunflint Trail, which runs west from here. Surrounded by Superior National Forest, it offers a variety of activites year round.

Tourism is the mainstay of the Grand Marais economy and has served it well. Natural beauty abounds here throughout the year. Visitors come to enjoy fishing, hunting, sailing, canoeing, bird watching, skiing, and snowmobiling.

The area's good ruffed grouse numbers mean a lot of weekend hunting activity. For better hunting and less pressure, check out aspen groves and areas of alder brush on a weekday. With less hunting pressure on them, spruce grouse are in fair supply and can be found in and around evergreen forests and cedar swamps. The least-hunted upland bird in the area is the woodcock, and their numbers are good. Look for them in the low-lying swampy areas before their mid-October migration.

There are good numbers of resident mallards, diving ducks, and some Canada geese. These resident flocks are only around in the early part of the hunting season, before they start their migration. Opportunities for hunting waterfowl abound on the area's many waterways, potholes, and lakes.

UPLAND BIRDS
Ruffed Grouse, Spruce Grouse, and Woodcock

WATERFOWL
Ducks and Geese

ACCOMMODATIONS
Lund's on the Scandinavian Riviera, P.O.Box 126 / 14 units / Motel and house-keeping cabins, color cable TV, gas fireplaces, in-room coffee, and refrigerators / Pets allowed / 218-387-2155 / $$-$$$

Nelson's Traveler Rest, P.O.Box 634 / 11 units / "Best in-town resort," with kitchens, microwaves, and some cabins with fireplaces (wood supplied) / Pets allowed / 218-387-1464 / $$-$$$

Many hunters walk forest service roads, such as this one near Grand Marais, in search of ruffed grouse.

CAMPGROUNDS AND RV PARKS

Grand Marais Recreation Area and RV Park, P.O.Box 820 / 300 sites / Tenting to full RV hookups, 4 bath houses, dumping station, ice, wood, RV supplies, an indoor pool, and whirlpool with sauna (fee for using the pool complex) / Pets allowed, but must at all times be in compliance with the Grand Marais leash law / 218-387-1712 or 1-800-998-0959

RESTAURANTS

Sven and Ole's, 9 West Wisconsin Street / Open 7 days, 11AM–1AM / Pizza place on the North Shore with sandwiches and an around-the-world tour of beer selections / 218-387-1713

Blue Water Cafe, Wisconsin Street and 1st Avenue West / Open Sun–Thurs, 6AM–8PM; Fri and Sat, 6AM–9PM / Serves breakfast all day long, homemade soups, and broasted chicken / 218-387-1597

Birch Terrace/Terrace Lounge, West Sixth Avenue and Hwy 61 / 1800s log mansion and truly a classic / Open Mon–Thurs, 5PM–9PM; Fri and Sat, 5PM–10PM / Known for its Lake Superior lake trout and barbequed ribs, great lounge / 218-387-2215

VETERINARIANS
Grand Marais Veterinary Clinic, Hwy 61 East / 218-387-2063

SPORTING GOODS
Holiday Station Store, 3 Hwy 61 West / 218-387-1043
Buck's Hardware Hank, Hwy 61 West / 218-387-2280

AUTO REPAIR
Wally's Service, 11 First Avenue West / 218-387-2044 or 218-387-2566
C.S. Service Inc., Hwy 61 / 218-387-1500

AIR SERVICE
Cook County Airport, Devil's Track Lake / 218-387-2721 / Small aircraft
Northwest Airlines, Duluth / 1-800-225-2525

MEDICAL
Cook County Northshore Hospital and Care Center / 218-387-1500

TAXIDERMIST
Bowe Taxidermy, 5905 East Superior Street, Duluth 55802 / 218-525-3695

FOR MORE INFORMATION
Grand Marais Chamber of Commerce
15 North Broadway
P.O. Box 1048
Grand Marais, MN 55604
218-387-2524 or 1-800-622-4014

William Peterson
Minnesota Department of Natural Resources Wildlife Section
P.O. Box 156
Grand Marais, MN 55604
218-387-3034

Duluth
Southern St. Louis and Carlton Counties

County Population:
    St. Louis–199,454
    Carlton–30,975
County Area:
    St. Louis–6,226 sq. mi.
    Carlton–860 sq. mi.
	Duluth Population–85,225
	October Temperature–53°
	County Acres in CRP:
	    St. Louis–448
	    Carlton–274
	WMAs–11 (6,949 acres)

At the end of Interstate 35 north of the Twin Cities and at the lower tip of Lake Superior sits Minnesota's "City by the Bay," Duluth. This port city has seen its fortunes swing back and forth throughout its history. From Duluth's ports on Lake Superior, ships have carried much of the grain from the Great Plains as well as iron ore from the Mesabi Iron Range.

Duluth is a wonderful city with a coastal feel and the gateway to Lake Superior's rugged North Shore. The lumber industry still plays a vital role in the economy, with papermills and other wood products companies producing a variety of goods.

Sportsmen and tourist dollars have reinvigorated Duluth, with many fine shops and restaurants to be enjoyed in and around the city. Sport fishing and hunting opportunities abound, along with boating, sailing, downhill skiing, cross-country skiing, and hiking, making this a destination for all seasons. North and west of Duluth are many acres of federal and state forest land that provide many of the opportunities to enjoy the activities mentioned above.

Ruffed grouse numbers are excellent and can be found in aspen groves and swampy areas with alder. There are very few spruce grouse, however woodcock numbers are good and experience very little pressure. If you plan to hunt in Superior National Forest, contact its headquarters for information about trails and hunting.

Early in the hunting season, look for mallards, wood ducks, and teal on the many potholes and lakes in the area. In particular, look for bodies of water still having wild rice or aquatic vegetation. Later in the season, ring-necked ducks migrate through the western edges of this region. There are some resident Canada geese flocks, but opportunities for hunting them are limited.

UPLAND BIRDS
Ruffed Grouse, Spruce Grouse, and Woodcock

Waterfowl
Ducks and Geese

ACCOMMODATIONS
AmericInn of Duluth and Proctor, 185 Hwy 2 / 68 units / Indoor pool, sauna, whirlpool, color TV, continental breakfast / Blackwoods Grill and Bar connected by heated corridor / Pets allowed / 218-624-1026 or 1-800-634-3444 / $$$

Best Western Edgewater, 2400 London Road / 284 units / Two indoor pools, sauna, whirlpool, color TV, free breakfast, and cocktails / Pets allowed / 218-728-3601 or 1-800-777-7925 / $$-$$$

Voyageur Lakewalk Inn, 333 East Superior Street / 40 units / In the heart of the restaurant district, 1 block from a casino, free continental breakfast, and color TV / Pets allowed / 218-722-3911 or 1-800-258-3911 / $$-$$$

CAMPGROUNDS AND RV PARKS

Skyline Court Motel, 4880 Miller Trunk, Hwy 53 and I-94 / This is a motel, but it has RV sites / Pets allowed / 218-727-1563 or 1-800-554-0621 / $-$$

Indian Point Campground, 75th Avenue West and Grand Avenue / 50 sites: 37 electric, 3 electric and water; 6 electric, water, and sewer, 7 drive thru's; tenting areas; showers; restrooms; dump station; laundromat; store; firewood; and ice / Pets on a leash / 218-624-5637 or 218-723-3337 / $

RESTAURANTS

21st Delight, 2125 West Superior Street / Open 7 days, 6:30am-8 pm / Good homestyle cooking in a friendly atmosphere / 218-727-5804

Buena Vista Restaurant, 1144 Mesaba Avenue / Open Sun–Thur, 7AM–9PM; Fri and Sat, 7AM–10PM / Overlooking Lake Superior / Great basic foods and good service / 218-722-9047

Fitger's Brewhouse, 600 East Superior Street / Open 7 days, 11AM–1AM / Duluth's only brewpub / Great soups and sandwiches / 218-726-1392

Grandma's Saloon and Grill, 522 Lake Avenue South or 2202 Maple Grove Road / Both of these grills are great places to eat and drink in a fantastic atmosphere / 218-727-4192 and 218-722-9313

Lake Avenue Cafe, 394 Lake Avenue South (DeWitt-Seitz Marketplace) / Open Sun –Thur, 11AM–9PM; Fri and Sat, 11AM–10PM / Owned by the chef / Has an out-of-the-ordinary touch for many different crossover styles of gourmet foods / 218-722-2355

Little Angie's Cantina and Grill, 1115 Buchanan Street / Southwestern wood-grilled foods giving one a true South of the Border flavor way up North / Great food and bar / 218-727-6112

VETERINARIANS

North Shore Veterinary Hospital, 6001 East Superior Street / 24 hours / 218-525-1937

Grand Avenue Veterinary Clinic, 5503 Grand Avenue / 24 hours / 218-628-0301

SPORTING GOODS

Marine General Sports, 1501 London Road / 218-724-8833 or 1-800-777-8557

Gander Mountain Store, 1307 Miller Trunk Hwy / 218-726-1100

Holiday Station Store, 5430 Grand Avenue / 218-624-5201

Typical forest setting just west of Duluth showing an area harvested of timber and the surrounding maturing forests grown back from previous cuts.

AUTO REPAIR

Freeway Amoco, I-35 / 24 hours / 218-722-0005
University Conoco and Carwash, 1624 Woodland Avenue / 218-724-0102

AIR SERVICE

Duluth Airport, 4701 Airport Drive / 218-727-2968
Northwest Airlines / 1-800-447-4747
American Airlines / 1-800-433-7300
Delta Airlines / 1-800-221-1212

MEDICAL

Duluth Clinic, 400 East Third Street / 218-722-8364
Saint Luke's Urgent Care, 1011 East First / 218-725-6095

TAXIDERMIST
Bowe Taxidermy, 5905 East Superior Street / 218-525-3695

FOR MORE INFORMATION
Duluth Chamber of Commerce
118 East Superior Street
Duluth, MN 55802
218-722-5501 or 1-800-438-5884

Bob Kirsch
Minnesota Department of Natural Resources Wildlife Section
1568 Hwy 2
Two Harbors, MN 55616
218-834-6619

Rich Staffon
1604 South Hwy 33
Cloquet, MN 55720
218-879-0883

Grand Rapids
Southern Itasca and Northeastern Cass Counties

County Population:
  Itasca–43,337
  Cass–24,531
County Area:
  Itasca–2,665 sq. mi.
  Cass–2,018 sq. mi.
	Grand Rapids Population–8,434
	October Temperature–50°
	County Acres in CRP:
	  Itasca–154
	  Cass–891
	WMAs–21 (14,727)

Grand Rapids is situated at the western end of the Mesabi Iron Range and US 2. This city's economy centers around the timber industry, and a paper mill and particle board plant are in operation. Grand Rapids is the birthplace of Judy Garland, home to the annual Ruffed Grouse Society National Hunt, and host city for the many resorts in the area.

Sharp-tailed grouse are found only on the eastern fringes of these counties, while spruce grouse can be found in and around the evergreen forest and cedar swamps of northern Itasca County. Excellent ruffed grouse and woodcock numbers are the real hunting opportunity here. Chippewa National Forest has excellent trail maps for hunters and hikers, and four trail maps are availble for areas managed by Itasca County.

Early in the hunting season, wood ducks and blue-winged teal are plentiful on the many lakes here. While mallards can be good throughout the season, diving ducks are considered the "bread-and-butter" species on lakes and potholes found to the west. Look for good numbers of ring-necked ducks in wild rice areas of Mud, Goose, Squaw, and Bowstring Lakes. There are some resident populations of Canada geese, however, they migrate fairly early.

UPLAND BIRDS
Ruffed Grouse, Woodcock, Sharp-tailed Grouse, and Spruce Grouse

WATERFOWL
Ducks and Geese

ACCOMMODATIONS
The Sawmill Inn, 2301 South Pokegama Avenue / 124 rooms / Color TV, large indoor pool, whirlpool, and a truly superior restaurant that is open 7 days a week / Pets allowed / 218-326-8501 or 1-800-804-8006 / $$-$$$

Americana Motel, 1915 West Hwy 2 / 17 units / Cable TV, in-room coffee, and some kitchenettes available / Pets allowed / 218-326-0369 or 1-888-326-0369 / $-$$

A mixture of fir and mature aspen trees northwest of Grand Rapids.

Pine Grove Motel, 1420 Fourth Street Northwest / 20 units / Cable TV and some kitchenettes / Pets allowed / 218-326-9674 / $-$$

CAMPGROUNDS AND RV PARKS
Shady Rest Cabins, HC-3, Box 786, Deer River 56636 / While this has cabins, it also has RV parking / Pets allowed / 218-246-8785 / $-$$

Sleepy Hollow Resort and Campground, HC-69, Box 28, Northome 56661 / 12 RV sites / Complete shower house, ice, hot tub, close to a supper club, and within the Chippewa National Forest / 218-897-5234 or 1-800-897-5234

RESTAURANTS
Bridgeman's Original Ice Cream Restaurant, 3331 West Fourth Street / Open Mon–Thur, 7AM–10PM; Fri and Sat, 8AM–10:30PM; Sun, 8AM–10PM / A family style restaurant featuring Bridgeman's ice cream treats / 218-326-5302

The Sawmill Inn, 2301 South Pokegama Avenue / 218-326-8501 / Excellent food, serving breakfast, and a wonderful lounge

VETERINARIANS
Grand Rapids Veterinary Clinic, 405 Southeast 13th Street / 24-hour / 218-326-0395 or 1-800-858-1312

SPORTING GOODS
God's Country Outfitters, 6652 Hwy 38 North / 218-326-9866
Pagel Gun Works, 1407 West Hwy 2 / 218-326-3003

AUTO REPAIR
Jack's Amoco Service Center, Hwy 2 West and Hwy 38 / 218-326-9855 or
1-800-259-9855
Jim's Auto Repair, 401 Northeast Fourth Street / 218-326-0214 or 1-800-454-0214

AIR SERVICE
Grand Rapids Itasca County Airport, 1500 Southeast Seventh Avenue /
218-326-0893 / Mesaba Airlines (Northwest Airlines) 1-800-225-2525

MEDICAL
Itasca Medical Center, 126 Southeast First Avenue / 218-326-3401

TAXIDERMIST
Elich Taxidermy / 218-326-9293

FOR MORE INFORMATION
Grand Rapids Area Chamber of Commerce
One Northwest Third Street
Grand Rapids, MN 55744
218-326-6619 or 1-800-472-6366

Jim Schneewels
Minnesota Department of Natural Resources Wildlife Section
1201 East Hwy 2
Grand Rapids, MN 55744
218-327-4428

Region 3 Map

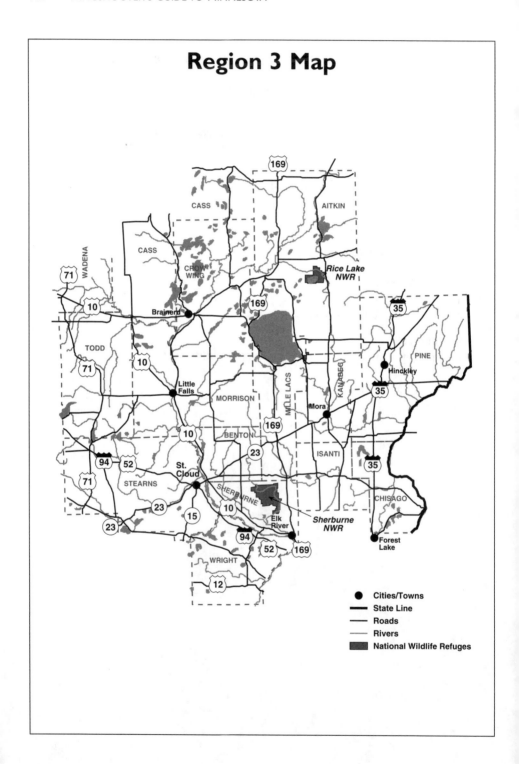

CASS

AITKIN

CASS

WADENA

CASS

(71)

CROW
WING

Rice Lake
NWR

(169)

(10)

Brainerd

(35)

TODD

(169)

PINE

(71)

(10)

Hinckley

Little
Falls

MORRISON

MILLE LACS

KANABEC

(35)

Mora

(169)

BENTON

(10)

ISANTI

(23)

(35)

(94)   (52)

St.
Cloud

(71)

STEARNS

SHERBURNE

CHISAGO

(23)

(15)

(10)

Elk
River

Sherburne
NWR

(23)

(94)

WRIGHT

(52)   (169)

Forest
Lake

(12)

● Cities/Towns
▬ State Line
— Roads
⋯ Rivers
▮ National Wildlife Refuges

Region 3

This region is rich in the history of the Indians, railroads, farms, iron mining, and resorts that characterize east central Minnesota. Located at the southern fringe of the great northern forests and iron mining ranges, this area is filled with opportunities for outdoor enthusiasts, including hunting and fishing—walleye abound in the many glacial lakes.

The abundance of game and other native foods attracted both the Dakota and Ojibway Indians to the area. Today, the Mille Lacs Indian Museum, located 10 miles north of Onamia on US 169, has excellent exhibits depicting how the Indians lived and survived in this region. It includes a life-size diorama showing the seasonal activities of 200 years ago as well as a computer display demonstrating the Ojibway language.

Many of the resorts in the Brainerd Lakes region have served visitors since the turn of the century, when trains brought people from the south to enjoy the area's forests and lakes. Fish seemed to be an unlimited resource back then, and there was even a commercial fishing industry that supplied fish to many restaurants around the country. Today, the trains carry coal, grains, and other products rather than tourists.

Giant white pine forests attracted the lumber and paper industries to the region, and they still play a role in the area's economy. All who are involved in forestry, including the lumber and paper companies, local landowners, and state and federal government agencies, are responsible for the stewardship of this resource, and have played a crucial role in maintaining a healthy wildlife population for all to enjoy.

Where the vast supplies of iron ore found in the Crosby area have been mined and played out, there are now many springfed lakes enjoyed by locals and tourists alike. Just north of Crosby, look for the Croft Mine Historical Park, an underground museum depicting the area's mining history.

As the forests give way to open country farther south, farms begin to dominate the countryside. Family farms are becoming much harder to maintain, but by turning to other crops, such as potatoes and poultry, they are still a vital part of this area's economy.

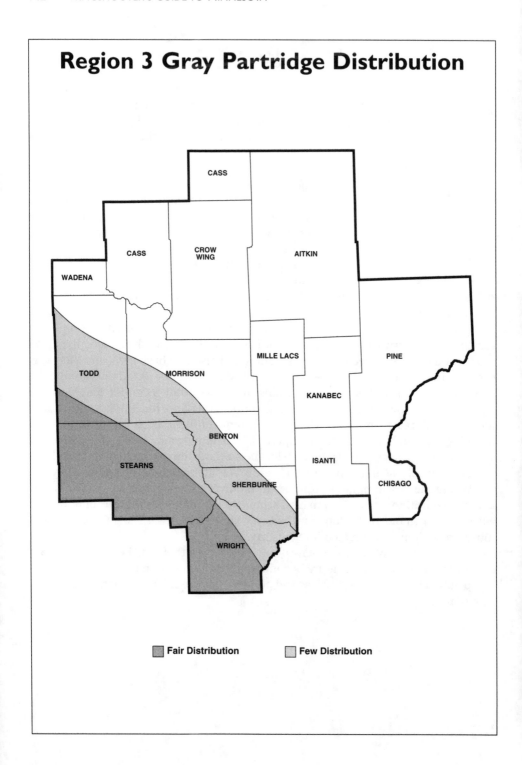

Region 3 Pheasant Distribution

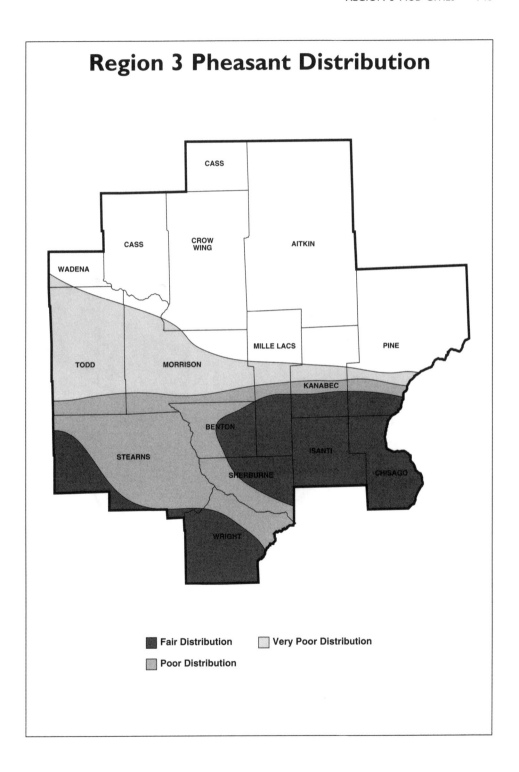

Fair Distribution

Very Poor Distribution

Poor Distribution

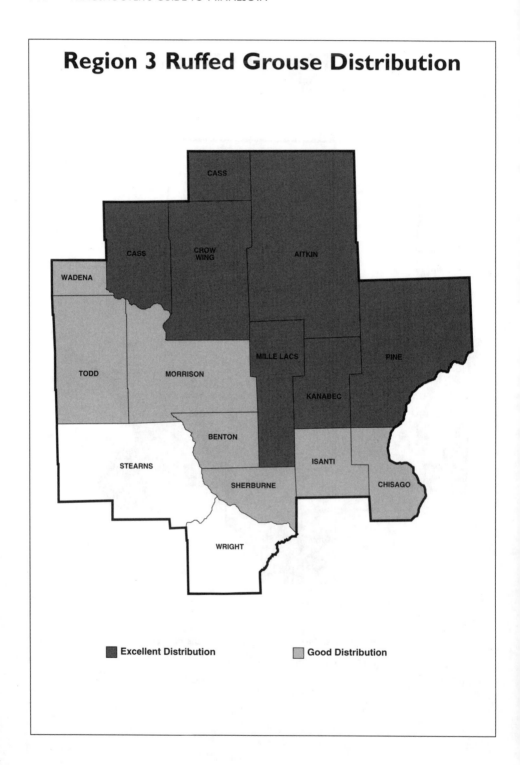

Region 3 Ruffed Grouse Distribution

CASS

CASS

CROW WING

AITKIN

WADENA

TODD

MORRISON

MILLE LACS

PINE

KANABEC

BENTON

STEARNS

ISANTI

SHERBURNE

CHISAGO

WRIGHT

Excellent Distribution

Good Distribution

Region 3 Sharp-tailed Grouse Distribution

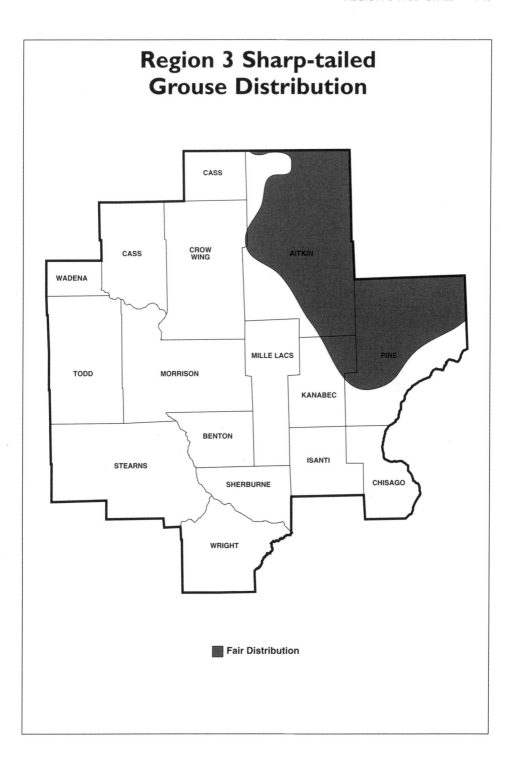

Fair Distribution

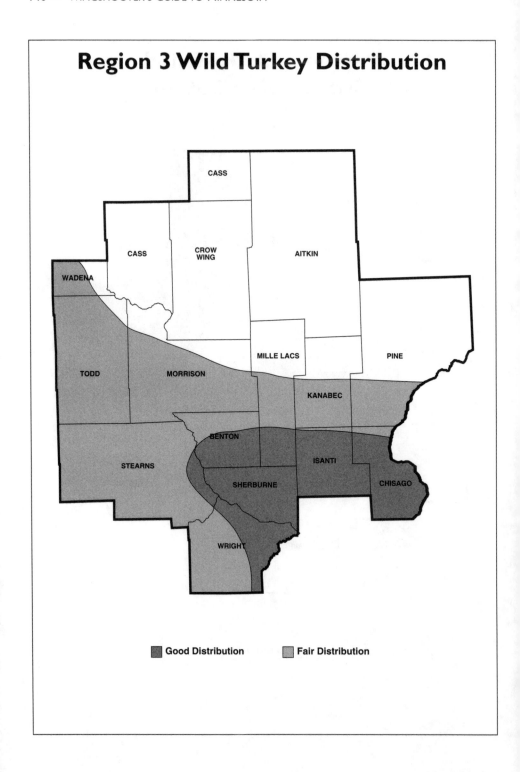

Region 3 Woodcock Distribution

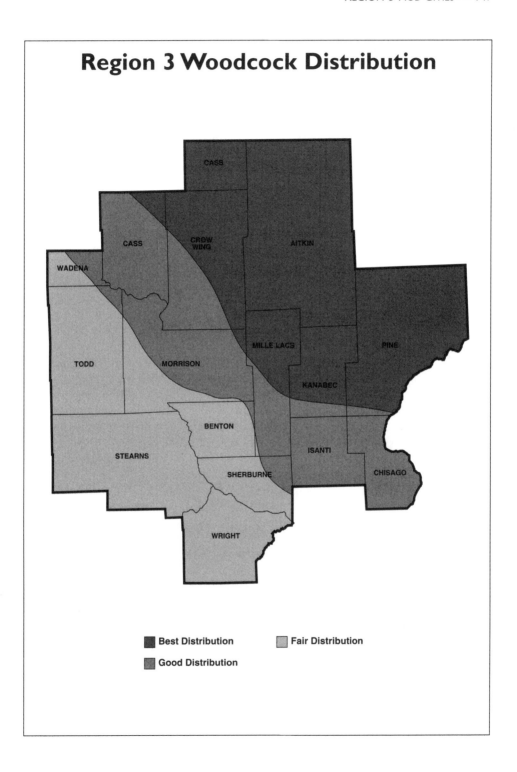

Best Distribution

Good Distribution

Fair Distribution

Brainerd
Southern Cass, Crow Wing, and Aitkin Counties

County Population:	Brainerd Population–13,160
Cass–24,531	October Temperature–50°
Crow Wing–50,578	County Acres in CRP:
Aitkin–13,949	Cass–154
County Area:	Crow Wing–673
Cass–2,665 sq. mi.	Aitkin–113
Crow Wing–997 sq. mi.	WMAs–47 (49,726 acres)
Aitkin–1,819 sq. mi.	

Brainerd is a four-season tourist mecca situated at the junction of State Highways 371 and 210. Once there was a major railcar repair facility here, and trees harvested in the area were transported on the many waterways for processing elsewhere. There is still a paper mill in Brainerd, and the timber industry has played a major part in creating the aspen groves so vital for ruffed grouse habitat.

Area resorts that first started to appear at the turn of the century play a major role in the Brainerd Lakes economy. All of the area's major resort and convention centers feature fishing, swimming, boating, cross-country skiing, and snowmobiling for year-round tourism. There are also several fine golf courses available, not to mention the Brainerd International Raceway, which brings in many national auto racing events.

Ruffed grouse numbers are very good and can be found in the aspen groves and lowland alder swamps along with some resident woodcock. The bulk of woodcock hunting comes when they migrate in the end of September and beginning of October. Look for fair numbers of sharp-tailed grouse in Aitkin County's brushland and bog areas—very few people hunt sharptails. Pheasant numbers are low in the southwestern portion of Crow Wing County.

Very healthy populations of mallards, blue-winged teal, and wood ducks can be found early in the season. Later, look for bluebills and goldeneyes on their southern migration. Jump shooting over potholes is very productive, with wildlife management areas and forest lands offering numerous opportunities.

Canada goose populations are fairly high and can be found on the rivers and lakes near agricultural areas. The Mississippi and Crow Wing Rivers have a number of backwater sites with standing wild rice, where geese like to congregate.

UPLAND BIRDS
Ruffed Grouse, Woodcock, Sharp-tailed Grouse, and Pheasant

WATERFOWL
Ducks and Geese

Low wetland areas, such as this one, are common north of Brainerd and provide a varied habitat that is suitable for ruffed grouse, woodcock, and waterfowl.

ACCOMMODATIONS

Econo Lodge, 2655 Hwy 371 South / 30 units / Complimentary breakfast, queen beds, and cable TV / Pets allowed / 218-828-0027 or 1-800-553-2666 / $-$$$

Riverview Inn, 324 West Washington Street / 68 units / Sauna, color cable TV, and suites available with microwave and refrigerator / Pets allowed / 218-829-8771 or 1-800-850-8771 / $-$$$

Hidden Haven Resort, Ruth Lake, P.O. Box 125, Emily 56447 / Modern house-keeping cabins / Pets welcome / 218-763-2255 / $$-$$$

CAMPGROUNDS AND RV PARKS

Highview Campground and RV Park, HC-83, Box 1084, Breezy Point 56472 / 100 full hookups / Showers, flush toilets, store, ice, and laundry / Leashed pets / 218-543-4526 / $-$$

Shing Wako Resort and Campground, HC-87, Box 9580, Merrifield 56465/ 32 sites /
Primitive to full hookups, new restrooms and showers, freezer service, wood,
ice, sanitation station, and grocery items / Pets allowed, but not in cabins /
218-765-3226

RESTAURANTS

Perkins Family Restaurant, 623 West Washington / 24 hours, 7 days a week /
Family style, breakfast, lunch, dinner, and a bakery on site / 218-829-9457
Morey's Fish House and Grille, Hwy 371 North / Open 7 days, 10AM–8PM /
"Casual dining in a gourmet-market setting" / Seafood, beer, wine, and
espresso / Will package and ship a wide variety of seafoods anywhere /
218-829-8248 or 1-800-548-9603
Zorbaz Pizza and Mexican Restaurant, 6401 Lost Lake Road, Lakeshore 56468 /
Open 7 days a week, 11AM–1AM / Wonderful pizza and Mexican food, full
liquor service, and casual surroundings / 218-963-4790
Iven's on the Bay, 5195 North Hwy 371 / Open 7 days a week, 5PM–10PM /
Seafood specialties, full liqour service, good food, and good service /
218-829-9872
The Boathouse Eatery, 1588 Quarterdeck Road West, Lakeshore 56468 / Open 7
days a week, 11AM–10PM / 100-item menu, great ribs, steaks, and seafood /
218-963-7537

VETERINARIANS

Companion Animal Care, 5425 County Road 45 South / 218-829-2422
Crosslake Veterinary Hospital, Crosslake / 218-692-4400

SPORTING GOODS

Holiday Station Stores, South Sixth Street and also on Hwy 25 North / 218-829-0984
and 218-828-0076
Mill's Fleet Farm, 300 Hwy 371 / 218-829-1565
Oasis Sport Shop, Pequot Lakes 56472 / 218-568-4426
Pamida, Hwys 210 and 25 / 218-829-1486

AUTO REPAIR

DJ's Auto Service, 1120 Northeast Mill Avenue / 218-829-8382
Brainerd Mobil, 321 Washington Street / 218-828-9515 or 1-888-828-9515
Tanner Motors, 703 West Washington Street / 218-829-3597 or 1-800-222-0434

AIR SERVICE

Brainerd Crow Wing County Airport, Hwy 210 East / 218-828-0572
Northwest Airlink (Northwest Airlines) 1-800-225-2525

MEDICAL

Saint Joseph's Medical Center, 523 North Third Avenue / 218-829-2861

TAXIDERMIST

Taxidermy by Dave Ringstrom, 6375 Hwy 25 North / 218-829-5666

A drumming log and droppings are a sure sign of ruffed grouse in the area.

FOR MORE INFORMATION

Brainerd Lakes Area Chamber of Commerce
124 North Sixth Street
Brainerd, MN 56401
218-829-2838 or 1800-450-2838

Marty Anderson
Minnesota Department of Natural
    Resources Wildlife Section
1601 Minnesota Drive
Brainerd, MN 56401
218-828-2555

Dave Dickey
P.O. Box 138
Aitkin, MN 56431
218-927-6915

Little Falls
Todd and Morrison Counties

County Population:	Little Falls Population–7,653
Todd–24,014	October Temperature–50°
Morrison–31,234	County Acres in CRP:
County Area:	Todd–10,389
Todd–942 sq. mi.	Morrison–4,634
Morrison–1,125 sq. mi.	WMAs–37 (13,007 acres)

Little Falls is the birthplace of Charles A. Lindbergh, first person to fly solo across the Atlantic Ocean. This small, friendly town sits on the banks of the Mississippi, just off State Highway 371, and is surrounded by farming country. It was originally called KaKaBikans (the little squarely cut-off rock) by the Ojibway because of its location on the Mississippi River where water used to tumble over a rock outcropping. It was the "little falls" on the mighty river that was eventually dammed for power production. Charles Weyerhaeuser started and operated a lumber company in Little Falls and a paper mill followed, which is still in operation today. Northern forests fueled part of the town's economy while farming made up the rest.

Ruffed grouse numbers have risen in areas holding aspen and in the alder brush lowlands. A few migrating woodcock can be found on the eastern edge of Morrison County, but they are not hunted much. An occasional Hungarian partridge can be found around and near abandoned buildings in southern Todd and Morrison Counties. Pheasant numbers are fair in and around swampy wildlife management areas in southern Todd County. Turkeys have been planted in some of the WMAs and have been surviving on hazelnut brush.

There are good resident populations of mallards, blue-winged teal, and wood ducks, and wetter years mean even better populations. While there aren't as many lakes in this area, there are many potholes and lowland waters. Later in the season, ring-necked ducks move through and use the same waters as the resident ducks.

Mostly Canada geese and a very few snow geese use the waterways for resting and the agricultural fields for feeding. Access to private land is rare here, so the WMAs that have food plots are the most productive feeding areas for hunters without connections here.

UPLAND BIRDS
Ruffed Grouse, Hungarian Partridge, Woodcock, Pheasant, and Turkey

WATERFOWL
Ducks and Geese

Farm ponds, such as this one near Little Falls, often hold a few resident ducks as well as some on their way south for the winter.

ACCOMMODATIONS

Cliffwood Motel, 1201 North County Road 76 / 19 units / Cable color TV, free coffee and ice / Pets allowed / 320-632-5488 / $-$$

Goodnight Inn, RR 6, Box 280 / 15 units / Color cable TV, some rooms with microwaves and refrigerators / Pets allowed with approval / 320-632-2989 or 1-800-575-0594 / $-$$$

CAMPGROUNDS AND RV PARKS

Fletcher Creek Campground, Route 5, Box 93A / Full hookups, hot showers, flush toilets, store, ice, firewood, laundry, and sanitation station / Pets allowed on leash and must be cleaned up after / 320-632-9636 or 1-800-337-9636 / $-$$

RESTAURANTS

The Kitchen Restaurant, 1201 First Avenue / Open 7 days a week, 6AM–11PM / Full service restaurant, breakfast served all day, Bridgeman's soda fountain, and espresso / 320-632-2384

Pete and Joy's Bakery, 121 East Broadway / Open at 5AM Mon–Sat / Fresh baked goods, soups, salads, sandwiches, coffee, and boxed lunches / 320-632-6388

Jerry's Supper Club, County Road 76 South / Mon–Sat, 4:30PM–10PM / Known for prime rib, barbecue ribs, salad bar, and full liquor service / 320-632-2501

VETERINARIANS

Little Falls Veterinary Clinic, 16571 Haven Road / 320-632-9216

Community Animal Hospital, 214 Second Street Northeast / 320-632-2994 or 1-800-806-2994

SPORTING GOODS

Pap's Sport Shop, 64 East Broadway / 320-632-5171

Wal-Mart, 1800 First Avenue North East / 320-632-3644

AUTO REPAIR

Doc's Auto Service, 104 Sixth Street Northeast / 320-632-3615

Bill's Standard Service, 200 First Street Southeast / 320-632-5311

AIR SERVICE

Little Falls Morrison County Airport / Small aircraft / 320-632-2413

Northwest Airlink, St. Cloud / 1-800-225-2525

MEDICAL

Centracare Clinic, 808 Third Street Southeast / 320-632-1099

St. Gabriel's Hospital, 815 Second Street Southeast / 320-632-5441

TAXIDERMIST

Sportsman's Image Taxidermy, 16515 203rd Street / 320-632-3558

FOR MORE INFORMATION

Little Falls Area Chamber of Commerce
200 First Street Northwest
Little Falls, MN 56345
320-632-5155 or 1-800-325-5916

Gary Johnson
Minnesota Department of Natural Resources Wildlife Section
Rt. 4, Box 19A
Little Falls, MN 56345
320-616-2468

Hinckley
Mille Lacs, Kanabec, and Pine Counties

County Population:	Hinckley Population–1,150
Mille Lacs–20,648	October Temperature–50°
Kanabec–14,030	County Acres in CRP:
Pine–23,582	Mille Lacs–244
County Area:	Kanabec–165
Mille Lacs–575 sq. mi.	Pine–156
Kanabec–525 sq. mi.	WMAs–26 (45,407 acres)
Pine–1,411 sq. mi.	

Lumberjacks and farmers settled Hinckley, established in 1885 along the banks of the Grindstone River. Its historic downtown still stands just off Interstate 35. The Great Hinckley Fire of 1894 destroyed the town and several surrounding communities and killed 400 people. For many years thereafter, the lumber industry was nonexistent, and farming became the mainstay of the area's economy.

Today, farming is still an important economic base, but timber has made a comeback. Aspen trees grown in the area are an important source for the paper industry. Also contributing to Hinckley's growth are tourism and the local Indian casino.

Mille Lacs Wildlife Management Area, consisting of 36,719 acres, is an excellent public hunting resource. Ruffed grouse numbers have increased in the WMA as well as in the rest of the region's counties and can be found in and around aspen groves. PRIM maps are a valuable asset in locating and using the huntable state and county lands of this region.

Wet years find good woodcock numbers in the abundant lowland areas. Few sharptail are found on public hunting land, and private property access is limited. This is also true of the few pheasant to be found in the southern part of Pine County. Turkeys are becoming more and more huntable in the lower portion of these three counties. Check with wildlife management areas and DNR wildlife managers for locations and numbers.

Resident duck populations are down after a few dry years that caused nesting problems. Normally, mallards, wood ducks, and green- and blue-winged teal would be numerous on the area's waterways and potholes. Some migrating birds provide hunting later in the season. Canada goose numbers are high and can be found in agricultural fields with limited access or resting on area lakes.

UPLAND BIRDS
Ruffed Grouse, Sharp-tailed Grouse, Woodcock, Turkey, and Pheasant

WATERFOWL
Ducks and Geese

This cover, found north of Hinckley, is perfect for finding ruffed grouse.

ACCOMMODATIONS

61 Motel, 1409 Hwy 23 North (Old Hwy 61) / 12 units / Color cable TV and restaurant nearby / Pets allowed / 320-245-5419 / $-$$

Super 8 Motel, Intersection I-35 and Hwy 23, Finlayson 55735 / 30 units just 10 minutes north of Hinckley / Laundry, whirlpool, RV parking, color TV, and free coffee and rolls in the morning / Pets allowed by permission / 320-245-5284 or 1-800-800-8000 / $$-$$$

CAMPGROUNDS AND RV PARKS

St. Croix Haven Campground, Rt.3, Box 385 / 92 sites / Indoor heated pool, water and electric hookups, adult lounge, restrooms, showers, and laundry / Pets welcome / 320-655-7989 or 1-800-280-0166 / $

RESTAURANTS

Tobie's Restaurant, P.O. Box 397 / 24 hours, 7 days a week / Over 50 years in the area, famous bakery, coffee shop, lounge, and fine dining area / 320-384-6174

Marge's Cafe, Old Hwy 61 South / Mon–Fri, 5AM–4PM; Sat, 5AM–3PM / Old style cafe with good, homestyle cooking / 320-384-6209

VETERINARIANS

Twin Pines Veterinary Clinic, 129 Main Street East / 320-384-7004

SPORTING GOODS

Banning Sport & Gun, I-35 & Hwy 23 Banning Junction / 320-245-5296 / 10 minutes north of Hinckley

AUTO REPAIR

Hinckley Automotive Inc., 320 Fire Monument Road / 320-384-0206

AIR SERVICE

Northwest Airlines, Duluth / 1-800-225-2525

MEDICAL

Mora Medical Center LTD, 302 Fire Monument Road / 320-384-6189

TAXIDERMIST

Ouverson Wildlife Taxidermy, Rt.2, Box 123 / 320-692-7763

FOR MORE INFORMATION

Hinckley Convention and Visitors Bureau
P.O. Box 197
Hinckley, MN 55037
320-384-0126 or 1-800-996-4566

Dick Tuszynski
Minnesota Department of Natural Resources Wildlife Section
Mille Lacs WMA
320-532-3537

Lee Hemness
P.O. Box 398
Hinckley, MN 55037
320-384-6148

St. Cloud
Stearns and Benton Counties

County Population:	St. Cloud Population–59,202
Stearns–130,574	October Temperature–50°
Benton–34,057	County Acres in CRP:
County Area:	Stearns–27,314
Stearns–1,345 sq. mi.	Benton–862
Benton–408 sq. mi.	WMAs-30 (4,909 acres)

St. Cloud, the city of granite, is situated on the Mississippi River between Interstate 94 on the west and US Hwy 10 on the east. One of Minnesota's larger cities, St. Cloud was literally built from the granite quarries encircling the area. It is a busy college town with many amenities for visitors.

Pheasant numbers here are good to fair and are best hunted in and around food-plot areas as well as the swamps and lowlands found on the wildlife management areas. There are few Hungarian partridge in this area. Ruffed grouse are sparse due to the lack of aspen, however alder brush and some of the lowland areas may hold a few birds. Turkey hunting is becoming more popular here, both on private land and on the wildlife management areas where they have been introduced. Hunting on private land is limited unless you have contacts in the area. PRIM maps will help you locate state or county lands that may hold a few birds.

Good resident populations of mallards, wood ducks, teal, widgeon and ringnecks are found on the few lakes with public access and on potholes found in wildlife management areas. Migrating ducks can offer good hunting in the same areas. Canada goose numbers are way up, but there is almost zero access on any of the private lands where they feed. They can be found resting on area rivers and other waters. These birds learn quickly, and once the shooting starts, they move into towns to rest.

UPLAND BIRDS
Pheasant, Ruffed Grouse, Turkeys, Hungarian Partridge, and Woodcock

WATERFOWL
Ducks and Geese

ACCOMMODATIONS
Super 8 Motel, 50 Park Avenue South / 68 units / Continental breakfast, cable color TV, and 24-hour Perkin's Restaurant next door / Pets allowed / 320-253-5530 or 1-800-800-8000 / $$-$$$

Budget Inn, I-94 and Hwy 24, 6 miles south of St. Cloud at Exit 178 / 27 units / Color TV, refrigerators, free coffee, whirlpool, sauna, and lounge / Pets allowed / 320-558-2221 or 1-800-950-7751 / $$-$$$

CAMPGROUNDS AND RV PARKS

St. Cloud Campground and RV Park, 2491 Second Street Southeast / 103 sites / Large, level pull-thrus, clean restrooms, showers, laundry, LP gas, wood, dump station, store, ice, and RV supplies / Call ahead for pets / 320-251-4463 / $

RESTAURANTS

Copper Lantern Restaurant, Hwy 10 and East St. Germain Street / Open 7 days a week, 6AM–12PM / Bakery, homemade soups, and standard family menu / 320-252-0672

D.B. Searle's, 18 South Fifth Avenue / Mon–Sat, 11AM–1PM; Sun, 3PM–10PM / Four-level restaurant, bar, great foods with an all American menu / 320-253-0655

O'Hara's Brew Pub and Restaurant, 3308 Third Street North / Open 7 days a week, 11AM–10PM / Fabulous on site brewed beers, wonderful variety of meals, special pastas, and many large screen TVs / 320-251-9877

VETERINARIANS

Clearwater Road Pet Hospital, 2703 Clearwater Road / 24-hour emergency service / 320-252-6700

SPORTING GOODS

Gander Mountain Retail Store, 614 Second Street South, Waite Park (west end of St. Cloud) / 320-654-6600

Scheel's Sports Shop, Crossroads Center / 320-252-9494

AUTO REPAIR

Firestone Tire and Service Center, 2701 West Division Street / 320-251-3210

Heartland Four Wheel Drive, 18 Seventh Avenue Northeast / 320-259-4791

AIR SERVICE

St. Cloud Airport, 1550 45th Avenue Southeast / Northwest Airlines / 320-251-8574 or 1-800-225-2525

MEDICAL

St. Cloud Hospital, 1406 Sixth Avenue North / 320-251-2700 or 1-800-835-6652

TAXIDERMIST

Schmidkunz Paul Wildlife Art Gallery, 1152 61st Avenue Southeast / 320-253-8197

FOR MORE INFORMATION

St. Cloud Area Convention
and Visitors Bureau
30 Sixth Avenue South
P.O. Box 487
St. Cloud, MN 56302-0487
320-656-3828 or 1-800-264-2940 Ext. 128

Mike Maurer
Minnesota Department of Natural
Resources Wildlife Section
4140 Thielman
St. Cloud, MN 56301
320-255-4279

Elk River
Sherburne and Wright Counties

County Population:	Elk River Population–14,667
Sherburne–56,682	October Temperature–50°
Wright–82,493	County Acres in CRP:
County Area:	Sherburne–666
Sherburne–437 sq. mi.	Wright–6,501
Wright–661 sq. mi.	WMAs–14 (4,202 acres)

Indians called the area "Wich a wan" (where two rivers join). An early settlement was built here at the confluence of the Elk and Mississippi Rivers. Today, Elk River sits just north of the Twin Cities at the same junction and with US 10 running through the heart of it. Its slogan is "where city and country flow together."

Turkey reintroduction efforts have been successful in the wildlife management areas, where pheasant numbers are good as well. With its proximity to a major metropolitan area, weekends receive much more hunting pressure than weekdays.

Ruffed grouse are scarce due to the small amount of preferred habitat, and Hun populations are just beginning to climb. Development has brought an overall loss of cover and habitat. Wildlife management areas offer the bulk of the remaining, very important habitat.

Potholes are the only real source for hunting mallard, teal, wood ducks, and late-season ringnecks in the two-county area. Some ducks are found on the rivers and streams, but access is limited.

Canada goose numbers are very high, but since their food is generally on private land, access is difficult. And even when they are found resting on the limited larger bodies of water, it doesn't take much shooting for these birds to move to safer stretches of water in town where hunting is not allowed.

UPLAND BIRDS
Pheasant, Ruffed Grouse, Hungarian Partridge, Turkey, and Woodcock

WATERFOWL
Ducks and Geese

ACCOMMODATIONS

AmericInn Motel, 17432 Hwy 10 / 42 units / Indoor pool, sauna, cable color TV, and free continental breakfast / Pets allowed / 612-441-8554 or 1-800-634-3444 / $$-$$$

Elk Motel, 13291 Hwy 10 Northwest / 16 units / Color cable TV, in-room coffee, refrigerators, and microwaves / Pets allowed / 612-441-2552

CAMPGROUNDS AND RV PARKS
Camp in the Woods, 14791 289th Avenue, Zimmerman 55398 / North of Elk River off Hwy 169 / 150 sites / Water, electric, 90 sites with sewer, flush toilets, showers, LP gas, and store / Pets on leashes / 612-389-2516 or 612-427-5050 / $

RESTAURANTS
Houle's Tally Ho Restaurant, 17069 Hwy 10 Northwest / Open 7 days a week, 6AM–9PM / Family atmosphere with your favorite comfort foods and homemade pies / 612-441-2708

Time Out Restaurant and Sports Bar, 19232 Evans Street / Open 7 days a week, 11AM–1AM / 12 large screen TVs, good American foods / 612-441-4443

VETERINARIANS
Elk River Animal Hospital, 15670 90th Street / 612-441-5111

SPORTING GOODS
Pro Sporting Goods, 6871 Hwy 10 Northwest, Ramsey / 612-576-1706

AUTO REPAIR
Champion Auto Stores, 720 Main Street / 612-441-5160
J R Tech Automotive, 279 Carson Avenue / 612-441-4653

AIR SERVICE
Northwest Airlines, Minneapolis/St. Paul / 1-800-225-2525

MEDICAL
Fairview Northland Clinic, 290 Main Street / 612-241-0373

TAXIDERMIST
Rich's Taxidermy, 14526 89th Street Northeast / 612-441-7170

FOR MORE INFORMATION
Elk River Area Chamber of Commerce
509 Hwy 10
Elk River, MN 55330
612-441-3110

Mike Maurer
Minnesota Department of Natural Resources Wildlife Section
4140 Thielman
St. Cloud, MN 56301
320-255-4270

Mora
Isanti and Chisago Counties

County Population:	Mora Population–2,999
Isanti–29,603	October Temperature–50°
Chisago–38,937	County Acres in CRP:
County Area:	Isanti–952
Isanti–439 sq. mi.	Chisago–616
Chisago–418 sq. mi.	WMAs-11 (4,506 acres)

Mora is located just off Interstate 35 about 50 miles north of the Twin Cities. Established as a railroad station in 1882, Mora has had a past centered first around logging and then farming. The Swedish immigrants who settled the area brought with them a hard work ethic, which holds true today in the area's diverse economy.

Pheasant populations are rising, and local wildlife management areas have been designed to accommodate the increased bird numbers. Ruffed grouse numbers are on the upswing, as well, but look for them in the alder brush lowlands in the WMAs rather than in their typical aspen habitat. During the peak of migration, woodcock numbers are fair and can be found in the same areas as grouse. Turkey populations are also on the increase in wildlife management areas.

As elsewhere, Canada goose numbers are very strong here. Accessible goose hunting is found primarily on the wildlife management areas with bodies of water, which is also where you will find mallards, wood ducks, and teals. Don't forget to check for public access on the area's lakes as well.

UPLAND BIRDS
Pheasant, Turkey, Ruffed Grouse, and Woodcock

WATERFOWL
Ducks and Geese

ACCOMMODATIONS
Ann River Motel, Hwy 65 / 23 units / Color cable TV, in-room coffee / Host to the Ruffed Grouse Dog Trails / Pets allowed / 320-679-2972

Motel Mora, 301 South Hwy 65 and 23 / 23 units / Color cable TV, in-room coffee, 2 kitchenette units, refrigerators and microwaves in some rooms / Pets allowed / 320-679-3262

CAMPGROUNDS AND RV PARKS
Riverview Campground, 764 Fish Lake Drive / 60 sites / Complete hookups for electric, sewer, and water; central bathroom and showers / Pets on leash / 320-679-3275

A set of decoys on a lake near Mora.

RESTAURANTS

Country Cottage Cafe, 108 South Union Street / Open Mon–Fri, 6AM–4PM; Sat, 7AM–Noon / Breakfast and real homecooked meals / 320-679-2419

Luigi's, 710 South Hwy 65 / Open Mon–Sat 11AM–9:30PM / Large portions, Italian cooking, and full bar / 320-679-4492

Freddie's, 810 South Hwy 65 / Open Sun–Thur 6AM–9PM; Fri and Sat 6AM–10PM / Full service family dining specializing in broasted chicken and barbecue ribs / 320-679-2811

VETERINARIANS

East Central Veterinarians, 2004 Mahogany Street / 320-679-4197

SPORTING GOODS

Jerry's Sport & Bait Shop, 71 North Hwy 65 / 320-679-2151

The Weapon Shop, 28 North Union Street / 320-679-2872

Holiday Station Store, 700 Hwy 65 South / 320-679-3856

Pamida, 340 Hwy 65 South / 320-679-5115

AUTO REPAIR
Glen's Tire and Automotive, 800 East Forest / 320-679-2500
Jerry's Service, 824 South Union and Hwy 65 / 320-679-2691

AIR SERVICE
Northwest Airlines, Minneapolis/St. Paul / 1-800-225-2525

MEDICAL
Kanabec Hospital, 300 Clark Street / 320-679-1212

TAXIDERMIST
Little Bit of Nature Taxidermy, 1890 South Hwy 65 / 320-679-0334

FOR MORE INFORMATION
Mora Area Chamber of Commerce
20 North Union Street
Mora, MN 55051
320-679-5792 or 1-800-291-5792

Dave Pauly
Minnesota Department of Natural Resources Wildlife Sections
800 Oak Savanna Lane Southwest
Cambridge, MN 55008
612-689-7108

A ruffed grouse has used this area and left a burrow in the deep snow.

Region 4 Map

- ● Cities/Towns
- ▬ State Line
- ▬ Roads
- ─ Rivers
- ▨ Indian Reservations
- ▰ National Wildlife Refuges

Region 4

Southwest Minnesota's landscape is made of tall-grass prairie and provides a vivid contrast to much of the rest of the state, where forest and water dominate the scenery. Once, buffalo, elk, deer, and prairie chickens thrived here, where the deep-rooted, tall grasses provided habitat and plenty of food. Some believe that the great northern forests would have covered this area if fires started by lightning and Native Americans hadn't prevented the forest's encroachment.

Once European settlers moved in, these prairies were planted with the wheat, corn, soybeans, and other food crops that dominate the landscape today. This region's economy is still driven mostly by agriculture.

There are fewer lakes here but there are more small prairie potholes and numerous rivers and creeks that flow southward. The Minnesota River Valley runs through the heart of this territory and is one of the main arteries of the Mississippi River. This land holds some of the most fertile soils to be found in Minnesota. Glaciers scraped topsoil from the north and deposited it along its southward path. Long stretches of gently rolling landscape are now dotted with farms as far as the eye can see.

Within this region, there are many wildlife management areas offering diverse hunting opportunities. Lac Qui Parle, one of the state's largest wildlife management areas at 31,238 acres, has some of the best duck and goose numbers in the state. There are special regulations that apply here, which means that the local Minnesota DNR office (320-734-4451) should be contacted before any hunting trip to the area.

With the variety of agricultural crops found here, it is well suited for pheasant, and in some areas, there are also fair numbers of Hungarian partridge. To find birds, look for tall grass, cattails, old farm sites, the edges of harvested fields, and wooded areas. Hunting access to private land can be difficult to find, but there are a few landowners who allow hunting. Once again, it helps to have local contacts.

If you want to use the services of a guide or outfitter, there are some available, particularly for goose hunting, and mostly found near the Lac Qui Parle Wildlife Management Area. Making use of such services can greatly improve your hunting success.

Many of the wildlife management areas have been designed to attract waterfowl migrating through the state. Some of the areas offer jump shooting opportunities.

Region 4 Gray Partridge Distribution

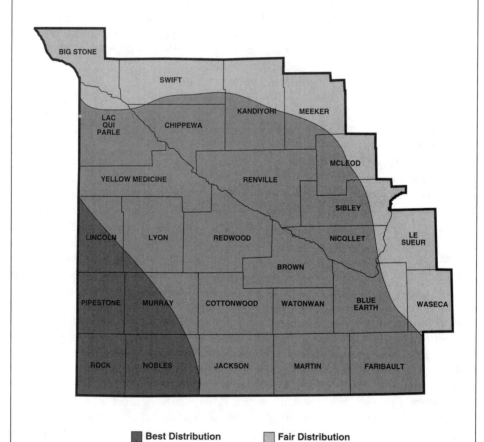

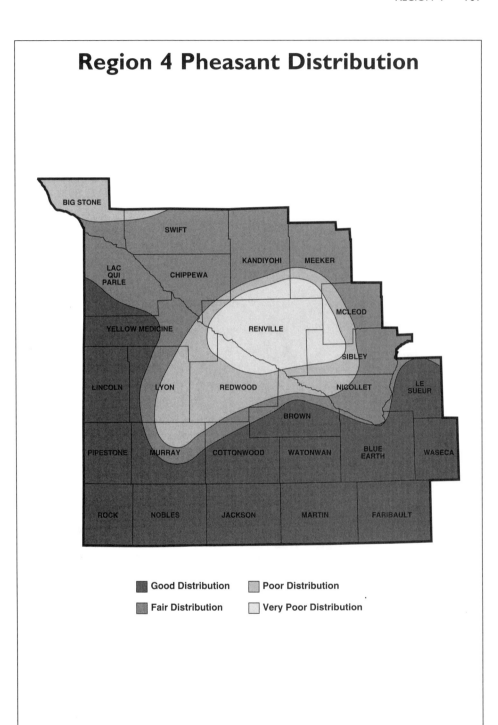

Region 4 Pheasant Distribution

Region 4 Wild Turkey Distribution

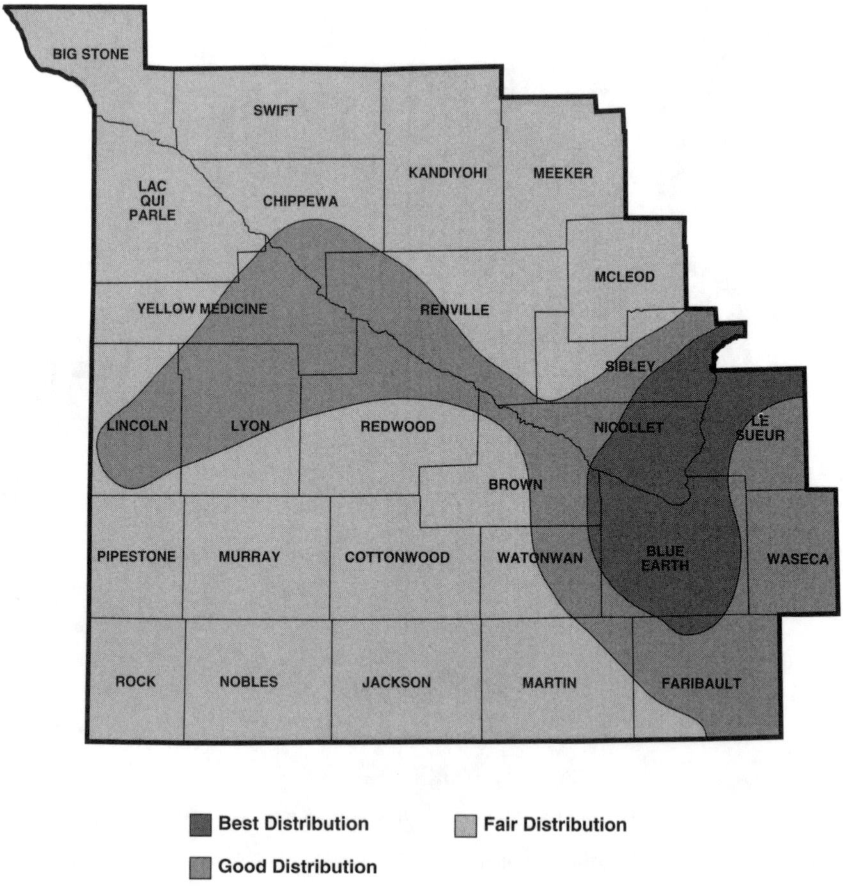

BIG STONE

SWIFT

LAC QUI PARLE

CHIPPEWA

KANDIYOHI

MEEKER

MCLEOD

YELLOW MEDICINE

RENVILLE

SIBLEY

LINCOLN

LYON

REDWOOD

NICOLLET

LE SUEUR

BROWN

BLUE EARTH

PIPESTONE

MURRAY

COTTONWOOD

WATONWAN

WASECA

ROCK

NOBLES

JACKSON

MARTIN

FARIBAULT

Best Distribution   Fair Distribution

Good Distribution

Region 4 Woodcock Distribution

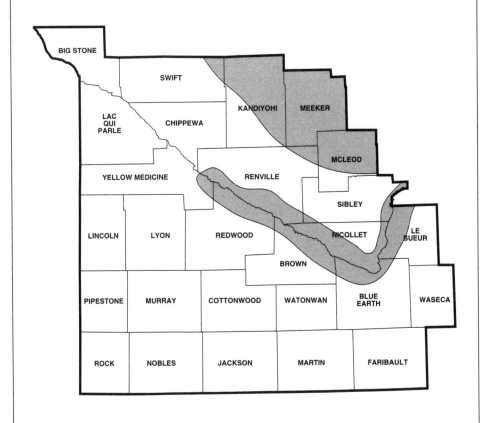

Fair Distribution

Benson
Big Stone, Swift, and Chippewa Counties

County Population:	Benson Population–3,235
Big Stone–5,915	October Temperature–55°
Swift–11,159	County Acres in CRP:
Chippewa–13,183	Big Stone–7,125
County Area:	Swift–26,248
Big Stone–497 sq. mi.	Chippewa–6,106
Swift–744 sq. mi.	WMAs–48 (41,454 acres)
Chippewa–583 sq. mi.	

Benson is located west of the Twin Cities at the crossroads of US 12 and State Highway 29. The town became one of the railroad's hubs for shipping locally grown grains to mills in the Twin Cities. Today, the rich farmland is still producing grain. While some of the area's wetlands have been drained for growing more crops, there is still an abundance of prairie lakes and potholes that support wildlife. Wildlife management areas are generally located around water but are also surrounded by agricultural fields, so that habitat is varied. Federal waterfowl areas are another important resource here, with tall grass and cattails surrounding the waters found in these refuges.

Huns are few and far between but can be found in and around short grasslands with brushy features. Turkey hunting is on the rise, mostly in Big Stone County, where permits are available. Contact the local wildlife manager for help in locating turkey populations.

Because of Lac Qui Parle and the surrounding WMAs, both ducks and geese are abundant. There is so much waterfowl hunting available in the area that you would not be able to hunt them all. It's wise to choose a few areas to hunt in advance of your trip. Jump shooting early in the morning or placing a decoy spread on a pond works well early and late in the season, when migrating flocks come through.

UPLAND BIRDS
Pheasant, Hungarian Partridge, and Turkey

WATERFOWL
Canada Geese and Ducks

ACCOMMODATIONS
Motel 1, East Highway 12 / 10 units, 6 units are efficiencies / Cable TV / Pets allowed / 320-843-4434 / $-$$

Super 8 Motel, West Highway 12 / 21 units / TV / Continental breakfast / Adjoining bar and grill / Pets allowed / 320-843-3451 / $$

CAMPGROUNDS AND RV PARKS
Ambush Park, West Highway 9 / Located on the Chippewa River / 7 RV sites and additional sites for tenting / Electric and water—all sites have picnic tables and fire rings; dump station, and hot showers / Pets allowed / 320-843-4775 / $$

RESTAURANTS
DeToy's Family Restaurant, 210 13th Street South / Open Mon–Fri, 6AM–9PM; Sat, 7AM–9PM; Sun, 8AM–9PM / Tuesday buffet, 5PM–8PM / Sunday noon buffet / Specialty is broasted chicken and specials for breakfast everyday / Setups for bring your own liquor / 320-843-4767
Benson Golf Club, West Highway 9 / Open 7 days a week, Noon–9PM / Specialty fine dining featuring steaks and prime rib / Full service bar / 320-842-7901

VETERINARIANS
Benson Veterinary Clinic, 1440 Minnesota Avenue / 24 hour service / 320-842-7501

SPORTING GOODS
Holiday Station Store, 314 14th Street / 320-843-2018
Our Own Hardware, 1221 Pacific Avenue / 320-842-7581
Pamida, 19th Street and Minnesota / 320-843-4252

AUTO REPAIR
Amundson Wayne Garage, RR3 / 320-843-4699
Jack's Auto, 1435 Utah Avenue / 320-842-4002

AIR SERVICE
City of Benson Airport / 320-843-4880 / Small aircraft only
Northwest Airlines, Minneapolis and St. Paul / 1-800-225-2525

MEDICAL
Swift County/Benson Hospital, 1815 Wisconsin Avenue / 320-843-4232 or 1-800-324-0787

TAXIDERMIST
Brunko Taxidermy Studio, 1120 Park Lane, Morris 56267 / 320-589-4589

FOR MORE INFORMATION
Benson Area Chamber of Commerce
1410 Kanas Avenue
Benson, MN 56215
1-800-568-5722

Dave Soehren
Minnesota Department of Natural Resources Wildlife Section
323 Schlieman Avenue
Appleton, MN 56208
320-289-2493

Willmar
Kandiyohi and Meeker Counties

County Population:	Willmar Population–18,831
Kandiyohi–41,652	October Temperature–55°
Meeker–21,711	County Acres in CRP:
County Area:	Kandiyohi–31,087
Kandiyohi–796 sq. mi.	Meeker–13,244
Meeker–609 sq. mi.	WMAs–27 (5,824 acres)

Willmar is located west of the Twin Cities at the junction of US 12 and US 71. The surrounding landscape is dotted with glacial lakes and is considered by many to be the buffer zone between the prairie to the south and the forest to the north. Willmar was founded as a major railroad hub for the north and western parts of the state.

Ruffed grouse populations are very limited here due to lack of habitat. This also seems to be the case for Hungarian partridge as well. South and west of Willmar is your best bet for finding any Hun activity. Pheasants rule the roost and their numbers are good. Hunting is done primarily on and around the wildlife management areas because there is little access to private land. In the northern parts of these counties, the big news is the boom in turkey populations. These birds are very adaptable and are utilizing foods such as buckthorn berries, basswood seeds, and leftover grains on area farms. Most birds are found on private land where access can be difficult but not impossible to find. As the population grows so should the number of farmers willing to let hunters on their property.

Dominating the waterfowl hunting are the ever-increasing numbers of Canada geese. Early in the season, hunt the resident geese and ducks on the many lakes, marshes, ponds, and waterways in the region. Later in the season, target migrating shovelers, teal, mallard, pintail, and wood ducks, which may move through very quickly. The wildlife management areas, with their excellent habitat, may hold migrating birds a little longer, depending on weather conditions. If there are high winds and early snow, ducks won't linger long.

UPLAND BIRDS
Pheasant, Hungarian Partridge, Ruffed Grouse, Turkey, and Woodcock

WATERFOWL
Canada Geese and Ducks

ACCOMMODATIONS
Colonial Inn, 1102 South First Street / 23 units / Cable TV / Refrigerators and microwaves / Whirlpool suites / Pet allowed / 320-235-4444 or 1-800-396-4445 / $-$$-$$$

A flock of Canada geese dropping into a farm field in southern Minnesota.

Hi-Way 12 Motel, 609 East Highway 12 / 14 units / Cable TV / Pets allowed / 320-235-4500 / $-$$

Lakeview Inn, North Business Highways 71 and 23 / 36 units / Cable TV, continental breakfast, restaurant, lounge, whirlpool suites / Pets allowed / 320-235-3424 or 1-800-718-3424 / $$-$$$

CAMPGROUNDS AND RV PARKS

Henderson's Lake Resort and Campgrounds, 11174 County Road 9 Northeast, Spicer 56288 / 13 sites / Electric and water hookups, hot showers, and restrooms / Pets allowed / 320-796-2979 / $

RESTAURANTS

All-A-Bord, 905 West Litchfield Avenue / Open 7 days a week, 11AM–8PM; Sun, 10AM–2PM / Buffet style eating in a unique surrounding / 320-235-5822

Blue Heron on the Green, 1000 26th Avenue Northeast / Open Tues–Sat, 11AM–1PM in the lounge; Tues–Sat, 5PM–9PM in the restaurant / Prime rib, seafood, chicken, and pastas are featured on the menu / 320-235-4448

McMillan's Restaurant, 2620 South Highway 71 / 7 days, 24 hours / Family dining with soups, pies, and a complete menu / 320-235-7213

VETERINARIANS
Willmar Pet Hospital, 1804 Southwest Trott Avenue / 320-235-1090

SPORTING GOODS
71 Bait and Sports, 5511 Highway 71 / 320-235-4097
Our Own Hardware, 1700 South First Street / 320-235-9000

AUTO REPAIR
Ed's Service Center, 919 Gorton Avenue Northwest / 320-235-5945
Halldin's, 1951 48th Avenue Northeast / 320-235-5202 or 1-800-829-5205

AIR SERVICE
Willmar Municipal Airport, Airport Drive / 320-235-4844 / Small aircraft only
Northwest Airlines, Minneapolis and St. Paul / 1-800-225-2525

MEDICAL
Rice Memorial Hospital, 301 Becker Avenue Southwest / 320-235-4543

TAXIDERMIST
Master Design Taxidermy, 4926 15th Street Northwest / 320-235-9999

FOR MORE INFORMATION
Willmar Area Chamber of Commerce
2104 East Highway 12
Willmar, MN 56201
320-235-0300

Montevideo
Lac Qui Parle and Yellow Medicine Counties

County Population:	Montevideo Population–5,516
Lac Qui Parle–8,644	October Temperature–55°
Yellow Medicine–11,638	County Acres in CRP:
County Area:	Lac Qui Parle–22,189
Lac Qui Parle–765 sq. mi.	Yellow Medicine–16,054
Yellow Medicine–758 sq. mi.	WMAs–64 (12,020 acres)

Montevideo is located 130 miles almost straight west of the Twin Cities on State Highway 7. It lies just southeast of Lac Qui Parle Wildlife Management Area where the Chippewa River flows into the Minnesota River. Farming and related agricultural industries dominate the economy in this fertile country. Fishing, hunting, and other outdoor activities are both welcome and promoted here. If you have any questions, you will find people willing to help you.

The Lac Qui Parle Wildlife Management Area is a major draw for hunting and can be very productive for both upland birds and waterfowl. As of 1998, upland bird numbers are low in comparison to other years. However, a few winters with more favorable conditions could see their numbers rebound. This area holds some prime habitat and should produce well in the future, especially if wild bird transplants from South Dakota are implemented.

Turkey hunting possibilities are the silver lining for those willing to put in some time and effort to find huntable populations on private and public lands. Once again, call the area wildlife manager for current information.

Lac Qui Parle and the surrounding wildlife management areas are a sure bet for geese and a wide variety of diving ducks. There is an abundance of hunting opportunity early in the season for ducks and geese. Later in the season, geese are more readily available.

UPLAND BIRDS
Pheasant, Hungarian Partridge, and Turkey

WATERFOWL
Canada Geese and Ducks

ACCOMMODATIONS

Fiesta City Motel, Junction 59, 212 and 7 West / 26 units / Kitchenette suites and cabins, cable TV, and in-room coffee / Pets allowed / 320-269-8896 or 1-800-472-6478 / $-$$

Hotel Hunt on Main, 207 North First Street / 51 rooms / Restaurant, lounge, sports bar, and grill / Pets allowed / 320-269-5554 or 1-888-430-4400 / $$-$$$

CAMPGROUNDS AND RV PARKS

Lagoon Park Campground, 103 Canton Avenue / 10 sites / 8 electric and water hookups / Pets allowed / 320-269-5527 / $

RESTAURANTS

Ja Mom's, 701 West Highway 212 / Open 7 days a week, 5:30AM–10PM / All-day specials catering to family needs / 320-269-6226

Main Street Restaurant, 207 North First Street / Open Tues–Fri, 6AM–10PM; Sat, 7AM–10PM, Sun, 8AM–2PM; Sunday brunch starting at 10:30AM / Located in the Hotel Hunt on Main / Nightly specials featuring specialty dishes / Lounge / 320-269-5554

VETERINARIANS

Veterinary Clinic of Clara City and Olivia, 1605 West Lincoln, Olivia / 320-523-5550

South 71 Veterinary Clinic, Highway 71 South / 24-hour service / 320-235-396

SPORTING GOODS

Mitlyng Bait, Lac Qui Parle Dam, Watson 56295 / 320-269-5593

DJ's Avis Sports, Southtown Plaza / 320-269-7265 or 1-800-281-7265

AUTO REPAIR

DJ's Champion Auto, Southtown Plaza / 320-269-7265 or 1-800-281-7265

Monte Tire and Service, 319 Canton Avenue / 320-269-9204

AIR SERVICE

Northwest Airlines, Minneapolis and St. Paul / 1-800-225-2525

MEDICAL

Chippewa County-Montevideo Hospital, 824 North Eleventh Street / 320-269-8877

TAXIDERMIST

Master Design Taxidermy, 4926 15th Street Northwest, Willmar / 320-235-9999

FOR MORE INFORMATION

Montevideo Area Chamber of Commerce
110 North First Street
Montevideo, MN 56265
320-269-5527 or 1-800-269-5527

Minnesota Department of Natural Resources Wildlife Section
Steve Merchant
National Guard Armory
504 Third Street
Madison, MN 56256
320-598-7641

Hutchinson
Rennville, McLeod, and Sibley Counties

County Population:
  Rennville–17,521
  McLeod–34,493
  Sibley–14,913
County Area:
  Rennville–983 sq. mi.
  McLeod–492 sq. mi.
  Sibley–589 sq. mi.
	Hutchinson Population–12,710
	October Temperature–55°
	County Acres in CRP:
	  Rennville–2,440
	  McLeod–2,194
	  Sibley–1,543
	WMAs–34 (4,311 acres)

The busy town of Hutchinson sits straight west of the Twin Cities at the junction of State Highways 7 and 15. This community was founded by a singing family, known as the Hutchinson Brothers, who where looking for a beautiful spot to build a town with their namesake. Their surveyor convinced them to build on the site that the town now occupies. Beautiful bluffs, a river valley, and forests to the north offer variety to the town's residents. In recent years, it was home to famous wildlife artist, Les Kouba, known for his generosity to many different wildlife organizations around the country.

Upland bird hunting in these counties means pheasant, and as of this book's printing, their numbers are very good. Wildlife management areas, with their abundant water, food, and cover, are the best places to hunt them. The agricultural areas surrounding WMAs offer pheasant even more food and cover, however, access to private land is limited and nonexistent during deer season.

This region supports very few ruffed grouse and Huns. What Hun action there is will be best found along planted strips of prairie grass late in the season. Turkey are also doing well here, and ever-increasing numbers can be found in Renville County. The future should see an increase in huntable turkey range in all of these counties.

Resident ducks, such as mallards and wood ducks, can be found early in the season in wildlife management areas and federal waterfowl production areas. As the season progresses, turn to migrating diving ducks, such as pintail and scaup among others. Canada geese provide good hunting throughout the season.

UPLAND BIRDS
Pheasant, Ruffed Grouse, Hungarian Partridge and Turkey

WATERFOWL
Canada Geese and Ducks

ACCOMMODATIONS
Economy Inn, 200 Highway 7 East / 22 units / Refrigerators, microwaves, coffee makers, and cable TV / Pets allowed / 320-587-2129 / $-$$-$$$

Setting out decoys on a prairie slough in southwestern Minnesota.

King Motel, Highways 7 and 22 West / 24 units / Cable TV, water and queen-sized beds / Pets allowed / 320-587-4743 / $$

CAMPGROUNDS AND RV PARKS
Masonic / West River Park, 900 Harrington / 45 tent, 9 full water and electric hookups / Restrooms, showers, and firewood / Pets allowed on leash / 320-587-2975

RESTAURANTS
Jonny's Restaurant and Sports Lounge, 101 Park Place / Open Mon–Sat, 11AM–11PM; Sunday brunch / California cuisine made from scratch / Seafood, Angus beef, and smoked foods / Full bar service / 320-587-0101

Lamplighter Lounge II Family Sports Bar and Grill, 1011 Highway 15 South / Open Mon–Sat, 11AM–1AM; Sun, 11AM–10PM / Homemade soups and chili, buffalo wings, pork chops, steaks, and salads / Children's menu / 13 TVs / Full bar / 320-587-1010

McCormick's Family Restaurant, Highway 15 South / Open Mon–Sat, 6AM–10PM; Sun, 7AM–10PM / Bakery and breakfast, lunch, and dinner specials / 320-587-4417

VETERINARIANS
Crow River Veterinary Clinic, 164 Fourth Avenue Northwest / 320-587-4888
Hutchinson Pet Hospital, 146 Main Street North / 320-587-3161

SPORTING GOODS
Crow River Outdoors, Inc., 903 Highway 15 South / 320-587-0464
Little Crow Shooting Sports, 1848 2B 202 Circle Street / 320-587-9829

AUTO REPAIR
Crow River Auto and Truck Repair, 1020 Highway 22 South / 320-587-3910
Christensen's Repair Shop, 204 Adams Street Southeast / 320-587-8214

AIR SERVICE
Hutchinson Municipal Airport (Butler Field), 16713 Highway 15 / 320-587-9910 /
    Small aircraft only
Northwest Airlines, Minneapolis and St. Paul / 1-800-225-2525

MEDICAL
Hutchinson Community Hospital, 1095 Highway 15 South / 320-234-5000

TAXIDERMIST
Bear Paw Taxidermy, 415 Adams Street / 320-587-2984

FOR MORE INFORMATION
Hutchinson Area Chamber of Commerce
206 Main Street North
Hutchinson, MN 55350
320-587-5252 or 1-800-572-6689

Don Schultz
Minnesota Department of Natural Resources Wildlife Section
1241 East Bridge Street
Redwood Falls, MN 56283
507-637-4076

Ken Verland
Regional Wildlife Manager
261 Hwy 15 South
New Ulm, MN 56073
507-359-6030

Redwood Falls
Lincoln, Lyon, Redwood, and Brown Counties

County Population:
   Lincoln–6,707
   Lyon–25,431
   Redwood–17,293
   Brown–28,006
County Area:
   Lincoln–537 sq. mi.
   Lyon–714 sq. mi.
   Redwood–880 sq. mi.
   Brown–611 sq. mi.
	Redwood Falls Population–5,197
	October Temperature–55°
	County Acres in CRP:
	   Lincoln–32,654
	   Lyon–12,941
	   Redwood–7,648
	   Brown–7,393
	WMAs–128 (4,707 acres)

Redwood Falls is located southwest of the Twin Cities at the junction of US 71 and State Highway 19, where it sits astride the banks of the Redwood River near its confluence with the Minnesota River. The terrain consists of high bluffs, river valley, and fertile farmland.

Richard Sears sold his first watch in Redwood Falls, and subsequently, the Sears and Roebuck Company got its start. Farming has been an integral part of this community since the 1800s, when farmers brought their crops to the city's mills, which were powered by the river.

Pheasant numbers are down at present due to recent severe winter seasons. But with some mild winters and an abundance of habitat on both private land and wildlife management areas, populations should rebound. On the bright side, Hun numbers have risen and can be found along brushy edges of prairie grasslands and in the stubble of harvested agricultural fields.

Turkey numbers are good, and they can be found along ridges of hardwood timber as well as feeding in and around farms. These birds are very opportunistic feeders and are doing far better than expected. While access to private land isn't abundant, don't let that keep you from asking for permission to hunt. Obtain current information on turkey hunting from the area wildlife manager.

While there is some early season Canada goose hunting in and around the waters found in the wildlife management areas, ducks are the more prevalent game species here. Hunt the resident populations of mallards and wood ducks early in the season. Later, diving ducks pass through on their migration and will stay as long as there is open water. At this time of year, ducks sometimes rely more heavily on food they find in grain fields than on the water plants they normally eat.

UPLAND BIRDS
Pheasant, Hungarian Partridge, and Turkey

WATERFOWL
Ducks and Canada Geese

ACCOMMODATIONS

Comfort Inn, 1382 East Bridge Street / 106 units / Cable TV, 12 units with whirlpool bath, continental breakfast / Pets allowed / 507-644-5700 or 1-800-221-2222 / $$$

Redwood Inn, Highway 19 and 71 / 30 units / Cable TV, restaurant and lounge, complementary breakfast / Pets allowed / 1-800-801-3521 / $-$$-$$$

CAMPGROUNDS AND RV PARKS

Jackpot Junction Casino Hotel Campground, P.O. Box 400, Morton 56270 / 40 full hookup units, paved drive and pads, restrooms and showers, dump station, and other RV services / Pets on leash allowed / 507-644-2645 or 1-800-946-2274 / $

RESTAURANTS

Country Kitchen, 1201 East Bridge Street / Open Sun–Thur, 6AM–11PM, Fri and Sat, 6AM–Midnight / Family foods / 507-637-3220

Valley Supper Club, North Redwood / Open Sun–Fri, 11AM–1:30AM, Sat, 5PM until closing / Bar and supper club with all around fine food / 507-637-5541

VETERINARIANS

Redwood Veterinarians, 300 Mill Street / 507-637-5206

SPORTING GOODS

Kahnke Gunworks, 206 West Eleventh Street / 507-637-2901

Holiday Station Store, East Highway 71 and 19 / 507-637-5003

AUTO REPAIR

Kike's Auto Service, 210 North Patten Street / 507-637-5893

Larry's Auto Center, 409 East Tin Street / 507-637-2234

AIR SERVICE

Redwood Falls Municipal Airport / 507-644-3590 / Small aircraft only
Northwest Airlines, Minneapolis and St. Paul / 1-800-225-2525

MEDICAL

Redwood Falls Hospital, 100 Fallwood Road / 507-637-2907 or 507-637-5888

TAXIDERMIST

Gewerth Taxidermy, 619 East Second Street / 507-637-5446

FOR MORE INFORMATION

Redwood Falls Area
 Chamber of Commerce
610 East Bridge Street
Redwood Falls, MN 56283
507-637-2828 or 1-800-657-7070

Don Schultz
Minnesota Department of Natural
 Resources Wildlife Section
1241 East Bridge Street
Redwood Falls, MN 56283
507-637-4076

Worthington
Pipestone, Murray, Rock, and Nobles Counties

County Population:
  Pipestone–10,427
  Murray–9,624
  Rock–9,966
  Nobles–20,570
County Area:
  Pipestone–466 sq. mi.
  Murray–705 sq. mi.
  Rock–483 sq. mi.
  Nobles–716 sq. mi.
	Worthington Population–10,461
	October Temperature–55°
	County Acres in CRP:
	  Pipestone–9,375
	  Murray–13,942
	  Rock–990
	  Nobles–3,470
	WMAs–86 (9,935 acres)

Minnesota's southwest corner holds rolling hills and fertile soil and its landscape is dominated by farms. Worthington, at the junction of Interstate 90 and US 59, is an agricultural community with processing plants for chicken and turkey. The railroad originally called this Okabena Station after Lake Okabena on the town's southwest side. Okabena means "nesting place of herons" in the Dakota language.

Wildlife management areas in the region hold fair numbers of pheasant and Hungarian partridge, which inhabit the borders of WMAs where there is short grass and brushy cover. Turkey populations are good and are increasing in Pipestone and Murray Counties. As in the rest of the state, turkey hunting is gaining in popularity. Turkeys use woody cover for roosting and feed in farm fields. Contact the local wildlife officer for up-to-date information on locating these birds.

Water in this area is primarily in the form of creeks and small rivers, however, the few prairie ponds and lakes offer jump shooting for pintails, mallards, and teal early in the season. Lakes provide better hunting for flocks of migrating diving ducks. The best goose hunting will be found on the western edge of Talcot Lake Wildlife Management Area containing 3,441 acres of waterfowl habitat.

UPLAND BIRDS
Pheasant, Hungarian Partridge, and Turkey

WATERFOWL
Canada Geese and Ducks

ACCOMMODATIONS
AmericInn Motel, 1475 Darling Drive / 43 units / Continental breakfast, cable TV, specialty rooms with microwaves, refrigerators, and whirlpools / Perkins Restaurant next door / Pets allowed / 507-376-4500 or 1-800-634-3444 / $$-$$$

Best Western Worthington Motel, Northeast Junction Highway 59 and 60 / 36 units / Cable TV, some units with microwaves and refrigerators, continental breakfast / Pets allowed / 507-376-4146 or 1-800-528-1234 / $-$$-$$$

Campgrounds and RV Parks
Olson Park Campground, P.O. Box 279 / 57 campsites, 30 sites with electric hookups / Located on Sunset Bay of Lake Okabena, restrooms, showers, firewood, grills, and picnic tables / Pets allowed on leash / 507-372-8650 / $

Restaurants
The Windmill Cafe, Highway 59 and 60 South / Open 7 days a week, 24 hours / Sunday noon buffet, breakfast any time, and home cooking all of the time / 507-376-5223

Gobbler, 1861 Oxford Street / Open daily, 6AM–11PM / Fresh roasted turkey daily and great homemade soups / 507-372-2200

Brandywine Restaurant, Ramada Inn, Highway 59 North / Open 7 days a week, 6:30AM–2PM and 5PM–10PM / Bar open Mon–Sat, 5PM–1:30AM / Sunday buffet both breakfast and dinner, specializing in steaks, walleye, and atmosphere / 507-327-2991

Veterinarians
Veterinary Medical Center, 600 Oxford Street / 507-372-2957 or 1-800-522-3276

Sporting Goods
K-Mart Store, 1635 Oxford Street / 507-372-2928
Coast-to-Coast Store, 312 Tenth Street / 507-376-4555

Auto Repair
Mark's Towing and Repair, 1566 Rowe Avenue / 507-372-7206
C&M Auto Service, 761 South Highway 59 and 60 / 507-376-4288

Air Service
Worthington Airport, Airport Road / 507-372-8658 / Small aircraft only
Northwest Airlines, Minneapolis and St. Paul / 1-800-225-2525

Medical
Worthington Regional Hospital, 1018 Sixth Avenue / 507-372-2941

Taxidermist
Lais Taxidermy Studio, 718 8th Avenue / 507-376-9459

For More Information
Worthington Area
  Chamber of Commerce
1121 Third Avenue
Worthington, MN 56187
507-372-2919 or 1-800-279-2919

Roy Peterson
Talcot Lake WMA
507-468-2248

Perry Loegering
Minnesota Department of Natural
  Resources Wildlife Section
2431 26th Street
Slayton, MN 56712
507-836-6919

Fairmont
Cottonwood, Watonwan, Jackson, and Martin Counties

County Population:
  Cottonwood–12,930
  Watonwan–11,750
  Jackson–11,750
  Martin–22,849
County Area:
  Cottonwood–640 sq. mi.
  Watonwan–435 sq. mi.
  Jackson–702 sq. mi.
  Martin–709 sq. mi.
	Fairmont Population–11,339
	October Temperature–55°
	County Acres in CRP:
	  Cottonwood–8,332
	  Watonwan–2,227
	  Jackson–6,550
	  Martin–1,738
	WMAs–58 (9,133 acres)

Fairmont is just north of the Iowa border at the junction of Interstate 90 and State Highway 15. It was originally called Fair Mount because of its excellent view of the rolling hills and string of lakes in the area. Before the influx of farmers who settled the area, a fort and a jail were established here. Farming remains the most important part the economy.

Pheasant numbers here are the best they have been in the last five years and are found on both public and private land. Hungarian partridge populations have risen also. The best place to find Huns is in and around wildlife management areas bordered by the stubble of harvested grain or by short grass. The area's increasing turkey populations are found mostly on private land along the Des Moines River Valley and northeast of Windom.

The large resident population of Canada geese provides good hunting in the early part of the season and can be found on harvested grain fields. Later in the season, look for large migrating flocks on prairie potholes and lakes. Resident mallards, teals, and wood ducks are good early in the season on potholes and lakes. Wigeon, pintail, and migrating mallards are a good bet later in the season on the same potholes and lakes.

UPLAND BIRDS
Pheasant, Hungarian Partridge, and Turkey

WATERFOWL
Ducks and Canada Geese

ACCOMMODATIONS
Highland Court Motel, 1245 Lake Avenue / 25 units / Cable TV, all ground-level units, some rooms with queen size bed, refrigerators, and microwaves / Pets allowed / 507-235-6686 / $$-$$$

Southern Minnesota wildlife management areas are good places to find pheasant because they are often located near waterways and have excellent cover.

Holiday Inn, I-90 and Highway 15 / 103 units, Holidome / Cable TV, laundry, Torge's All American Bar and Grill / Pet allowed / 507-238-4771 or 1-800-HOLIDAY / $$$

CAMPGROUNDS AND RV PARKS
Flying Goose Campground, Route 2, Box 274 / 100 sites / Full hookups, showers, restrooms, and laundry / Pets on leash / 507-235-3458 / $

RESTAURANTS
The Ranch Family Restaurant, Highway 15 / Open 7 days a week, 6AM–11PM / Home style foods, soup and salad bar / Cocktail lounge / 507-235-3044

El Rodeo and Las Maracas Cantina, 62 Downtown Plaza / Open Mon, 4PM–11PM , Tues–Sun, 10AM–11PM / Family dining and carryout, Mexican and American food / Cocktails in the "Las Maracas Cantina"

VETERINARIANS
Fairmont Veterinary Clinic, 1275 Highway 15 South / 507-238-4456

SPORTING GOODS
K-Mart, 1215 North State Street / 507-235-8080
Zanke's Hook'um Tackle, 445 Lake Avenue / 507-235-6931

AUTO REPAIR
Richard's Auto Repair and Towing, 200 South Park Street / 507-235-5800

AIR SERVICE
Fairmont Regional Airport, Highway 16 East, RR2, Box 331 / 507-238-8739 / Small aircraft and United Express from the Twin Cities - 1-800-241-6522

MEDICAL
Fairmont Community Hospital, Highway 15 and Johnson Street / 507-238-4254

TAXIDERMIST
Tim Hecht Taxidermy, 806 East Fourth Street / 507-238-2762

FOR MORE INFORMATION
Fairmont Area Chamber of Commerce
206 North State Street
Fairmont, MN 56031
507-235-5547 or 1-800-657-3280

Randy Marki
Minnesota Department of Natural Resources Wildlife Sections
Route 2, Box 245
Windom, MN 56101
507-831-2917

Mankato
Blue Earth, Waseca, Faribault, Nicollet, and Le Sueur Counties

County Population:
  Blue Earth–55,286
  Waseca–18,626
  Faribault–16,548
  Nicollet–29,965
  Le Sueur–24,939
County Area:
  Blue Earth–752 sq. mi.
  Waseca–423 sq. mi.
  Faribault–714 sq. mi.
  Nicollet–452 sq. mi.
  Le Sueur–449 sq. mi.

Mankato Population–31,850
October Temperature–58°
County Acres in CRP:
  Blue Earth–3,876
  Waseca–4,611
  Faribault–1,230
  Nicollet–2,032
  Le Sueur–12,693
WMAs–58 (11,503)

Situated at the confluence of the Blue Earth and Minnesota Rivers, Mankato is built in the mile-wide river valley and the surrounding hills and bluffs. US 169 and US 14 meet here, as well. Before the railroad, waterways provided the best means of transport, and Mankato's location helped it to flourish and grow. While farming is still a vital part of the economy, the city is also home to four colleges and a number of industries. Even though Mankato has grown to be a good-sized city, it still doesn't take long to leave the city behind and find yourself in a rural setting.

Pheasant numbers have been on the increase, and local wildlife management areas and their surrounding farms are excellent places to hunt them. While there is more hunting pressure due to larger communities, good bird populations and numerous wildlife management areas provide sufficient hunting opportunities.

Hungarian partridge are also doing well and are found on the fringes of wildlife management areas where there is short grass or stubble from harvested grain. Here again, turkeys are flourishing on private farmland with wooded river areas nearby.

This is a transitional landscape, from prairie and potholes to lakes, rivers, and forest. There are good numbers of resident ducks, both dabblers and divers, early in the hunting season. Wildlife management areas provide good hunting opportunities, as they do throughout the state. Besides the WMAs, there are lakes northeast of Mankato that shouldn't be overlooked.

Goose populations are high and huntable throughout the season both in fields and on water. Because the geese are so numerous, some area farmers are happy to have hunters thin the flocks for them, so knock on a few doors.

German shorthairs can keep up the pace on a long day of pheasant hunting.

UPLAND BIRDS
Pheasant, Hungarian Partridge, and Turkey

WATERFOWL
Duck and Canada Geese

ACCOMMODATIONS
Holiday Inn, 101 East Main Street, P.O. Box 3386 / 151 units / Cable TV, restaurant and lounge, laundry / Pets allowed / 507-345-1234 or 1-800-HOLIDAY / $$$

Kato Economy Inn, 1255 Range Street (Highway 169) / 54 units / Cable TV / Pets allowed / 507-388-1644 or 1-800-822-2521 / $-$$-$$$

CAMPGROUNDS AND RV PARKS
Daly Park Blue Earth County Park, 35 Map Drive / 74 mobile sites, 52 electric, tent sites, 2 bath houses with showers / 126 acres on the shores of Lura Lake / Pets allowed on leash / 507-524-3000 or 507-625-3281 / $

Land of Memories Campground, P.O. Box 3368 / 42 sites / Electrical hookups, dump station / Located at the confluence of the Minnesota and Blue Earth Rivers / Pets allowed on leash / 507-387-8649

RESTAURANTS

Happy Chef Restaurant, Highway 169 North and 14 Junction / Open 7 days a week, 24 hours / Breakfast anytime and daily specials / Saturday and Sunday breakfast buffet / 507-388-2953

Bobby Joe's Pub, 253 Belgrade Avenue / Open 7 days a week / Food: 7AM–10:30PM; Bar: 8PM–1AM / Casual dining and daily specials / 507-388-8999

Stoney's Restaurant, North Riverfront and Madison Avenue / Featuring steaks, walleye, and Italian cuisine / Full bar / 507-387-4813

VETERINARIANS

Minnesota Valley Pet Hospital, 505 Madison Avenue / 507-345-5900

SPORTING GOODS

Sportsman's Specialties, 14 Deerwood Trail, North Mankato 56003/ 507-947-3956 or 1-800-786-6713

Scheel's All Sport, River Hills Mall / 507-386-7767

AUTO REPAIR

Superior Auto Repair, 409 Patterson / 507-387-5717

Bernie's One Stop Service, 501 Riverfront / 507-345-6678

AIR SERVICE

Mankato Regional Airport / 507-625-6006 / Small and commercial aircraft

American Airline / American Eagle, 1-800-433-7300

Delta Airlines Inc. / 800-221-1212

MEDICAL

Immanuel St. Joseph's-Mayo Health System, 1025 Marsh / 507-625-4031

TAXIDERMIST

Authentic Taxidermy, 1904 South Riverfront Drive / 507-625-4443

FOR MORE INFORMATION

Mankato Area Chamber of Commerce
112 Riverfront Drive
P.O. Box 999
Mankato, MN 56002
507-345-4519 or 1-800-657-4733

Regions 5 and 6 Map

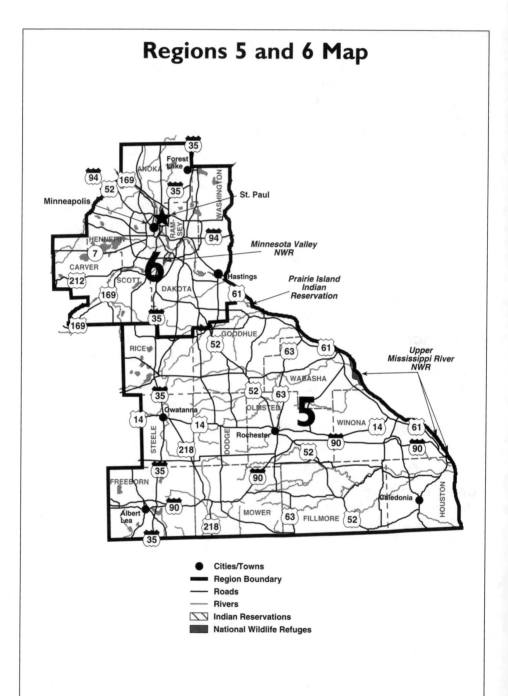

Forest Lake

ANOKA

WASHINGTON

Minneapolis

St. Paul

Minnesota Valley
NWR

HENNEPIN

RAM-
SEY

CARVER

Prairie Island
Indian
Reservation

SCOTT

DAKOTA

Hastings

Upper
Mississippi River
NWR

GOODHUE

RICE

WABASHA

OLMSTED

Owatonna

WINONA

STEELE

Rochester

DODGE

FREEBORN

Caledonia

HOUSTON

Albert
Lea

MOWER

FILLMORE

● Cities/Towns
▬ Region Boundary
— Roads
— Rivers
▨ Indian Reservations
▨ National Wildlife Refuges

Regions 5 and 6

These two regions comprise what is known as the hill country of Minnesota. High bluffs and riverbottom farm country are found in the southern two-thirds and flatter terrain is found around the Twin Cities area.

This region is generally warmer and wetter than the rest of the state. Hardwood trees dominate many of the woods in these two regions. Also found here are two poisonous snakes: the common timber rattlesnake and the very rarely seen massasauga. Timber rattlers are found in the rocky outcroppings of bluffs, and massasauga are found in the Mississippi River's backwaters.

Along the Mississippi River from St. Paul to La Crescent, one finds Minnesota's oldest communities, which are rich in history. The Mississippi and other major rivers in the state carried many of the westward bound settlers and much of its commerce before the railroads were built.

Agriculture, timber, and other commerce continue to use the mighty Mississippi for transporting goods. The many locks and dams were built to aid tugboats and barges navigate the river and have created a variety of backwaters for both resident and migrating waterfowl. The treelined bluffs and farmland are home to an evergrowing population of turkeys. Farms also provide pheasant habitat as well. Limited numbers of Hungarian partridge can be found in the southwestern portion of Region 5, as well as a thin strip along the Mississippi River Valley where migrating woodcock may also be seen in mid-October.

Regions 5 and 6 Gray Partridge Distribution

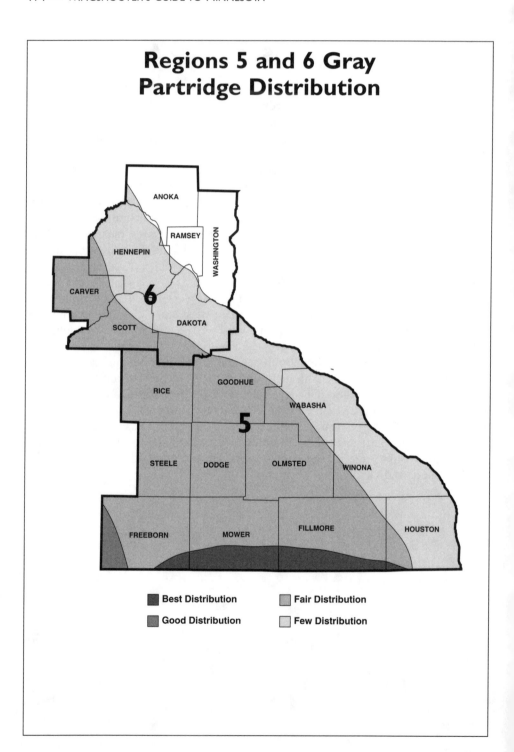

Regions 5 and 6 Pheasant Distribution

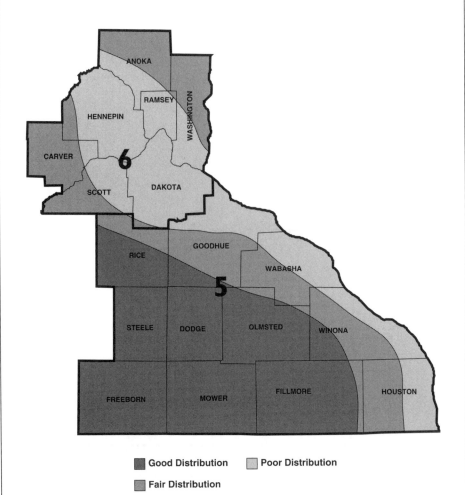

Good Distribution Poor Distribution
Fair Distribution

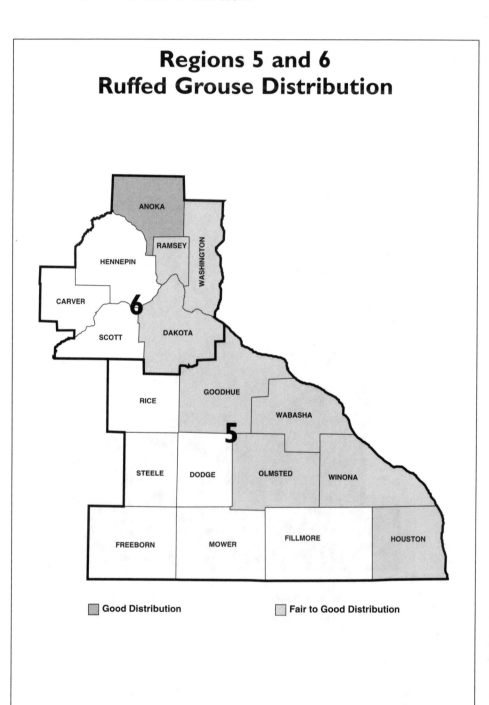

Regions 5 and 6
Ruffed Grouse Distribution

ANOKA

RAMSEY

WASHINGTON

HENNEPIN

CARVER

6

SCOTT

DAKOTA

GOODHUE

RICE

WABASHA

5

STEELE

DODGE

OLMSTED

WINONA

FREEBORN

MOWER

FILLMORE

HOUSTON

☐ Good Distribution   ☐ Fair to Good Distribution

Regions 5 and 6 Wild Turkey Distribution

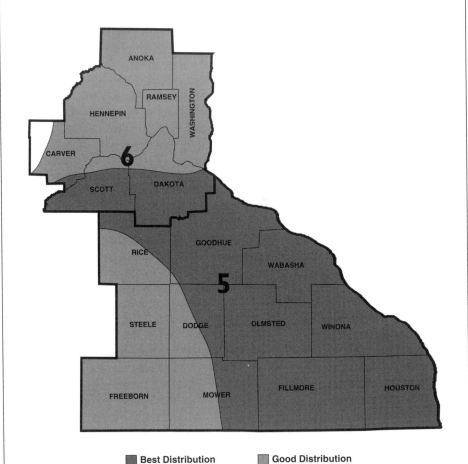

Best Distribution
Good Distribution

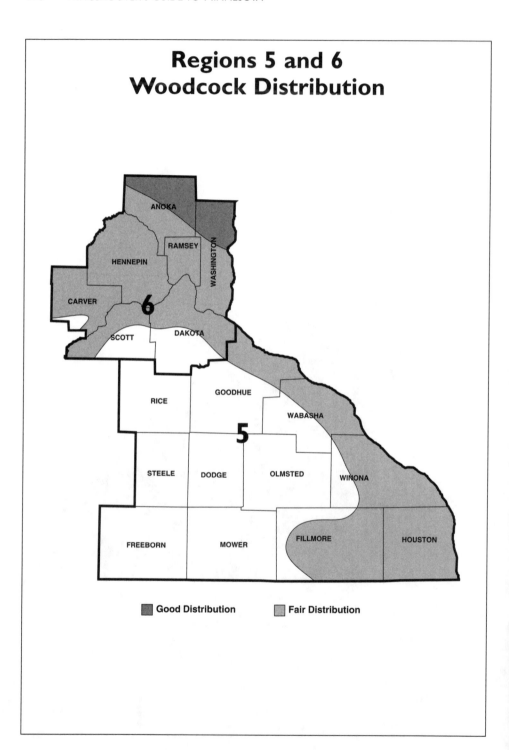

Regions 5 and 6
Woodcock Distribution

Owatonna
Rice, Steele, Dodge, and Goodhue Counties

County Population:	Owatonna Population–20,920
Rice–53,514	October Temperature–60°
Steele–32,320	County Acres in CRP:
Dodge–17,122	Rice–15,825
Goodhue–42,987	Steele–7,316
County Area:	Dodge–2,780
Rice–498 sq. mi.	Goodhue–8,240
Steele–430 sq. mi.	WMAs–15 (1,975 acres)
Dodge–440 sq. mi.	
Goodhue–759 sq. mi.	

About an hour south of the Twin Cities, at the junction of Interstate 35 and US 14, one will find Owatonna, named after an Indian princess who was said to have had her health restored by drinking from the springs at Mineral Springs Park.

In 1866 the Minnesota Central and the Saint Peter and Winona Railways met here and ensured that Owatonna would be a commercial transportation hub. Located on the eastern edge of the prairie, agriculture plays an important role in the area's economy. There are lakes to the north and west and rivers to the south and east.

Although the wildlife management areas are designed primarily as wetland habitat for waterfowl production, they also provide good habitat and cover for pheasant. The agricultural land surrounding the WMAs is also suitable pheasant country, and landowners can be cooperative if hunters ask permission and respect the landowner's rules.

Hungarian partridge populations are small here but can experience a fair amount of fluctuation from year to year. Shortgrass areas and the stubble of harvested grain fields are the best places to find these birds. This is the edge of the woodcock's migratory flyway, and it is rare to come across them. Turkeys provide the bulk of upland bird hunting here, and hunters with good landowner relations are achieving high success ratios. Look for habitat that has wooded areas for roosting and containing the nuts on which they feed. If such habitat is located adjacent to farm fields, that is even better.

Mallards, teal, and wood ducks are the most numerous of the resident ducks found on the smaller wetlands early in the season. Late in the season on larger bodies of water there will be good action on large flocks of divers and dabblers. Check out Chubb and Bullsby Lakes as well as the other lakes and potholes on the edge of the prairie.

Greater Canada geese flourish here and can be found throughout the season depending on the weather. Quality hunting can be found on the eastern edge of Goodhue County as well as the Mississippi River's backwaters and the large, open expanses of water preferred by both geese and ducks.

A ruffed grouse searches for buds on this aspen tree during winter.

UPLAND BIRDS
Pheasant, Hungarian Partridge, Ruffed Grouse, Turkey, and Woodcock

WATERFOWL
Ducks and Canada Geese

ACCOMMODATIONS

Best Budget Inn, I-35 and US 14, R5 / 30 units / Perkins and Happy Chef Restaurants adjacent / Cable TV, microwave, and refrigerators available / Pets allowed with permission / 507-451-0776 / $$-$$$

Budget Host Inn, 745 State Avenue / 27 units / Cable TV / Restaurant and coffee shop adjacent / Pets allowed with permission / 507-451-8712 or 1-800-BUD-HOST / $$

CAMPGROUNDS AND RV PARKS

Owatonna Campground, Inc., 2554 Southwest 28th Street / 185 sites, 55 with sewer, water, and electric, 120 with water and electric / Camping cabin, camp store, and LP gas / Pets allowed on leash with advanced permission / 507-451-8050 or 1-888-922-CAMP / $

RESTAURANTS

Jerry's Supper Club, 203 North Cedar Avenue / Open Mon–Thur, 11AM–2PM and 5PM–9:30PM; Fri and Sat, 11AM–2PM and 5PM–10:30PM / Complete bar / American foods specializing in steaks and seafood / 507-451-6894

Happy Chef Restaurant, I-35 and US 14 / Open 7 days a week, 24 hours / Breakfast anytime and daily specials / Saturday and Sunday breakfast buffet / 507-451-8613

VETERINARIANS

Owatonna Veterinary Services, 2121 Cedar Avenue / 507-451-0960

SPORTING GOODS

Cabela's Retail Store, 3900 Cabela Drive / 507-444-0528

Coast to Coast Hardware, 121 Oakdale Street / 507-451-7978

AUTO REPAIR

Crown Auto Service Center, 1120 Hoffman Drive / 507-455-3080

Gleason's Automotive, 505 West North Street / 507-455-0203

AIR SERVICE

Owatonna Municipal Airport, 3400 West Frontage Road / 507-444-2448 / Small aircraft only

Northwest Airlines, Minneapolis and St. Paul / 1-800-225-2525

MEDICAL

Owatonna Hospital, 903 South Oak Avenue / 507-451-3850 or 507-455-7632

TAXIDERMIST

Hidden Creek Taxidermy, 3819 Dane Road / 507-451-2784

FOR MORE INFORMATION

Owatonna Area Chamber of Commerce
320 Hoffman Drive
Owatonna, MN 55060
507-451-7970 or 1-800-423-6466

Jeanine Varland
Minnesota Department of Natural Resources Wildlife Section
8485 Rose Street
Owatonna, MN 55060
507-455-5841

Albert Lea
Freeborn and Mower Counties

County Population:
  Freeborn–32,429
  Mower–37,575
County Area:
  Freeborn–709 sq. mi.
  Mower–712 sq. mi.
	Albert Lea Population–18,009
	October Temperature–60°
	County Acres in CRP:
	  Freeborn–6,412
	  Mower–1,105
	WMAs–13 (1,587 acres)

The city of Albert Lea lies southwest of the Interstate 35 and 90 junction. This is corn country, and agriculture is a major portion of the local economy. This area had been a prime hunting ground for the Dakota Indians before the advent of the white settlers. The town was founded in 1855 and named after Lt. Albert Miller Lea.

Settlers came to the area to farm its rich soil, planting wheat as well as corn. In the 1860s the railroad came through Albert Lea. With readily available transportation to markets, the town prospered. This rolling countryside has not only been good farming land but has become good wildlife habitat as well.

Currently, pheasant numbers are better here than in other parts of the state. Farmland adjacent to wildlife management areas provide good early-season hunting, since hunting pressure within the WMAs pushes the birds outside. There are some Hungarian partridge in the area, however, their numbers are so low that you wouldn't plan a hunt around them. As they have in other parts of the state, turkeys have thrived here, mostly on private land. Because turkey hunters have been responsible while hunting on private land, owners are generally receptive to hunters asking permission.

Around the edges of the few prairie potholes and wetlands of this region, resident mallards, teal, and wood ducks can be found early in the season. Later, good numbers of migrating dabblers and divers are found on larger bodies of water, such as Lake Geneva and Bear Lake. These birds stay until weather forces them to move south.

Numerous Canada geese are found in the area, especially feeding in harvested fields and resting near bodies of water. While larger lakes hold the bulk of the flocks, they can also be found on smaller wetlands and streams.

UPLAND BIRDS
Pheasant, Hungarian Partridge, and Turkey

WATERFOWL
Ducks and Geese

ACCOMMODATIONS
Super 8 Motel, 2019 East Main Street / 60 units / Cable TV / Free coffee and donuts / Pets allowed / 507-377-0591 or 1-800-800-8000 / $$-$$$

Days Inn of Albert Lea, 2306 East Main Street / 126 units / Cable TV, courtyard restaurant and lounge, indoor pool, coffee makers in the rooms / Pets allowed / 507-373-6471 / $$-$$$

CAMPGROUNDS AND RV PARKS

Hickory Hills Hideaway Campground, Rt.1 Box 166-A / 80 sites / Electric and water hookups, dump station, restrooms, lodge with ice and pop / Pets allowed / 507-852-4555

RESTAURANTS

Trumble's, 1811 East Main Street / Open 7 days a week, Sun–Fri, 6AM–10PM; Sat, 6AM–11PM / Breakfast, lunch, and dinner specials daily, serving family meals, fresh baked pies, and pastries / 507-373-2638

Philly's Bar and Grill, 804 East Main Street / Open 7 days a week, 11AM–1AM / Sports bar with full service, American foods / 507-373-2450

VETERINARIANS

Skyline Veterinary Clinic, 1410 West Main Street / 507-373-8175

SPORTING GOODS

Skyline Trustworthy Hardware, Skyline Mall / 507-373-7467

Coast to Coast Hardware, 2525 Bridge Avenue / 507-373-8636

AUTO REPAIR

Ken's Service, 2020 Pioneer Trail / 507-377-2099

Albert Lea Oil, 525 East Main Street / 507-373-7712

AIR SERVICE

Albert Lea Airport, Inc., 400 Airport Road / 507-373-0608 / Small aircraft only

Northwest Airlines, Minneapolis and St. Paul, 1-800-225-2525

MEDICAL

Naeve Hospital-Mayo Health System, 404 Fountain Street / 507-373-2384

TAXIDERMIST

Gary's Life-like Taxidermy, RR 1 Box 62 / 507-373-8437

FOR MORE INFORMATION

Albert Lea / Freeborn County Chamber of Commerce
202 North Broadway
Albert Lea, MN 56007
507-373-3938 or 1-800-345-8414

Jeanine Varland
Minnesota Department of Natural Resources Wildlife Section
8485 Rose Street
Owatonna, MN 55060
507-455-5841

Caledonia
Fillmore and Houston Counties

County Population:	Caledonia Population–2,957
Fillmore–20,969	October Temperature–60°
Houston–19,330	County Acres in CRP:
County Area:	Fillmore–15,179
Fillmore–861 sq. mi.	Houston–12,806
Houston–558 sq. mi.	WMAs–4 (780 acres)

Caledonia is situated at the intersection of State Highways 44 and 76 in far southeast Minnesota. Sitting in a valley, Caledonia was once considered an afterthought to the town of Brownsville. But in the late 1800s, a fire decimated Brownsville, and Caledonia became the county seat. The town thrives today and is still essentially a farming community. It is considered the wild turkey capital of Minnesota.

Good pheasant numbers coupled with less hunting pressure make this a worthwhile destination. Private land access is good but don't overlook state lands that can be found on PRIM maps.

While this is mostly farm country, there are some forested areas containing birch and aspen that attract grouse. Numbers here aren't quite as good as farther north, but the population remains fairly consistent. While grouse are generally found among aspen and alder, they feed mostly on oak bud flowers, berries, and greens.

Hungarian partridge and quail are both present here, and hunters should be certain of what they are shooting. Quail are not present in the sustainable numbers needed for a hunting season. Huns can be found in shortgrass and stubble fields.

As mentioned, turkeys are flourishing in this region and are found on both private and state land. They will most likely be found among the hills and bluffs that have oak trees, especially if there is farmland nearby. While access to private land is good, remember that it is a privilege rather than a right to hunt on private land.

With little or no lakes or ponds in the area, the best place to find waterfowl is on rivers, especially oxbows, and on Mississippi River backwaters. Wood ducks and teal can be found here, and mallards feed in farm fields near rivers. Migratory diving ducks, such as canvasbacks, are found on the Mississippi's more open backwaters.

Canada geese are the most abundant migratory birds found in this region, and they linger here as long as there is open water. At first, they feed in harvested fields and then move to river vegetation later in the season.

UPLAND BIRDS
Pheasant, Hungarian Partridge, Ruffed Grouse, Turkey, and Woodcock

WATERFOWL
Ducks and Canada Geese

ACCOMMODATIONS
Crest Motel and Supper Club, Highways 44 and 76 / 25 units / Cable TV / Adjoining supper club / Pets allowed / 507-724-3311 or 1-800-845-0904 / $$

CAMPGROUNDS AND RV PARKS
Dunromin' Park Campground, Rt. 1, Box 146 / 106 sites, 88 with electricity and water hookups / Dump station, restrooms, showers, store, and laundry / Pets on leash / 1-800-822-2514 / $

RESTAURANTS
Redwood Cafe, Highways 44 and 76 / Open Mon–Fri, 5:30AM–8PM; Sat, 5:30AM–5PM; Sun, 6AM–2PM / Small town cafe with something for everyone, homestyle cooking for breakfast and lunch, and dinners with specials / 507-724-2270

The Crest Supper Club, Highways 44 and 76 / Open Tues–Sat, 5PM–10PM / Lounge open 5PM –1AM / Specialties are barbecue ribs and prime rib, Friday fish fry, and seasonal Sunday brunch / 507-724-3311 or 1-800-845-0904

VETERINARIANS
Caledonia Veterinary Service, 126 West Main Street / 507-724-3380

SPORTING GOODS
Coast to Coast Hardware, 223 South Kingston / 507-724-3986
Hardware Hank, 208 East Main Street / 507-724-3935

AUTO REPAIR
Weichert Motors, 114 South Pine Street / 507-724-3300
Ellingson Motors, 205 North Kingston / 507-724-3963

AIR SERVICE
Rochester International Airport, Helgerson Drive Southwest, Rochester 55902 / 507-282-2328 / Northwest Airlines: 1-800-225-2525 / United Airlines: 1-800-241-6522

MEDICAL
Franciscan-Skemp Health Care/Caledonia Clinic, 701 North Sprague / 507-724-3353

TAXIDERMIST
Peterson Taxidermy and Outdoors, 407 East Cedar, Houston / 507-846-3129

FOR MORE INFORMATION
Caledonia Area Chamber
 of Commerce
City Hall, Main Street
Caledonia, MN 55921
507-724-5477

Nick Gulden
Minnesota Department of Natural
 Resources Wildlife Section
411 Exchange Building
Winona, MN 55987
507-453-2950

Rochester
Wabasha, Olmsted, and Winona Counties

County Population:	Rochester Population–78,276
Wabasha–20,721	October Temperature–60°
Olmsted–116,537	County Acres in CRP:
Winona–49,485	Wabasha–8,581
County Area:	Olmsted–15,023
Wabasha–525 sq. mi.	Winona–7,873
Olmsted–653 sq. mi.	WMAs–11 (31,667 acres)
Winona–626 sq. mi.	

Rochester is approximately an hour and a half southeast of the Twin Cities on US 52. What started as a small trading center in the early 1800s has developed into a major commercial and industrial center. Despite all the industry, the area around the city is still mostly farm country interspersed with the woods and river valleys sporting buttes and rock formations that give the area a distinctive look.

The Mayo Clinic, considered by many to be among the largest medical complexes in the world, started in 1863 when William W. Mayo opened his practice in Rochester. Later, his two sons, William J. and Charles H., expanded the family practice, and gradually it developed into the world-famous medical facility known for its innovative techniques and treatments.

Presently, pheasant numbers are fair, and access to area farms can be found with persistence and through honoring the landowner's rights. While there are only a few wildlife management areas, they should not be overlooked as turkey and grouse habitat. The Whitewater Wildlife Management Area, northeast of Rochester, is an especially good choice, since it has some areas specifically designed with these two species in mind. Sometimes referred to as the "banana belt," this area has numerous south-facing slopes that provide excellent feeding areas for birds. Food consists of ironwood, birch, and elm buds, as well as berries when available.

Huns are very rare in this region, however, some might be found in Wabasha County in shortgrass areas and stubble of harvested grain fields. Woodcock are present only briefly in the last week of September and first week of October. Look for them in the creeks and riverbottoms where worms are available in the moist soil.

Look for the area's limited duck population on Mississippi River backwaters located on the eastern edges of Wabasha and Winona Counties. Wood ducks, mallards, and blue-winged teal are the predominant species. Migrating divers, especially canvasbacks, can be found later in the season on the more open water channels.

The area's best waterfowl hunting is provided by Canada geese. There is excellent late-season action for geese, and the area's numerous guides can provide heated pits and decoys. Goose hunting remains good as long as there is running water in the rivers.

*This is an example of the bluff country east and north of Rochester,
where turkey reintroduction has been very successful.*

UPLAND BIRDS
Pheasant, Hungarian Partridge, Ruffed Grouse, Woodcock, and Turkey

WATERFOWL
Ducks and Canada Geese

ACCOMMODATIONS

Motel 6, 2107 Frontage Road West / 107 units / Satellite TV and free morning
coffee / Pets allowed / 507-282-6625 or 1-800-4-MOTEL 6 / $$-$$$

Holiday Inn, 1630 South Broadway / 196 units / Three Crowns dining room,
Viking Lounge / Cable TV, some kitchenette units available / Pets allowed /
507-288-1844 / $$$

CAMPGROUNDS AND RV PARKS

Rochester / Marion KOA, 5232 65th Avenue Southeast / Multiple electrical and
water hookups / Fenced-in pet area / 507-288-0785

Wazionja Campground, 6450 120th Street Northwest, Pine Island 55963 / 100
sites / Water and electric hookups, dump station, restrooms, showers, and
laundry / Pets on leash / 507-356-8594

RESTAURANTS

Canadian Honker Restaurant, 1204 Southwest Second Street / Open 7 days a week, 7AM–9PM / Wide variety of homestyle cooking / 507-282-6572

Grandma's Kitchen, 1514 North Broadway / Open Mon–Sat, 6AM–8PM / Homemade soups and pies, daily specials / 507-289-0331

John Barley Corne, 2780 Highway 63 South / Open Mon–Fri, 11AM–2PM for lunch; 5PM to closing for dinner / Specializing in steaks, prime rib, and seafood / Full bar and lounge / 507-285-0178

The Smiling Moose, 1829 Highway 52 North / Open 7 days a week, 11AM–1AM / Featuring 23 different specialty burgers; also steaks and other dinners on the menu / Large variety of tap beers and full bar / 507-288-1689

VETERINARIANS

Northern Valley Animal Clinic, 1303 Circle Drive East / 507-282-0867

SPORTING GOODS

Gander Mountain, Crossroads Shopping Center, 1201 Broadway Avenue South / 507-289-4224

Wild Goose Sports, 1117 Broadway North / 507-289-2520

Fleet Farm, 3551 Broadway South / 507-281-1130

AUTO REPAIR

Meyer's Auto Repair, 410 Sixth Avenue Southeast / 507-285-0551

Midwest Auto and Repair, 972 Fourteenth Avenue Southwest / 507-289-7978

AIR SERVICE

Rochester International Airport, Helgerson Drive Southwest / Complete commercial and small aircraft / 507-282-2328

Northwest Airlines, Minneapolis and St. Paul / 1-800-255-2525

United Airlines, Minneapolis and St. Paul / 1-800-241-6522

MEDICAL

Saint Mary's Hospital, 1216 Second Street Southwest / 507-255-5123 or 507-255-55901

TAXIDERMIST

Smitty's Taxidermy, 2012 Fifth Avenue Northeast / 507-286-7437

FOR MORE INFORMATION

Rochester Area Chamber
of Commerce
220 South Broadway
Rochester, MN 55904
507-288-1122 or 1-800-634-8277

Mike Tenney or Tony Stegen
Minnesota Department of Natural
Resources Wildlife Section
2300 Silver Creek Road Northeast
Rochester, MN 55901
507-280-5069 or 507-285-7435

Hastings
Carver, Scott, and Dakota Counties

County Population:	Hastings Population–17,268
Carver–61,377	October Temperature–58°
Scott–75,009	County Acres in CRP:
Dakota–332,657	Carver–1,990
County Area:	Scott–2,010
Carver–357 sq. mi.	Dakota–2,859
Scott–357 sq. mi.	WMAs–12 (8,127 acres)
Dakota–570 sq. mi.	

The river town of Hastings sits on the edge of the Mississippi River about 22 miles southeast of the Twin Cities on US 61. The town's original name was Oliver's Grove until the 1800s. Henry Hastings Sibley won a drawing by land speculators and later became the first governor of the state. Hastings is still a hub for river travel and commerce, with scenic views stretching as far as the eye can see up and down the river.

Southern Scott County offers some of the best pheasant hunting opportunities in the region. Currently, Pheasants Forever and the Department of Natural Resources are purchasing land in order to bolster pheasant numbers. Wildlife management areas in these three counties provide some pheasant hunting, but with their proximity to the Twin Cities, hunting will be better on weekdays. In southeastern Dakota County, turkey and ruffed grouse hunters can find some access in the Richard J. Dorer Memorial Hardwood State Forest. The low wetland areas of Gores Pool Wildlife Management Area along the Mississippi River is the best bet for hunting migrating woodcock. There are also very limited numbers of pheasant and better numbers of ruffed grouse and turkey to be found here.

Look for good numbers of mallard, teal, and wood ducks in the wildlife management areas found in these counties. They can also be found on stretches of the Mississippi that aren't within the Upper Mississippi National Wildlife and Fish Refuge. Some smaller lakes and ponds in Scott and Dakota Counties hold both ducks and geese. Be aware that lakes located near towns may be subject to city ordinances prohibiting gunfire—check with local officials.

Gores Pool Wildlife Management Area on the eastern edge of Dakota County offers the best all-around waterfowl hunting. This backwater of the Mississippi River holds not only resident ducks and geese, it also attracts large numbers of migrating waterfowl that stay as long as there is open water.

UPLAND BIRDS
Pheasant, Ruffed Grouse, Woodcock, and Turkey
WATERFOWL
Ducks and Canada Geese

The great, wide Mississippi River near Red Wing, breaking into many channels and backwaters that support a rich supply of diverse waterfowl species.

ACCOMMODATIONS

AmericInn, 2400 Vermillion Street / 44 units / Cable TV, laundry, some rooms with microwave and refrigerator / Pets allowed / 612-437-8877 / $$-$$$

CAMPGROUNDS AND RV PARKS

Greenwood Campground, 13797 190th Street / 91 sites, 68 with sewer / Dump stations, flush toilets, and showers / Pets on leash / 612-437-5269 / $

RESTAURANTS

Bierstube, 109 West 11th Street / Open Sun–Thur, 11AM–11PM; Fri and Sat, 11AM –Midnight / Fine German restaurant featuring a mixture of steaks, Reuben sandwiches, brats, and more / 612-437-8259

Levee Cafe, 100 Sibley Street / Open 7 days a week, 11AM–1AM / Family and fine dining with everything made from scratch / Daily specials / Breakfast on weekends, 8:30AM–Noon, and Sunday brunch from 10AM–2PM / 612-437-7577

Perkins Family Restaurant, 1206 Vermillion Street / Open 24 hours, 7days a week / Family dining and onsite bakery / 612-437-5028

VETERINARIANS

Hastings Veterinary Clinic, 3150 Red Wing Boulevard / 612-437-5101

SPORTING GOODS
John's Outdoor Store and Taxidermy, 120 Third Street West / 651-437-7421

AUTO REPAIR
Auto Doctor, 1370 South Frontage Road / 612-437-9699
Downtown Tire and Auto, 320 Vermillion Street / 612-437-6400

AIR SERVICE
Northwest Airlines, Minneapolis and St. Paul / 1-800-255-2525
United Airlines, Minneapolis and St. Paul / 1-800-241-6522

MEDICAL
Regina Memorial Hospital, 1175 Nininger Road / 612-480-4100

TAXIDERMIST
John's Outdoor Store and Taxidermy, 120 Third Street West / 612-437-7421

FOR MORE INFORMATION
Hastings Area Chamber of Commerce
119 West Second Street
Hastings, MN 55033
612-437-6775 or 1-888-612-6122

Diane Regenscheid
Minnesota Department of Natural Resources Wildlife Section
100 South Fuller Street, #155
Shakopee, MN 55379
612-496-7686

Forest Lake
Hennepin, Ramsey, Washington, and Anoka Counties

County Population:	Forest Lake Population–6,691
Hennepin–1,075,907	October Temperature–58°
Ramsey–497,423	County Acres in CRP:
Washington–187,475	Hennepin–925
Anoka–285,271	Ramsey–None
County Area:	Washington–828
Hennepin–557 sq. mi.	Anoka–295
Ramsey–156 sq. mi.	WMAs–9 (26,727 acres)
Washington–392 sq. mi.	
Anoka–424 sq. mi.	

Forest Lake, about 30 miles northeast of the Twin Cities via US 61 or Interstate 35, was organized as a township in 1874 and incorporated 20 years later in 1893. With the advent of the railroad, it became an outlet for the agricultural and dairy products produced in the area. Today, it serves as an escape for those who work in the Twin Cities.

Wildlife management areas in this area hold very limited pheasant numbers, and with their proximity to the metropolitan area, weekends see a great deal of pressure. Mickelson, Lamprey Pass, and Carlos Avery Wildlife Management Areas offer the best ruffed grouse and turkey hunting.

Carlos Avery, which is one of the state's largest wildlife management areas, has some woodcock available in early October in and around the lowland areas. When hunting these birds, remember that grouse feed on buds and berries, turkey feed on nuts and grains, and woodcock feed on worms.

Even though Carlos Avery is a prime waterfowl area, don't overlook the other WMAs in this area. Potholes and lakes attract migrating waterfowl, but since many have towns on or near the water, they are quite often subject to in-town firearm ordinances. Mallards, teal, and wood ducks offer the best early-season hunting, with diving ducks appearing later during their migration.

Canada geese are very populous in this area, but once the season gets under way they learn quickly to stay within city limits where they can't be hunted. This means hunt in the early days of the season if you want to have any luck at all. As the season progresses, flocks get increasingly larger within the metropolitan areas.

UPLAND BIRDS
Pheasant, Ruffed Grouse, Woodcock, and Turkey

WATERFOWL
Ducks and Geese

ACCOMMODATIONS

AmericInn Motel, 1291 West Broadway / 45 units, cable TV, indoor pool, spa, free continental breakfast / Pets allowed / 651-464-1930 or 1-800-634-3444 / $$$

Forest Lake Motel, 7 Northeast Sixth Avenue / 15 units / Cable TV and in-room coffee / Pets allowed / 651-464-4077 or 1-800-470-4077 / $$$

CAMPGROUNDS AND RV PARKS

Timm's Marina and Campground, 9080 North Jewel Lane / 30 sites / Water and electrical or full hookups / Dump station, hot showers, restrooms, store, and laundry / Pets on leash / 651-464-3890 or 651-464-9965 / $

RESTAURANTS

My Place Restaurant, 7 Lake Street North / Open Mon–Sat, 6:30AM–7PM; Sun, 7AM–4PM / Cozy family style restaurant overlooking Forest Lake / Daily specials with fresh soups and desserts / Breakfast bar on Sunday / 651-464-4776

Vannelli's on the Green, located at Castlewood Golf Course / Open 7 days a week, Sun Thur, 10AM–10PM; Fri and Sat, 10AM–11PM / Lounge and bar open 10AM–1AM / Italian specials and Sunday brunch 10AM–2PM / 651-464-8435

VETERINARIANS

South Shore Veterinary Hospital, 380 West Broadway / 651-464-4210 / 24 hour emergency service

SPORTING GOODS

Coast to Coast Hardware, 814 South Lake Street / 651-464-6673

Forest Lake Sports and Tackle, 1007 West Broadway / 651-464-1200

Mike's Sporting Goods, 6625 North Lake Boulevard / 651-464-1557

AUTO REPAIR

Car Tunes Etc., 24061 Greenway Road / 651-464-7014

Jim's Service Center, 108 Southwest 12th Street / 651-464-6925

AIR SERVICE

Forest Lake Airport, 5385 North Scandia Trail / 651-464-4522 / Small aircraft only

Northwest Airlines, Minneapolis and St. Paul / 1-800-255-2525

United Airlines, Minneapolis and St. Paul / 1-800-241-6522

MEDICAL

Forest Lake Clinic, 1540 South Lake Street / 651-464-7100

TAXIDERMIST

O'Brien's Taxidermy, 9620 189th Avenue / 651-464-4460

FOR MORE INFORMATION

Forest Lake Area Chamber
of Commerce
92 South Lake Street
P.O. Box 474
Forest Lake, MN 55025
651-464-3200

Bob Welsh
Minnesota Departmentof Natural
Resources Wildlife Section
Carlos Avery Wildlife Management Area
Forest Lake, MN 55025
651-296-5200

Twin Cities Travel Hub

Minneapolis

The name, Minneapolis, is a combination of the Dakota word for water ("minne") and the Greek word for city ("polis"), and with 18 lakes in the city, it is an appropriate name. There are a wealth of cultural and recreational activities available as well as a naturally beautiful landscape. Minnesota's largest city with 368,383 residents, it is the upper Midwest's center for finance, industry, trade, and transportation. The city comprises 59 square miles with 5 square miles of water.

The city was founded as a grain-processing center, utilizing the power from St. Anthony Falls. From the large mills established in the early 1800s came the international corporations of Pillsbury, General Mills, and Cargill, which still have their headquarters in Minneapolis. Today, the city is home to a variety of businesses, including graphic arts, electronics, transportation, banking, insurance, machinery and metal fabricating, plastics, computers, and publishing. And of course, it is home to the Mall of America in Bloomington.

With a large contingent of sports enthusiasts who not only watch sports but participate in them, the city offers many ways for people to engage in their favorite sports activities. Warm weather opportunities include softball leagues, golfing, jogging, biking, roller skating, boating, sailing and swimming, and winter activities include ice skating, ice fishing, skiing, snowmobiling, and ice sailing.

The list of services following is just a fraction of what this metropolitan has to offer. We have listed 12 accommodations at the beginning of the list that we know are presently accepting dogs. This is not to say that there aren't others, and we suggest you call if one of the other accommodations listed suits your needs better. Also, there is a wealth of dining choices, including many ethnic restaurants. If you wish to find a particular kind of restaurant, you can always ask at the motel desk for a recommendation or flip through the yellow pages.

ACCOMMODATIONS

Best Western Normandy Inn, 405 South 8th Street (55404) / 612-370-1400 / Dogs allowed

Crown Sterling Suites–Centre Village, 425 South 7th Street (55415) / 612-333-3111 / Dogs allowed

Crowne Plaza Northstar Hotel, 618 South 2nd Avenue (55402) / 612-338-2288 / Dogs allowed

Holiday Inn Metrodome, 1500 Washington Avenue (55454) / 612-333-4646 / Dogs allowed

Marquette Minneapolis, 710 Marquette Avenue (55402) / 612-333-4545 / Dogs allowed

Metro Inn & Café, 5637 Lyndale Avenue South (55419) / 612-861-6011 / Dogs allowed

Minneapolis Hilton and Towers, 1001 Marquette Avenue (55402) / 612-376-1000 / Dogs allowed

Minneapolis Marriott City Center, 20 South 7th Street (55402) / 612-349-4000 / Dogs allowed

Radisson Hotel Metrodome, 615 Washington Avenue (55414) / 612-379-8888 / Dogs allowed

Radisson Plaza Hotel, 35 South 7th Street (55402) / 612-339-4900 / Dogs allowed

Regal Minneapolis Hotel, 1313 Nicollet Mall (55403) / 612-332-6000 / Dogs allowed

Sheraton Minneapolis Metrodome, 1330 Industrial Boulevard (55413) / 612-331-1900 / Dogs allowed

Aqua City Motel, 5739 Lyndale Avenue South (55419) / 612-861-6061 / Dogs allowed

Budgetel Inns, 6415 James Circle North (55430) / 612-561-8400 / Dogs allowed
7815 Nicollet Avenue (55420) / 612-881-7311 / Dogs allowed

Country Inns & Suites by Carlson, 155 Coon Rapids Boulevard Northwest (55433) / 612-780-3797
2221 Killebrew Drive (55425) / 612-854-5555

Days Inn Bloomington, 8000 Bridge Road (55437) / 612-831-9595
1501 Freeway Boulevard (55430) / 612-566-4140

Exel Inn of Minneapolis, 2701 East 78th Street (55425) / 612-854-7200 / Dogs allowed

Fairfield Inn of Bloomington, 2401 East 80th Street (55425) / 612-858-8475

Golden Valley Inn, 4820 Highway 55 (55422) / 612-588-0511

Hawthorn Suites Hotel, 3400 Edinborough Way (55435) / 612-893-9300 / Dogs allowed

Holiday Inn Express Airport, 814 East 79th Street (55420) / 612-854-5558

Hyatt Regency Minneapolis, 1300 Nicollet Avenue (55403) / 612-370-1234

Super 8 Motel Bloomington, 7800 2nd Avenue South (55420) / 612-888-8800 / Dogs allowed

Thunderbird Hotel, 2201 East 78th Street (55425) / 612-854-3411 / Dogs allowed

Wyndham Garden Hotel, 4460 West 78th Street (55435) / 612-831-3131 / Dogs allowed

RESTAURANTS

Anthony's Wharf Seafood Restaurant, 201 Main Street Southeast (55414) / 612-378-7058

Baja Tortilla Grill, 2300 Hennepin Avenue (55405) / 612-374-9900

Best Steak House, 5455 Nicollet Avenue (55419) / 612-824-1300

Billabong Aussie Grill & Pub, 5001 West 80th Street (55437) / 612-844-0655

Bridgeman's Original Ice Cream Restaurant, 6201 Brooklyn Boulevard (55429) / 612-537-9411

Brothers Deli, 607 Marquette Avenue (55402) / 612-341-8007
Cactus Creek Steak Outfitters & Saloon, 905 Hampshire Avenue South (55426) /
    612-546-5366
Cracker Barrel Old Country Store, 1501 James Circle North (55430) / 612-560-6808
Denny's Restaurant, 8850 University Avenue Northwest (55448) / 612-786-7840
Figlio, A Restaurant & Bar, Calhoun Square, 3001 Hennepin Avenue (55408) /
    612-822-1688
Fuddrucker's, 8955 Springbrook Drive Northwest (55433) / 612-780-2909
The Great Steak & Fry Company, 40 South 7th Street (55402) / 612-333-3990
J.D. Hoyt's Steak House, 301 Washington Avenue (55440) / 612-338-1560
Jimmy's Steaks & Spirits, 3675 Minnehaha Avenue (55406) / 612-729-9635
Minnesota Smokehouse Restaurant, 500 East Lake Street (55408) / 612-824-0558
Napa Valley Grille, Mall of America (55440) / 612-858-9934
Nicollet Island Inn Restaurant, 95 Merriam Street (55401) / 612-331-3035
O'Brien's Decoy Pub & Smokehouse, 815 Hennepin Avenue (55403) /
    612-623-3671
Perkins Family Restaurants & Bakery, University Avenue & Osborn (55440) /
    612-574-1670
Planet Hollywood, Mall of America (55425) / 612-854-7827
Sbarro–The Italian Eatery, 40 South 7th Street (55402) / 612-370-97077
Joe Senser's Sports Grill & Bar, 4217 West 80th Street (55437) / 612-835-1191
Old Spaghetti Factory, 233 Park Avenue (55415) / 612-341-0949
Sportsman's Restaurant, 9939 Bluebird Street Northwest (55433) / 612-755-6680
Stonehouse Bar & Grill, 2700 Highway 88 (55418) / 612-788-7499
Stuart Anderson's Cattle Company Restaurant, 4470 West 78th Street (55435) /
    612-835-1225
Tortilla Grill, 2300 Hennepin Avenue (55405) / 612-374-9900
Totem Pole Dining Room, 2201 East 78th Street (55425) / 612-854-4422

VETERINARIANS
Brookview Animal Hospital, 7926 Highway 55 (55427) / 612-546-2323
Central Animal Hospital, 2700 Central Avenue Northeast (55418) / 612-781-6941
Lyndale Animal Hospital, 2544 Lyndale Avenue South (55405) / 612-872-4674
Northwest Animal Hospital, 2045 Merrimac Lane North (55447) / 612-475-2448
Oak Knoll Animal Hospital, 7202 Minnetonka Boulevard (55426) / 612-929-0074

SPORTING GOODS
Gander Mountain Store, 8030 Wedgewood Lane (Maple Grove) / 612-420-9800
                            1780 County Road 42 (Burnsville) / 612-435-3805
                            4900 South Hwy 101 (Excelsior) / 612-474-4133
                            4445 Nathan Lane North (Plymouth) / 612-553-1050
                            250 57th Avenue Northeast (Fridley) / 612-571-8830
                            40 West 84th Street (Bloomington) / 612-881-0575

A flock of mallards on the Rum River near the Carlos Avery Wildlife Management Area.

Galyan's, 11260 Wayzata Boulevard (Minnetonka) / 612-525-0200
      1700 West 78th Street (Richfield) / 612-869-0200
Burger Brothers Outdoor Outfitters, 9801 Lyndale Avenue South (Bloomington) /
612-884-8842
American Army and Navy Surplus Store, 28 North 4th Street (55401) /
612-333-8325
Capra's Sporting Goods, 8565 Central Avenue Northeast (55434) / 612-780-4557
Frontiersman Guns, 6925 Wayzata Boulevard (55426) / 612-544-3775
Gun Shop & Pawnbroker, 7529 Lyndale Avenue South (55423) / 612-861-2727
Holiday Stores & Stations, 4445 Nathan Lane North (55442) / 612-553-1041
      57th & University Avenues (55440) / 612-571-1900
      8341 Lyndale Avenue South (55420) / 612-881-2691
Recreational Equipment Inc., 710 West 98th Street (55420) / 612-884-4315

AUTO REPAIR

Amigo Service Center Inc., 3544 Lyndale Avenue South (55408) / 612-822-6088
Barry's Towing, 3341 43rd Avenue South (55406) / 612-722-7337
Bob's Towing, 5311 Green Valley Drive (55437) / 612-831-3632
Carlson's Amoco Certicare, 4205 West Broadway Avenue (55422) / 612-537-6035
Cedar Towing & Garage Service, 1921 East 24th Street (55404) / 612-721-6645
Clausen's Mobil Servicenter, 22 East Franklin Avenue (55404) / 612-874-1905
Conoco Express Service, 3701 Central Avenue Northeast (55421) / 612-788-1113
Fisher Towing Service, 1022 Hennepin Avenue (55403) / 612-338-6953
Gary's Towing, 2924 Jersey Avenue (55440) / 612-925-3083
Herb's Servicenter, County Roads 6 & 101 (55440) / 612-473-1525
Lyndale Auto Service, 2801 Lyndale Avenue South (55408) / 612-872-6934
Madison Towing, 3021 4th Avenue South (55408) / 612-824-1055
Miller Towing Inc., 2935 Pleasant Avenue (55408) / 612-827-5591
Minnesota Towing Inc., 8011 Grand Avenue South (55420) / 612-884-4827
North Suburban Towing, 5170 West Broadway Avenue (55429) / 612-535-2201
Northeast Towing Service, 6519 Central Avenue Northeast (55432) /
    612-571-2660
Quality Towing Service Inc., 10360 Grand Avenue South (55420) / 612-861-3793
Rescue Towing, 1224 Highway 10 Northeast (55432) / 612-784-7030
Southtown 76 Service Center Towing, 7744 Penn Avenue (55440) / 612-861-4610
Youngstedt's Amoco Servicenters, 5925 Excelsior Blvd (55416) / 612-929-5257

AUTO RENTAL

Alamo Rent-a-Car, Minneapolis/St. Paul International Airport (55440) /
    612-726-5323
Americar Car & Van Rental Systems, I-494 & 12th Avenue (55440) /
    612-866-4918
Avis Rent-a-Car, Minneapolis/St. Paul International Airport (55440) /
    612-726-5263
Budget Car & Truck Rental, Minneapolis/St. Paul International Airport (55440) /
    612-727-2000
Dollar Rent-a-Car, Minneapolis/St. Paul International Airport (55420) /
    612-854-3003 or 800-800-4000
Enterprise Rent-a-Car, 6801 Wayzata Boulevard (55426) / 612-542-8535
Sears Car & Truck Rental, 5 Twin City Locations (55440) / 612-727-2600
Thrify Car Rental, 2401 East 79th Street, Bloomington (55425) / 612-854-8080
Wilkins Car Stores Rental Systems, I-494 & 12th Avenue (55440) / 612-866-4918

MEDICAL

Abbott Northwestern Hospital, 1801 Nicollet Avenue (55403) / 612-863-1000 /
    Emergency: 612-863-4233
Mercy Hospital, 4050 Coon Rapids Boulevard Northwest (55433) / 612-421-8888
Methodist Hospital, 6500 Excelsior Boulevard (55426) / 612-932-5000

Unity Hospital, 550 Osborne Road Northeast (55432) / 612-421-2222 /
Emergency Service: 612-780-6844
University of Minnesota Hospital (55440) / 612-626-3000

TAXIDERMISTS

Ed's Taxidermy, 11500 Northwest North Heights Drive (55440) / 612-757-6710
Jim's Taxidermy, 9727 5th Street Northeast (55434) / 612-786-5978
Little Bit of Nature Taxidermy Studio, 11220 Terrace Road Northeast (55434) /
612-754-2144
North Country Taxidermy, 12889 Crooked Lake Boulevard Northwest (55448) /
612-757-7620
James A. Riley, 9727 5th Street Northeast (55434) / 612-786-5978

FOR MORE INFORMATION
Greater Minneapolis Chamber of Commerce
81 South 9th Street
Minneapolis, MN 55402
612-370-9141

St. Paul

French settlers from the Winnipeg area formed the beginnings of what is now St.
Paul in the 1840s. They took shelter at Fort Snelling before they were forced to move
south to what is now Lowertown but was known then as Upper Town. Separated by a
swamp, it was really two settlements that grew due to the increased river traffic. By
1849, settlers began to pour in, and when Minnesota became a territory with St. Paul
as its capitol, it grew even faster.

By 1870, railroads had become the dominant means of transportation. River
trade slowed down until it became nonexistent when the Minnesota Valley Railroad
opened. The city is still a center for trade and industry.

St. Paul was considered one of the most progressive cities of its time, with the
grand architecture of the Cathedral of St. Paul, excellent bridges spanning the
Mississippi River, beautiful mansions, large parks and wetlands, Battle Creek Indian
village, and Indian burial mounds. Today, the city is host to a classic zoo, arboretum,
Como Park Conservatory, historic mansions open to the public, Minnesota State
Historical Society, and the Science Museum of Minnesota.

ACCOMMODATIONS
Best Western Kelly Inn-State Capitol, 161 St. Anthony Avenue (55103) /
651-227-8711 / Dogs allowed
Exel Inn of St. Paul, 1739 Old Hudson Road (55106) / 651-771-5566 / Dogs
allowed
Crown Sterling Suites St. Paul, 175 East 10th Street (55101) / 651-224-5400 /
Dogs allowed
Days Inn Civic Center, 175 West 7th Street (55102) / 651-292-8929 / Dogs
allowed

Ramada Hotel St. Paul, 1870 Old Hudson Road (55119) / 651-735-2333 / Dogs allowed

Sheraton Inn Midway, St. Paul, 400 Hamline Avenue North (55104) / 651-642-1234 / Dogs allowed

Best Western Maplewood Inn, 694 White Bear Avenue North (55106) / 651-770-2811

Best Western Yankee Square Inn, 3450 Washington Drive (55122) / 651-452-0100

Comfort Inn Roseville, 2715 Long Lake Road (55113) / 651-636-5800

Country Inns & Suites by Carlson, 2905 Snelling Avenue North (55113) / 651-628-3500

Country Inns & Suites by Carlson, 4940 Highway 61 North (55110) / 651-429-5393

Days Inn St. Paul East Maplewood, 285 Century Avenue North (55119) / 651-738-1600

Emerald Inn of Maplewood, 2025 County Road D East (55109) / 651-777-8131

Fairfield Suites by Marriott, 3635 Crestridge Drive (55122) / 651-686-0600

Hampton Inn Eagan (Near Mall of America), 3000 Eagandale Place (55121) / 651-688-3343

Hampton Inn Minneapolis/St. Paul North ,I-694 & Lexington Avenue (55101) / 651-482-0402

Holiday Inn Express, 1010 Bandana Boulevard West (55108) / 651-647-1637

Holiday Inn St. Paul, North Roseville, 2540 Cleveland Avenue North (55113) / 651-636-4867

Midwest Guest Suites, 1687 Century Circle (55125) / 651-735-8127

Northridge Emerald Inn, 1125 Red Fox Road (55112) / 651-484-6557

Ramada Hotel Minneapolis St. Paul, 2540 Cleveland Avenue North (55113) / 651-636-4567

Red Roof Inn, 1806 Wooddale Drive (55125) / 651-738-7160

Super 8 Motel Roseville, 2401 Prior Avenue North (55113) / 651-636-8888

Travel Inn, 149 University Avenue East (55101) / 651-227-8801

Yankee Square Inn, 3450 Washington Drive (55122) / 651-452-0100

RESTAURANTS

Applebee's Neighborhood Grill, University Avenue & Snelling (55101) / 651-642-9757

Baker's Square Restaurant & Bakery, 3088 White Bear Avenue North (55109) / 651-770-9070

Blue Fox Bar & Grill, 3833 Lexington Avenue North (55126) / 651-483-6000

Bridgeman's Original Ice Cream Restaurant, 4560 South Robert Trail (55123) / 651-455-0220

Caravelle Restaurant, 799 University Avenue West (55104) / 651-292-9324

Cattle Company Restaurant, 2750 Snelling Avenue North (55113) / 651-636-4145

Chi Chi's Mexican Restaurant, 3069 White Bear Avenue North (55109) / 651-770-6888

Chula Vista Mexican Restaurant, 1741 Robert Street South (55118) / 651-552-8457

A good retriever is worth its weight in gold.

Cracker Barrel Old Country Store, 1424 Weir Drive (55125) / 651-730-1233
Denny's Restaurant, 3050 White Bear Avenue North (55109) / 651-777-6497
Embers Restaurant, 1700 Snelling Avenue North (55113) / 651-645-8802
Fritz's Bar & Grill, 3883 Beau D Rue Drive (55122) / 651-452-7520
Great Steak & Fry, 30 7th Street East (55101) / 651-290-2428
The Italian Oven, 1786 Minnehaha Avenue East (55119) / 651-735-4944
Lindey's Prime Steak House, 3610 Snelling Avenue North (55112) / 651-633-9813
Main Event Sports Bar & Grill, 790 County Road D West (55112) / 651-636-2901
Mancini's Char House, 531 7th Street West (55102) / 651-224-7345
Olive Garden Italian Restaurant, 1525 County Road C West (55113) / 651-638-9557
Perkins Restaurant, 1544 University Avenue West (55104) / 651-659-0772
Quail on the Hill Restaurant, 371 Selby Avenue (55102) / 651-291-1236
Shannon Kelly's, 395 Wabasha Street North (55102) / 651-292-0905
Tuscany Grill, 1047 Hudson Road (55106) / 651-774-0811
Zantigo Mexican Restaurant, 565 Snelling Avenue (55101) / 651-646-5900

VETERINARIANS
Hudson Road Animal Hospital, 2942 Leyland Place (55125) / 651-738-9533
Roseville Animal Hospital, (55101) / 651-633-4881
Skadron Animal Hospital, 992 Caren Court (55118) / 651-454-1144

SPORTING GOODS

Gander Mountain Store, 1657 West County Road C (Roseville) / 651-633-7343
7150 Valley Creek Plaza (Woodbury) / 651-735-6101
East Side Gun Shop, 935 Arcade Street (55106) / 651-771-9776
Galyan's, 8292 Tamarack Village (Woodbury 55125) / 651-731-0200
Kern's Hunting Supply, (55101) / 651-222-4442
Sport Mart Inc., 1750 Highway 36 West (55113) / 651-638-3000

AUTO REPAIR

A-1 Car Starting & Towing, 760 Bush Avenue (55106) / 651-776-1902
Amoco Certicare Service & Towing, 1581 White Bear Avenue North (55106) /
651-771-0302
Auto Transport, 2754 Helen Street North (55109) / 651-773-4100
Budget Towing Inc. of St. Paul, 846 Earl Street (55106) / 651-771-8817
Century Avenue Service, 9 Century Avenue North (55119) / 651-738-9323
D & D Towing Service Inc., 1217 Frost Avenue (55109) / 651-772-8697
Damage Free Towing, 35 Little Canada Road East (55117) / 651-483-2029
East Metro Towing & Recovery, 1581 White Bear Avenue North (55106) /
651-774-2869
Freeway Towing, 201 5th Avenue Southwest (55112) / 651-633-5525
Jal Amoco Service, 2421 Larpenteur Avenue West (55113) / 651-645-5971
Jim's Towing, 1035 Oxford Street North (55103) / 651-487-1223
Kelly's Auto Repair, 760 Bush Avenue (55106) / 651-776-1902
Maplewood Amoco, 1987 County Road D East (55109) / 651-777-9818
Snelling Auto Service, 666 Snelling Avenue North (55104) / 651-644-9329
Tom's Mobil Service, 1935 Rice Street (55113) / 651-489-9897
United Towing, 2332 Stillwater Road (55119) / 651-731-6316

AUTO RENTAL

Agency Rent-a-Car, 2233 University Avenue West (55114) / 651-645-5937
Altra Auto Rental, 2905 Country Drive (55117) / 651-731-5118
Budget Car & Truck Rental, 1413 Hunting Valley Road (55108) / 651-727-2000
Car Temps Rent-a-Car, 1751 County Road B West (55113) / 651-639-0759
Dollar Rent-a-Car, 2575 Fairview Avenue North (55113) / 651-636-2923
Enterprise Rent-a-Car, 900 University Avenue West (55104) / 651-228-0088
Ford Rent-a-Car System, 2777 Snelling Avenue North (55113) / 651-636-8200
Practical Rent-a-Car, 2575 Fairview Avenue North (55113) / 651-636-8091
Sears Car & Truck Rental, 1413 Hunting Valley Road (55108) / 651-727-2600
Snappy Car Rental, 2437 Rice Street, (55113) / 651-486-2700
Thrifty Car Rental Burnsville/Eagan, 2105 Cliff Road (55122) / 651-452-2544

MEDICAL

Health East Bethesda Lutheran Hospital, 559 Capitol Boulevard (55103) / 651-232-2295

Healtheast St. Johns Hospital, 1575 Beam Avenue (55109) / 651-232-7000 / Emergency: 651-232-3348

Midway Hospital, 1700 University Avenue West (55104) / 651-232-5000

St. Johns Hospital, 1575 Beam Avenue (55109) / 651-232-7000

United Hospital St. Paul, 333 Smith Avenue North (55102) / 651-220-8000

TAXIDERMISTS

A-1 Taxidermy Inc., 2529 7th Avenue East (55109) / 651-777-1659

Bear Taxidermy, (55101) / 651-426-3339

Mark L. and Roger N. Dickinson, Taxidermists, 4140 Hodgson Road (55126) / 651-484-0769

G.H. Lensing, Taxidermy, 627 White Birch Drive (55126) / 651-483-8994

White Bear Taxidermists, 4911 Long Avenue (55110) / 651-429-3432

FOR MORE INFORMATION

St. Paul Area Chamber of Commerce
332 Minnesota Street
St. Paul, MN 55101
651-223-5000

South St. Paul Chamber of Commerce
450 View Street
St. Paul, MN 55102
651-451-2266

Minnesota Public Recreation
Information Maps (PRIM)

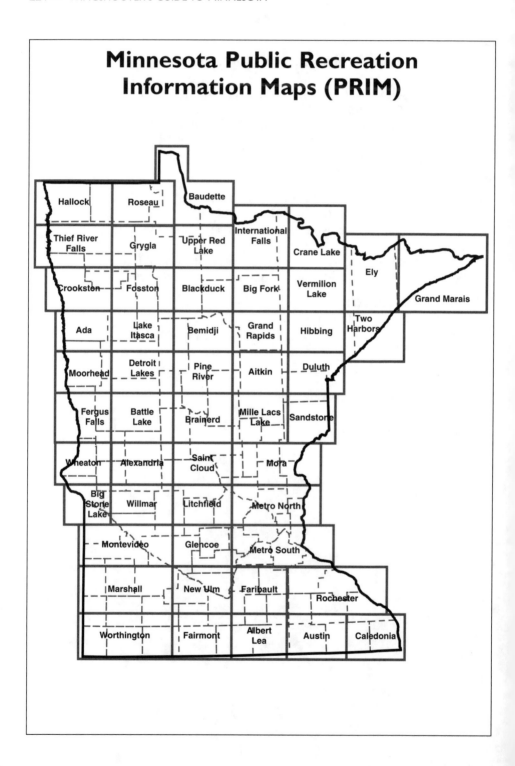

Finding Hunting Land in Minnesota

Finding a great place to hunt can be as challenging and exciting as the actual hunt. Individuals hunting in Minnesota will find that this isn't nearly as difficult as it is in states with little public land. For example, Texas has only 2 percent of its total land area open to public hunting. Compare that to Minnesota's 23 percent (more than 11 million acres), almost all of which is open to public hunting.

Minnesota's most commonly hunted public lands are the state wildlife management areas (WMAs), state forests, national forests, federal waterfowl production areas (WPAs), national wildlife refuges (NWRs), and in some counties (primarily in the north and northeast), county administered and state lands that don't fit any of the above categories.

The following information goes into more detail on Minnesota public hunting lands and gives sources of information and maps. Be sure to read the most current Minnesota Hunting Regulations booklet for restrictions or special regulations pertaining to any of these lands.

PRIM Maps

Public Recreation Information Maps (PRIMs) offer the most up-to-date information on federal, state, and county lands and their recreational facilities. Each map displays parks, forests, scientific and natural areas (SNAs), waterfowl production areas, refuges, and wildlife management areas. Each type of land (federal, state, county) is color coded. In addition, the maps show facilities such as state trails, campgrounds, DNR offices, etc. There are 51 PRIMs covering the entire state.

PRIMs can be purchased at DNR Regional Offices, Minnesota State Parks, and some DNR Area Forestry Offices. Also, look for them in major sporting goods stores. Complete sets are available at the DNR Gift Shop and Minnesota's Bookstore.

While these maps are not yet available online, the DNR's website does include a map showing all 51 areas and their boundaries, and you can download and mail or fax an order. The current cost for each map is $4.95 plus Minnesota sales tax and a shipping and handling charge.

These are generally the best source of information available to a hunter at this time.

DNR Giftshop
500 Lafayette Road
St. Paul, MN 55101
651-297-6157 or Fax 651-297-3618
Toll Free 888-646-6367
Website: www.dnr.state.us/engineering/prim/index.html

STATE WILDLIFE MANAGEMENT AREAS (WMAs)

Minnesota has 1,034 WMAs, ranging in size from 10 to 250,461 acres. These are wetlands, uplands, or woods owned and managed for wildlife by the Department of Natural Resources. Hunting is open to the public during regular hunting seasons. The DNR's "Guide to Minnesota Wildlife Lands" shows the location and size of each WMA and lists the larger areas that have resident managers and detailed maps. These maps are free and available from the source listed below. For specific information on a particular WMA, contact the nearest DNR Area Wildlife Office. To order:

Guide to Minnesota Wildlife Lands
DNR Information Center
500 Lafayette Road
St. Paul, MN 55155
651-296-6175
Toll Free 888-646-6367

Some wildlife management areas use corn cribs, such as this one, to feed the many different species of wildlife to be found within their boundaries.

Carlos Avery Wildlife Management Area

- ● **Town**
- —— **Roads**
- - - - **Trails**
- ····· **Unimproved Roads**
- —— **Rivers**
- ▓▓ **Lakes**
- - - - **County Line**
- Ⓟ **Parking**
- ▓▓ **Wildlife Management Area**
- ▨▨ **Sanctuary**

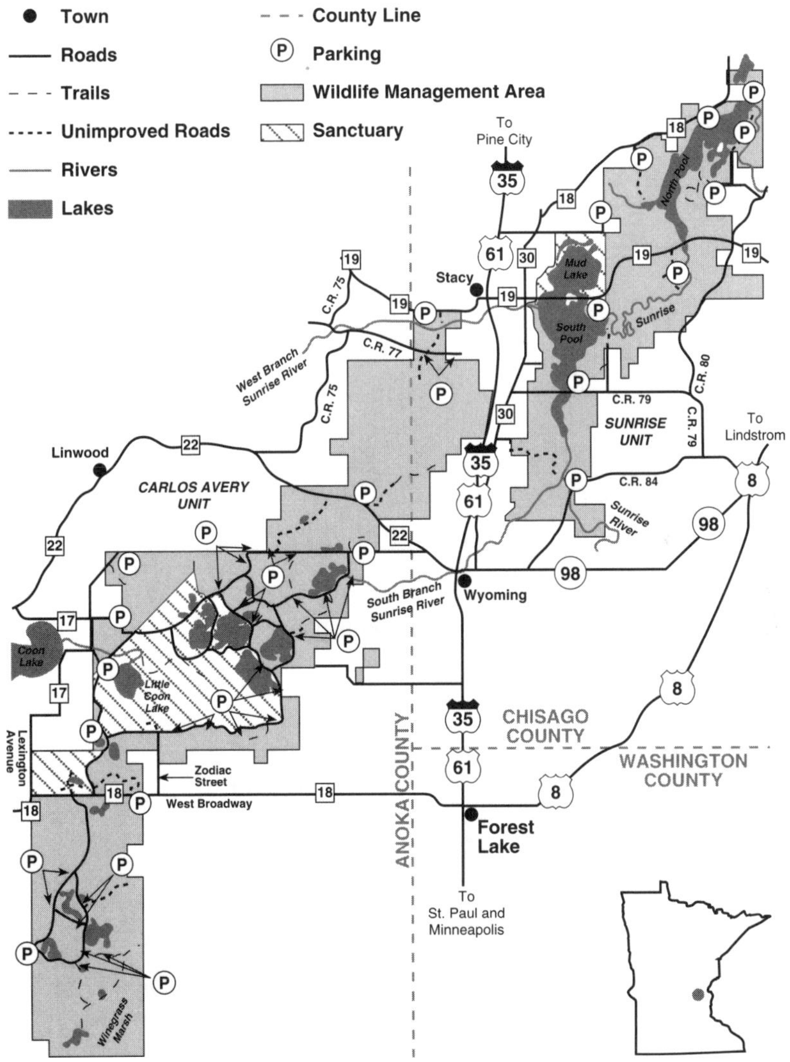

This 23,000-acre WMA is located 30 miles north of the Twin Cities near Forest Lake. Around one-third of the area is upland and two-thirds wetland, which are approximately one-half shallow marsh and one-half open water, providing excellent habitat for waterfowl. There are over 20 miles of trails and 57 miles of roads providing access to this area. For more information, contact: Carlos Avery WMA, 18320 Zodiac Street, Forest Lake, MN 5025; 612-296-5290.

Red Lake Wildlife Management Area

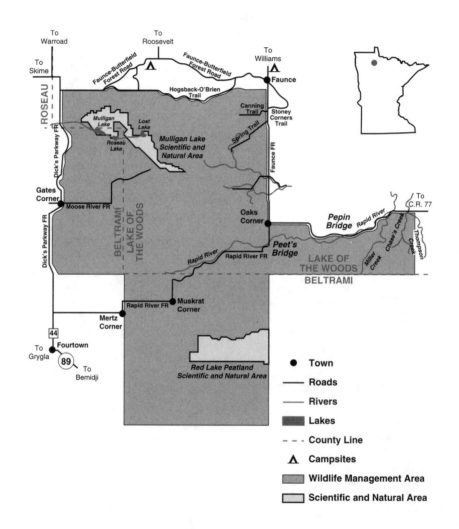

At 250,461 acres, this is the largest WMA in Minnesota. It is located within the Beltrami Island State Forest in northern Minnesota. There is much diversity of habitat in the forests and bogs, and ruffed grouse and woodcock are plentiful. Spruce grouse are also common here. For more information, contact: Red Lake WMA, Norris Camp, P.O. Box 100, Roosevelt, MN 56673; 218-783-6861.

Mille Lacs Wildlife Management Area

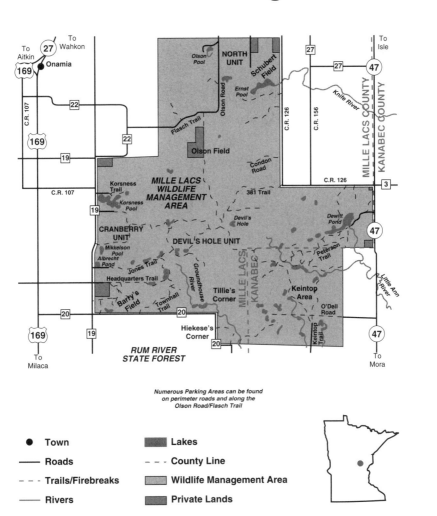

Located approximately 90 miles north of the Twin Cities, this 39,000-acre unit offers a variety of opportunities in its forests and bogs. With over 50 miles of roads and 100 miles of trails, access is very good throughout the area. Since 1966, the University of Minnesota has conducted a long-term ruffed grouse survey here. Researchers are studying responses of grouse to the habitat created by various clearcutting patterns. The mix of aspens and northern hardwoods create openings and edge cover that benefit ruffed grouse. Ducks are also plentiful. For more information, contact: Mille Lacs WMA, Rt. 2, Box 217, Onamia, MN 56359; 612-532-3537.

Lac Qui Parle Wildlife Management Area

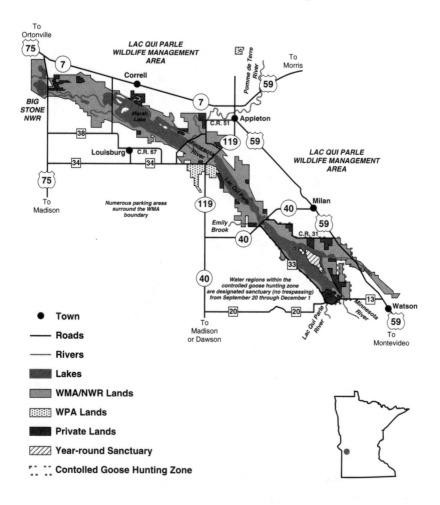

This unit contains two large lakes and numerous marshes and impoundments in its 31,000 acres. It is located in western Minnesota, near Montevideo. Lac Qui Parle Lake, at 6,400 acres, and Marsh Lake, at 5,100 acres, are the most prominent features. Goose hunting is very popular here, as over 150,000 Canada geese may be in the area in the fall. There is a Controlled Hunting Area within the unit, limiting hunters to designated hunting stations. Duck hunting is also excellent here, and pheasants are present in huntable numbers throughout the marshlands. For more information, contact: Lac Qui Parle WMA, Route 1, Box 23, Watson, MN 56295; 612-734-4451.

Whitewater Wildlife Management Area

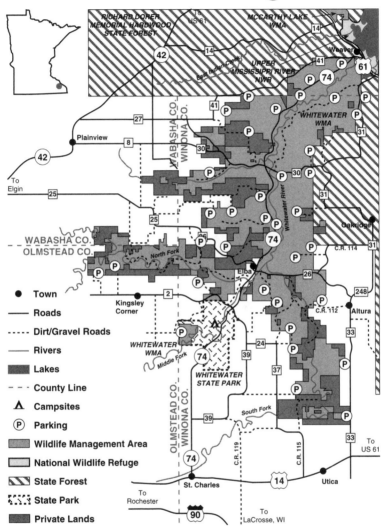

Legend:
- ● Town
- — Roads
- ---- Dirt/Gravel Roads
- ~~~ Rivers
- ▨ Lakes
- – – – County Line
- ⛰ Campsites
- Ⓟ Parking
- ▨ Wildlife Management Area
- ▨ National Wildlife Refuge
- ▨ State Forest
- ▨ State Park
- ▨ Private Lands

Located in southeastern Minnesota, this 27,000-acre unit offers a variety of hunting opportunities, with good populations of ruffed grouse, turkey, and waterfowl. The area is managed with a mix of prescribed burnings, food plots, and selective logging to renovate the grass stands and provide openings in the forest that grouse and turkey broods need. Fourteen natural and artificial wetlands provide good waterfowl habitat, as well. For more information, contact: Whitewater WMA, Rt. 2, Box 333, Altura, MN 55910; 507-932-4133.

Talcot Lake Wildlife Management Area

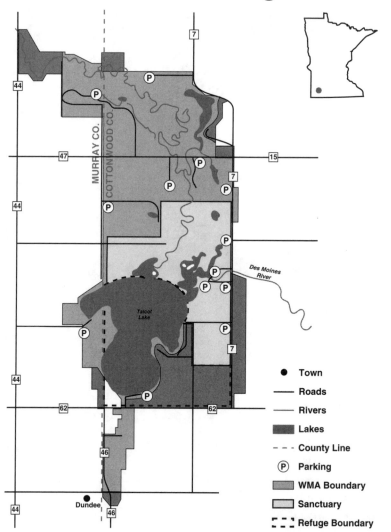

Town
Roads
Rivers
Lakes
County Line
P Parking
WMA Boundary
Sanctuary
Refuge Boundary

This 4,000-acre WMA was established in southwest Minnesota in 1957. Talcot Lake and the surrounding marshes provide excellent habitat for mallards, blue-winged teal, and wood ducks. Geese are also abundant but require close management. Pheasants and gray partridge are present in good numbers. Prescribed burning, planting of food plots, and tight management of wetland water levels all contribute to excellent wildlife habitat here. For more information, contact: Talcot Lake WMA, Dundee, MN 56126; 507-468-2248.

Following is a listing of WMAs (out of a total of 1,034) that are 1,000 or more acres in size. They are listed by the Department of Natural Resources Regions and by county within each region. Check with the DNR Regional Wildlife Offices and Area Wildlife Offices—the counties they oversee follow the WMA list. Be sure to check the most recent copy of "Minnesota Hunting and Trapping Regulations" handbook for restrictions or special regulations that may apply to some WMAs.

Wildlife Management Areas of 1,000 Acres or More

REGION 1

ROSEAU AND LAKE OF THE WOODS COUNTIES

Unit Name	Acres	Nearest Town	Directions
Roseau River	74,540	Pine Creek	3 mi west on CR 3
Roseau Lake	5,023	Roseau	3 mi west on SR 11, 5 mi north on CR 123
Nereson	2,910	Greenbush	2.5 mi south on SR 32, 10 mi east on CR 106
Palmville	3,454	Wannaska	2 mi south on SR 89, 6½ mi east on CR 8
Skime	1,170	Skime	½ mi north CR 9, ½ mi west on CR 18

KITTSON AND MARSHALL COUNTIES

Unit Name	Acres	Nearest Town	Directions
Thief Lake	64,292	Gatze	8 mi north & west on CR 6, 3 mi north on CR 48
Beaches	33,266	Lancaster	6 mi east & 1 mi north on CR 4, 1 mi east on CR 48
Skull	7,472	Lancaster	6 mi east & 4 mi north on CR 4, 1 mi east on township road
Twin Lakes	8,660	Karlstad	1 mi northeast on SR 11
Caribou	8,986	Lancaster	6 mi east, 4 mi north & 1 mi east on CR 4, 2 mi north on CR 51, 2 mi east on township road
Devils Playground	1,400	Karlstad	2 mi north on CR 14, ¼ mi west on trail
Halma Swamp	2,681	Halma	3 mi west on CR 7
Pelan	2,520	Karlstad	9 mi east on CR 7, 2 mi north on trail
East Park	10,218	Strandquist	2½ mi east, 1 mi south, & 1 mi east on CR 29, 1 mi east on township road

Labs work well in grouse cover.

KITTSON AND MARSHALL COUNTIES (continued)

Unit Name	Acres	Nearest Town	Directions
Eckvoll	6,440	Grygla	6 mi west on SR 89, 1½ mi south & west on SR 219, & 2 mi north on township road
Elm Lake	15,760	Holt	4 mi east on CR 7, 3½ mi south on CR 12, 4 mi east on CR 120
Huntley	6,314	Middle River	1 mi west on CR 6, ½ mi north on township road
Espelie	3,567	Grygla	2 mi south on CR 54, 2 mi west on township road
Florian	1,525	Florian	3 mi east on CR 6
Grygla	3,560	Grygla	5 mi north on CR 54
Moylan	1,446	Grygla	6 mi west on SR 89,1¾ mi south on township road
Sem	2,830	Grygla	6 mi south on CR 54

PENNINGTON AND POLK COUNTIES

Unit Name	Acres	Nearest Town	Directions
Chicog	1,624	Melvin	1 mi south on township road
Erskine	1,149	Erskine	1½ mi north on CR 208
Liberty	1,360	Fertile	5 mi west CR 1
Maple Meadows	1,360	Fertile	5½ mi north on SR 32, 1½ mi east on CR 41
Pembina	3,738	Euclid	3½ mi northwest on US 75, 8 mi east on CR 21
Polk	2,724	Erskine	1½ mi north on CR 208

BELTRAMI AND CLEARWATER COUNTIES

Unit Name	Acres	Nearest Town	Directions
Red Lake	250,461	Faunce	12 mi west on state forest road
Moose River	14,367	Fourtown	9 mi north & west on CR 44, 1 mi north on township road
Morph Meadows	5,020	Pennington	2½ mi north on CR 39, 2½ mi east on township road, 4 mi north on national forest road, ½ mi east on trail
Wapiti	33,710	Grygla	5 mi north on CR 54
Wolf Trail	7,221	Fourtown	3 mi west on SR 89, 2 mi south on CR 707
Benville	1,120	Grygla	3 mi east on SR 89, ½ mi north on CR 703
Carmelee	3,807	Grygla	5 mi south on CR 54, 1¼ mi east on CR 2 & 42
Fireweed	2,278	Fourtown	2 mi south on CR 709
Gun-Dog	1,321	Fourtown	2¼ mi west on SR 89
Lee	2,192	Grygla	5½ mi south on CR 54, 5 mi east on CR 2 & 42
Willow-Run	3,454	Grygla	5½ mi south on CR 54, 1½ mi east on CR 2
Old Red Lake Trail	1,082	Leonard	2 mi west on SR 223, 1 mi south on CR 85

NORMAN AND MAHNOMEN COUNTIES

Unit Name	Acres	Nearest Town	Directions
Neal	1,278	Syre	2¼ mi west on CR 39
Bejou	1,533	Bejou	2 mi west on CR 1
Vanose	1,966	Bejou	7 mi east on CR 1, ½ mi south on trail

NORMAN AND MAHNOMEN COUNTIES (continued)

Wambach	1,280	Mahnomen	5 mi north on US 59, 1½ mi east on township road
Waubun	1,754	Waubun	3 mi west on SR 113, ½ mi on township road

HUBBARD AND CASS COUNTIES

Unit Name	Acres	Nearest Town	Directions
Meadow Brook	5,767	Motley	3½ mi north on SR 64, 3 mi east on CR 34, & 6 mi north on CR 35
Mud Goose	3,254	Ball Club	1 mi east on US 2, 5 mi southwest on CR 18 & 3
Crow Wing Chain	3,150	Hubbard	8 mi east on SR 87

CLAY AND BECKER COUNTIES

Unit Name	Acres	Nearest Town	Directions
Barnesville	1,098	Barnesville	4 mi east on SR 34, 3½ mi north on CR 31and 6
Felton	1,014	Felton	2½ mi east on SR 34
Hubbel Pond	3,276	Rochert	½ mi northeast on township road

WILKIN, WADENA, AND OTTERTAIL COUNTIES

Unit Name	Acres	Nearest Town	Directions
Mantson	1,661	Rothsay	12 mi west on CR 26
Rothsay	3,066	Rothsay	6 mi west on CR 26, 2 mi north on CR 15, 2 mi east on township road
Burgen Lake	2,190	Nimrod	5 mi north on CR 27
Elmo	1,201	Henning	2 mi south on CR 65, 5 mi east on CR 134
Inman	1,220	Henning	2 mi south on CR 65, 5 mi east on CR 134
Orwell	1,992	Fergus Falls	5 mi south on CR 1, 3½ mi west on CR 2

REGION 2

KOOCHICHING, ITASCA, AND NORTHEASTER CASS COUNTIES

Unit Name	Acres	Nearest Town	Directions
Dishpan	1,460	Wirt	5 mi west on CR 29, 2 mi northwest on CR 26, 2 mi northwest on national forest road 2227

NORTHERN ST. LOUIS AND NORTHERN LAKE COUNTIES

Unit Name	Acres	Nearest Town	Directions
Canosia	2,074	Pike Lake	2 mi east on CR 9, 2½ mi north on CR 284

SOUTHERN ST. LOUIS AND CARLTON COUNTIES

Unit Name	Acres	Nearest Town	Directions
Blackhoof River	1,736	Scotts Corner	4½ mi south on CR 3

REGION 3

SOUTHERN CASS, CROW WING, AND AITKIN COUNTIES

Unit Name	Acres	Nearest Town	Directions
Grayling	7,635	McGregor	1 mi east on SR 210, 2½ mi north on CR 73
Kimberly	8,496	McGregor	4 mi west on SR 210, 4 mi south on township road
Moose Willow	18,092	Hill City	3 mi south on US 169, 5 mi east on state forest road
Ripple River	5,765	Bennettville	1 mi east & north on township road
Aitkin	2,947	Aitkin	4 mi northeast on US 169, ½ mi east on CR 56
Birchdale	1,303	Emily	6½ mi east on CR 1, 1½ mi south on CR 106

TODD & MORRISON COUNTIES

Unit Name	Acres	Nearest Town	Directions
Grey Eagle	1,340	Grey Eagle	3 mi west on CR 98
Staples	1,440	Staples	1½ mi south on SR 210, ½ mi east on CR 7, 2½ mi south on township road
Little Elk	1,480	Randall	3 mi west on CR 9, 3½ mi west on CR 11, ½ mi west on township road

MILLE LACS, KANABEC, AND PINE COUNTIES

Unit Name	Acres	Nearest Town	Directions
Mille Lacs	36, 719	Onamia	7 mi south on US 169, 2 mi east on township road
Kunkel	2,165	Princeton	4 mi west on SR 95
Ann Lake	1,613	Ogilive	4½ mi north on SR 47

SHERBURNE AND WRIGHT COUNTIES

Unit Name	Acres	Nearest Town	Directions
Suconnix	1,021	Clearwater	4 mi south on SR 24, 1½ mi southeast on township road

ISANTI AND CHISAGO COUNTIES

Unit Name	Acres	Nearest Town	Directions
Dalbo	2,178	Dalbo	2½ mi north on SR 47, 3½ mi west on CR 16

REGION 4

SWIFT AND CHIPPEWA COUNTIES

Unit Name	Acres	Nearest Town	Directions
Lac qui Parle	31,238	Milan	2½ mi southeast on US 59, 2 mi south on CR 32, ½ mi west on CR 33
Danvers	2,298	Benson	6 mi west on CR 20

RENVILLE, MCLEOD, AND SIBLEY COUNTIES

Unit Name	Acres	Nearest Town	Directions
Ras-Lynn	1,258	Stewart	7 mi north on CR 7, 1 mi west on CR 27, 1 mi north on township road

LINCOLN, LYON, AND REDWOOD COUNTIES

Unit Name	Acres	Nearest Town	Directions
Coon Creek	1,050	Russell	4 mi west & ½ mi north on CR 66

COTTONWOOD, WATONWAN, JACKSON, AND MARTIN COUNTIES

Unit Name	Acres	Nearest Town	Directions
Talcot Lake	3,441	Dundee	1 mi north on CR 19, 1½ mi east on SR 62, 3 mi north on CR 7

BLUE EARTH, WASECA, AND FAIRBAULT COUNTIES

Unit Name	Acres	Nearest Town	Directions
Walnut	2,094	Wells	5½ mi south on SR 22, 2 mi west on US 109

REGIONS 5 AND 6

GOODHUE AND WABASHA COUNTIES

Unit Name	Acres	Nearest Town	Directions
White Water	27,325	Elloa	2½ mi north on SR 74
McCarthy	2,886	Kellogg	4 mi southeast on US 61

CARVER, SCOTT, AND DAKOTA COUNTIES

Unit Name	Acres	Nearest Town	Directions
Gores Pool #3	6,249	Hastings	3 mi southeast on CR 54

HENNEPIN, RAMSEY, WASHINGTON, AND ANOKA COUNTIES

Unit Name	Acres	Nearest Town	Directions
Carlos Avery	23,291	Forest Lake	6 mi west on CR 2 & CR 18
Lamprey Pass	1,320	Forest Lake	¼ mi south on I-35 to junction of CR 23

Minnesota Department of Natural Resources Regions

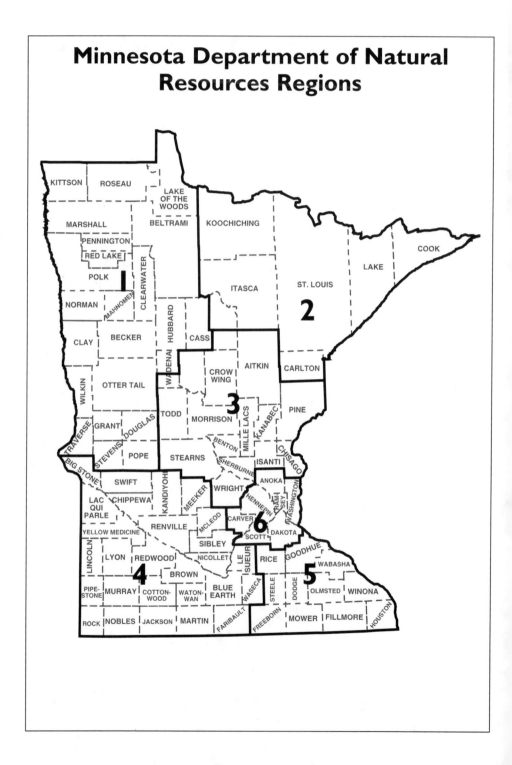

DEPARTMENT OF NATURAL RESOURCES AREA WILDLIFE OFFICES

Region 1	Area Covered
Baudette	Lake of the Woods County
Bemidji	Beltrami, Hubbard, and Clearwater Counties
Crookston	Polk and Red Lake Counties
Detroit Lakes	Norman, Mahnomen, and Becker Counties
Fergus Falls	Clay, Wilken, and Ottertail Counties
Glenwood	Grant, Douglas, Pope, Stevens, and Traverse Counties
Karlstad	Kittson and Northern Marshall Counties
Middle River	Thief Lake Wildlife Management Area
Park Rapids	Becker, Hubbard, and Northwest Cass Counties
Roosevelt	Red Lake Wildlife Management Area
Roseau	Roseau River Wildlife Management Area
Thief River Falls	Pennington and Southern Marshall Counties

Region 2	Area Covered
Cloquet	Carlton and Southern St. Louis
Ely	Northeast St. Louis and Northern Half of Lake Counties
Eveleth	West and West Central St. Louis County
Grand Marais	Cook County
Grand Rapids	Itasca and Northeast Cass Counties
International Falls	Koochiching and Northwest St. Louis Counties
Two Harbors	Eastern St. Louis and Southern Half of Lake Counties

Region 3	Area Covered
Aitkin	Aitkin County
Brainerd	Crow Wing, Wadena, and Southern/Southeastern Cass Counties
Cambridge	Isanti, Chisago, and Mille Lacs Counties
Hinckley	Pine and Kanabec Counties
Little Falls	Todd, Morrison, and Wright Counties
Onamia	Mille Lacs Wildlife Management Area
St. Cloud	Stearns, Sherburne, and Wright Counties

Region 4	Area Covered
Appleton	Big Stone and Swift Counties
Dundee	Talcot Lake Wildlife Management Area
Madison	Lac qui Parle and Yellow Medicine Counties
Mankato	Blue Earth, Waseca, and Faribault Counties
Marshall	Lincoln and Lyon Counties
Nicollet	Nicollet, Le Sueur, Sibley, and McLeod Counties
Redwood Falls	Renville, Redwood, and Brown Counties
Slayton	Pipestone, Murray, Rock, and Nobles Counties

Watson . . . . .Lac qui Parle Wildlife Management Area
Willmar . . . . .Chippewa, Kandiyohi, and Meeker Counties
Windom . . . . .Cottonwood, Watonwan, Jackson, and Martin Counties

Region 5	**Area Covered**

Altura . . . . .Whitewater Wildlife Management Area
Owatonna . . . . .Freeborn, Steele, Rice, and Dodge Counties
Rochester . . . . .Mower, Olmstead, Goodhue, and Wabasha Counties
Winona . . . . .Winona, Fillmore, and Houston Counties

Region 6	**Area Covered**

Forest Lake . . . . .Carlos Avery Wildlife Management Area
Forest Lake . . . . .Anoka, Washington, and Northwest Hennepin Counties
St. Paul . . . . .Ramsey and Hennepin Counties
Shakopee . . . . .Dakota, Scott, and Carver Counties

Addresses and telephone number for area wildlife offices can be found in Appendix X, Minnesota Information Sources.

STATE FORESTS

Minnesota has 57 state forests that contain 3.2 million acres of state land, most of which is open to hunting. In addition, there are 1 million additional acres of land outside state forest boundaries that are also managed by the Division of Forestry. Ruffed grouse, woodcock, wild turkey, and waterfowl can all be found in these forest lands.

Some state forests contain game refuges that may be closed to some or all forms of hunting. Others are posted as closed to hunting because of a recreation site. Check current hunting regulations for more information on game refuges. Please note that there are *private* lands interspersed with state forest land in all parts of the state. Always ask permission before entering private land.

Most state forest lands are not posted or identified in any way. In southeastern Minnesota, most land in the Richard J. Dorer Memorial Hardwood Forest is posted with signs outlining the boundary of state land. Because the majority of state forest lands are not marked, hunters need to obtain the appropriate PRIM map, state forest maps for the forest in which you want to hunt, or a county plat book that includes a particular state forest. PRIM maps and most state forest maps are available from the DNR sources listed below. County plat books are available from county courthouses. In addition, the Department of Tourism's free state highway map shows the location of the state forests, though not in as much detail as other maps.

There are about 2,000 miles of state forest roads that provide access to state forests. Please obey posted signs and do not drive on roads that are posted to prohibit motor vehicle use. Some state forest roads are closed in the spring and fall so that traffic won't damage the road surface. Call ahead or stop by the appropriate DNR area forest office to find out whether a road is open or not.

Sources for State Forest Maps
State Forest Maps, PRIM Maps, Outdoor Recreation Maps and Brochures
DNR Information Center
500 Lafayette Road
St. Paul, MN 55155-4040
651-296-6157 or 888-646-6367
Fax 651-297-3618
www.dnr.state.mn.us

Official Minnesota State Highway Map
Minnesota Department of Tourism
Travel Information Center
500 Metro Square
121 Seventh Place
St. Paul, MN 55101-2146
651-296-5029 (Twin Cities area) or 800-657-3700 (U.S. or Canada)
www.exploreminnesota.com

State Forest Area Offices

Office Address	State Forests Covered
2220 Bemidji Avenue Bemidji, MN 56601 218-755-2890	Buena Vista, Mississippi Headwaters, Welsh, Lake, Paul Bunyan (North Unit)
Hwy 92 North, RR1, Box 22 Bagley, MN 56621-9801 218-694-2146	White Earth
1101 East Lake Street, P.O. Box 43 Warroad, MN 56763-2407 218-386-1304	Lost River, Beltrami Island (West Part)
Hwy 89 South, RR Box 34A Wannaska, MN 56727 218-425-7793	Beltrami Island (West Part)
Hwy 11 and Second Avenue Route 1, Box 1001 Baudette, MN 56623 218-634-2172	Beltrami Island (East Part) Pine Island (Northwest Part)
1st Street West & Summit Avenue Box L Blackduck, MN 56630-0345 218-835-6684	Pine Island, Red Lake, Blackduck, Big Fork, Buena Vista, Bowstring
607 West 1st Street, Box 113 Park Rapids, MN 56470-1311 218-732-3309	Two Inlets, Smoky Hills, Paul Bunyan, Badoura
P.O. Box 823 Detroit Lakes, MN 56502-0823 218-847-1596	White Earth
Box 157 Deer River, MN 56636 218-246-8343	Golden Anniversary, Battleground
Box 95 Effie, MN 56639 218-743-3694	Big Fork, Pine Island, Koochiching, George Washington
1208 East Howard Street Hibbing, MN 55746 218-262-6760	Sturgeon River George Washington

State Forest Area Offices (continued)

4652 Hwy 53, P.O. Box 306 Orr, MN 55771 218-757-3274	Kabetogama
Tower, MN 55790 218-753-4500	Sturgeon River, Kabetogama, Bear Island
1604 South Hwy 33 Cloquet, MN 55720 218-879-0880	Cloquet Valley (West Part), White Face River, Fond du Lac
120 State Road Two Harbors, MN 55616 218-834-6602	Finland, Cloquet Valley (East Part)
Grand Marais, MN 55604 218-387-1075	Grand Portage, Pat Bayle
Little Fork, MN 56653 218-278-6651	Pine Island, Koochiching, Smoky Bear
1601 Minnesota Drive Brainerd, MN 56401 218-828-2565	Pillsbury, Crow Wing
Box 6 Backus, MN 56434 218-947-3232	Lyons, Huntersville, Foot Hills
Box 27 Pequot Lakes, MN 56472 218-568-4566	Land O'Lakes, Emily, Remer
926 2nd Street Northwest Aitkin, MN 56431 218-927-4040	Solana, Wealthwood
P.O. Box 9 Hill City, MN 55748 218-694-2476	Hill River, Savanna
701 South Kenwood, Route 2 Moose Lake, MN 55767 218-485-5400	Nemadji, General Andrews, D.A.R.
P.O. Box 74 Hinckley, MN 55037 320-384-6146	Snake River, St. Croix, Chengwatana, Rum River

State Forest Area Offices (continued)

Office Address	State Forests Covered
800 Oak Savanna Lane Southwest Cambridge, MN 55008 612-689-7100	Sand Dunes
3725 12th Street North, Box 370 St. Cloud, MN 56301 320-255-4276	Birch Lakes, Rum RIver
Box 278 Lewiston, MN 55952 320-523-2183	Richard J. Dorer Memorial Hardwood State Forest (Winona County)
603 North Sprague Street Caledonia, MN 55921 612-724-5261	Richard J. Dorer Memorial Hardwood State Forest (Houston County)
900 Washington Street Northwest Box B Preston, MN 55965 320-765-2740	Richard J. Dorer Memorial Hardwood State Forest (Fillmore County)
1801 South Oak Lake City, MN 55041 612-345-3216	Richard J. Dorer Memorial Hardwood State Forest (Goodhue and Wabasha Counties

Minnesota State Forests
Distribution and Amount of Ownership

Forest Number	State Forest	County	Total Acres	Amount State Owned	Percent Owned
75 to 100 Percent State Owned					
1	Emily	Crow Wing	640	640	100.0
2	Insula Lake	Lake	485	485	100.0
3	Lake Isabelle	Lake	66	66	100.0
4	Nemadji	Pine/Carlton	96,270	90,270	93.7
5	Smokey Bear	Koochiching	12,238	10,997	89.8
6	Red Lake	Beltrami	66,055	59,257	89.7
7	Solana	Aitkin	68,176	58,091	85.2
8	Snake River	Kanabec	9,160	7,758	84.6
9	Beltrami Island	Belt/L.O.W./Roseau	669,032	505,054	75.6
50 to 74 Percent State Owned					
10	Birch Lake	Stearns	637	477	74.8
11	Battleground	Cass	12,868	9,413	73.1
12	Pine Island	Koochiching	878,039	641,136	73.0
13	General Andrews	Pine	7,540	5,361	71.1

	50 to 74 Percent State Owned (continued)				
14	Fond Du Lac	Carlton/St. Louis	62,145	42,400	68.2
15	Hill River	Aitkin	111,392	24,854	67.1
16	Lost River	Roseau	97,500	63,400	65.0
17	St. Croix	Pine	42,105	26.046	61.8
18	Koochiching	Koochiching	565,582	345,064	61.0
19	Smokey Hills	Becker	23,791	14,429	60.6
20	Wealthwood	Aitkin	14,053	8,279	58.9
21	Land O'Lakes	Cass/Crow Wing	50,895	29,971	58.8
22	Paul Bunyan	Hubbard	102,440	59,931	58.5
23	Chengwatana	Pine/Chisago	28,004	16,119	57.5
24	D.A.R.	Pine	640	360	56.2
25	Savanna	Aitkin/St. Louis	218,451	121,193	55.4
26	Whiteface	St. Louis	4,480	2,480	55.3
27	Pillsbury	Cass	14,756	7,883	53.4
28	Two Inlets	Becker	26,225	13,850	52.8
29	Rum River	Kanabec/Mille Lacs	33,180	16,612	50.0
	25 to 49 Percent State Owned				
30	Sand Dunes	Sherburne	10,805	5,366	49.6
31	Huntersville	Wadena/Hubbard	33,222	14,459	43.5
32	Burntside	St. Louis	62,782	24,673	39.2
33	Foothills	Cass	45,125	17,556	38.9
34	Lyons	Wadena	14,720	5,529	37.5
35	Sturgeon River	St. Louis	142,868	52,155	37.2
36	Welsh Lake	Cass	16,336	6,058	37.0
37	White Earth	Mahnomen/Clearwater	113,338	41,617	36.7
38	Big Forks	Itasca	124,270	45,293	36.4
39	Blackduck	Itasca/Beltrami	123,116	41,375	33.6
40	Finland	Lake of Woods/Cook	307,648	102,519	33.3
41	Grand Portage	Cook	98,700	32,661	33.0
42	George Wash.	Itasca	306,838	95,818	31.2
43	Badoura	Hubbard	15,224	4,400	28.9
44	Bowstring	Itasca/Cass	414,090	118.083	28.5
45	Golden Anniv.	Itasca	6,811	1,811	26.5
	I to 24 Percent State Owned				
46	Pat Bayle	Cook	170,644	39,716	23.2
47	Kabetogama	St. Louis	697,363	155,365	22.2
48	Miss. Headwaters	Belt/Hubbard/Clear.	44,919	9,170	20.4
49	Crow Wing	Crow Wing	31,307	6,266	20.0
50	Romer	Cass	12,774	2,440	19.1
51	Northwest Angle	Lake of Woods	79,169	14,399	18.1
52	Buena Vista	Beltrami	104,073	18,480	17.7
53	Bear Island	Lake of Woods/St. Louis	141,187	24,877	17.6
54	Lake Jeanette	St. Louis	10,725	1,357	12.6
55	Cloquet Valley	St. Louis	316,467	39,628	12.5
56	R.J. Dorer	Various	1,006,819	42,000	4.2

Following are 13 maps for the largest of Minnesota's state forests. For more information on these forests, contact the offices listed on pages 244–246.

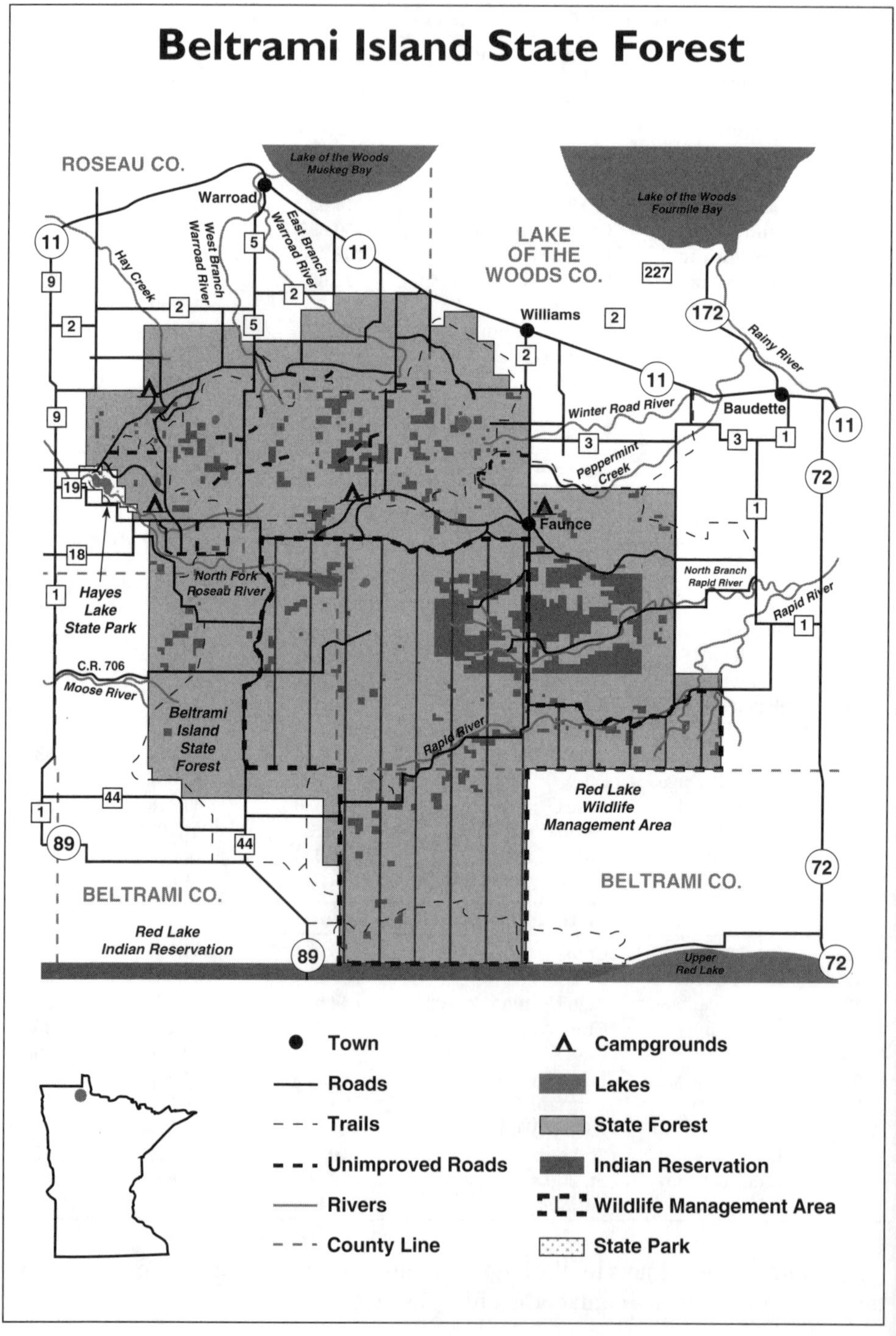

Beltrami Island State Forest

ROSEAU CO.

Lake of the Woods
Muskeg Bay

Warroad

LAKE
OF THE
WOODS CO.

Lake of the Woods
Fourmile Bay

11

West Branch
Warroad River

East Branch
Warroad River

Hay Creek

5

11

2

5

9

2

227

2

Williams

2

172

Rainy River

11

9

Winter Road River

3

Baudette

3

1

11

72

19

Peppermint
Creek

1

Faunce

18

1

Hayes
Lake
State Park

North Fork
Roseau River

North Branch
Rapid River

1

Rapid River

1

C.R. 706

Moose River

Beltrami
Island
State
Forest

Rapid River

Red Lake
Wildlife
Management Area

44

1

89

44

72

BELTRAMI CO.

Red Lake
Indian Reservation

BELTRAMI CO.

89

Upper
Red Lake

72

●	Town	⋀	Campgrounds
—	Roads	▨	Lakes
- - -	Trails	▨	State Forest
▬ ▬ ▬	Unimproved Roads	▧	Indian Reservation
——	Rivers	⌐⌐⌐	Wildlife Management Area
- - -	County Line	▨	State Park

Foothills State Forest

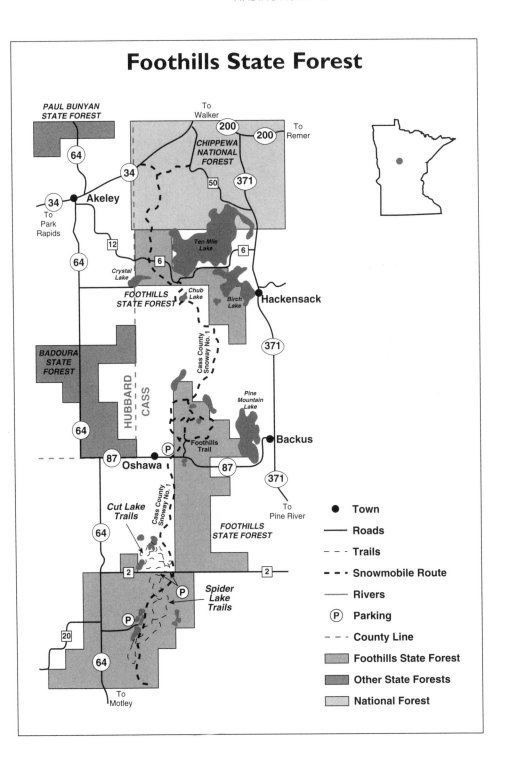

George Washington State Forest

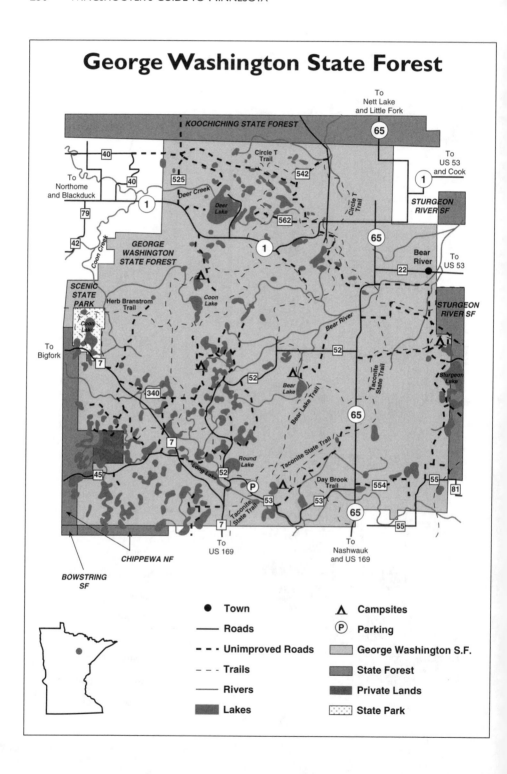

Hill River State Forest

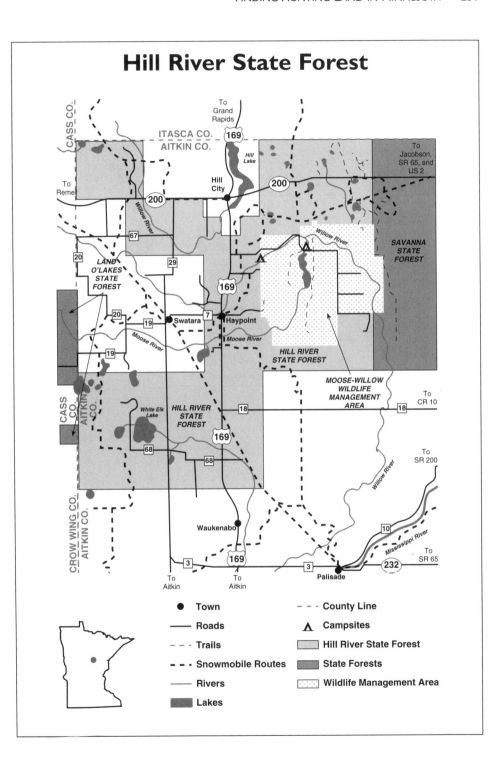

Town ●   **County Line** - - -
Roads ——   **Campsites** Λ
Trails - - -   **Hill River State Forest**
Snowmobile Routes - ▪ -   **State Forests**
Rivers ——   **Wildlife Management Area**
Lakes

Huntersville State Forest

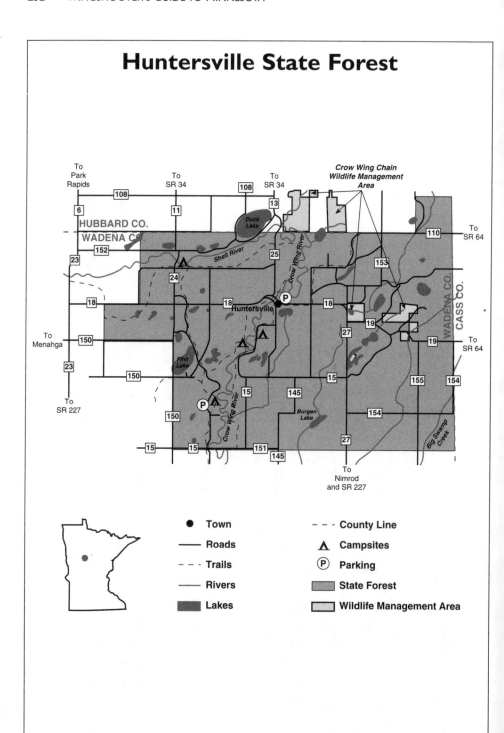

Town
Roads
Trails
Rivers
Lakes

County Line
Campsites
Parking
State Forest
Wildlife Management Area

Kabetogama State Forest

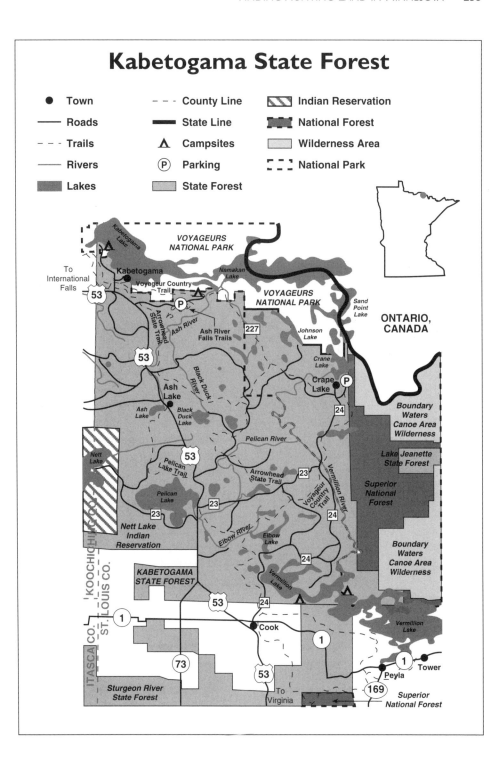

- ● Town
- —— Roads
- - - - Trails
- —— Rivers
- ▨ Lakes
- - - - County Line
- ▬ State Line
- ▲ Campsites
- Ⓟ Parking
- State Forest
- ▨ Indian Reservation
- ▨ National Forest
- Wilderness Area
- ⌐ ¬ National Park

VOYAGEURS NATIONAL PARK

To International Falls

53

Kabetogama Lake

Kabetogama

Voyageur Country Trail

Namakan Lake

VOYAGEURS NATIONAL PARK

Sand Point Lake

ONTARIO, CANADA

Ⓟ

Ash River

Ash River Falls Trails

227

Johnson Lake

Arrowhead State Trail

53

Black Duck River

Ash Lake

Crane Lake

Crape Lake

Ⓟ

Ash Lake

Black Duck Lake

Boundary Waters Canoe Area Wilderness

Pelican River

24

Nett Lake

Pelican Lake Trail

53

Arrowhead State Trail

23

Lake Jeanette State Forest

Superior National Forest

Pelican Lake

23

Voyageur Country Trail

Vermillion River

Nett Lake Indian Reservation

23

Elbow River

Elbow Lake

24

Boundary Waters Canoe Area Wilderness

KABETOGAMA STATE FOREST

53

24

Vermillion Lake

ITASCA CO. | KOOCHICHING CO.

ST. LOUIS CO.

1

Cook

1

Vermillion Lake

73

53

1

Tower

Peyla

To Virginia

169

Sturgeon River State Forest

Superior National Forest

Koochiching State Forest

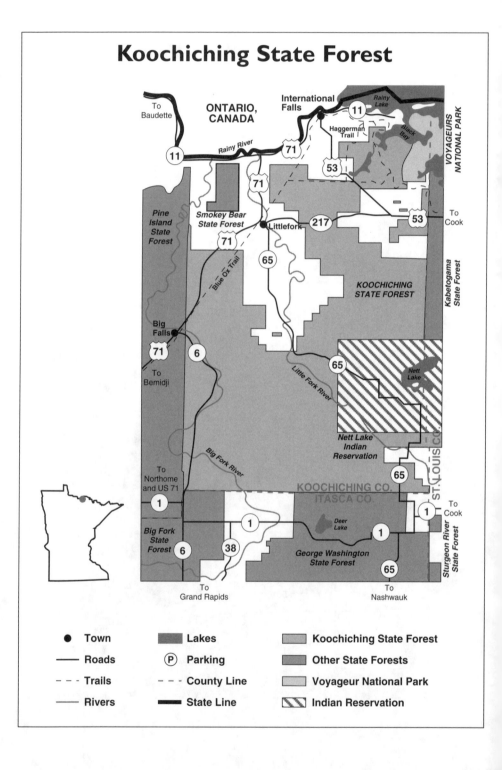

Town
Roads
Trails
Rivers

Lakes
(P) Parking
County Line
State Line

Koochiching State Forest
Other State Forests
Voyageur National Park
Indian Reservation

Land O'Lakes State Forest

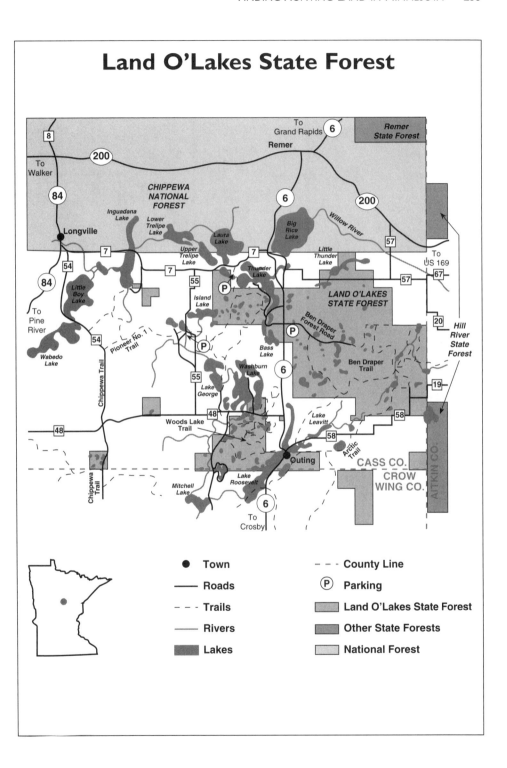

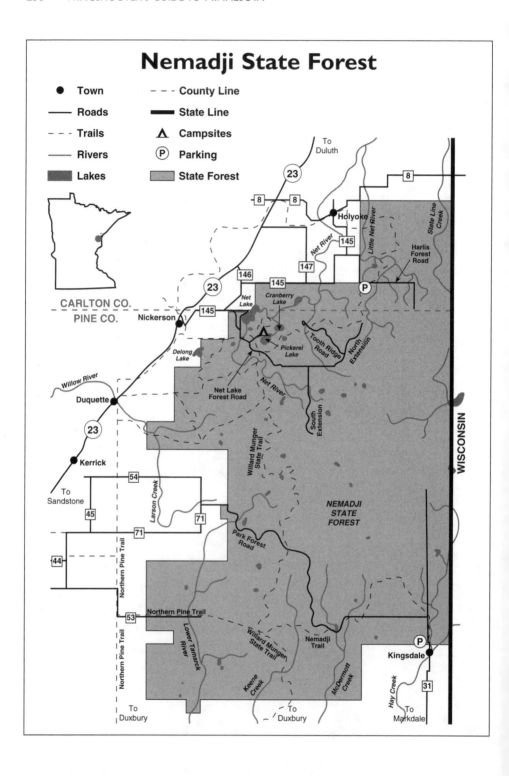

Nemadji State Forest

- ● Town
- ── Roads
- - - - Trails
- ── Rivers
- ▓ Lakes
- - - - County Line
- ━━ State Line
- ▲ Campsites
- Ⓟ Parking
- ▓ State Forest

Pillsbury State Forest

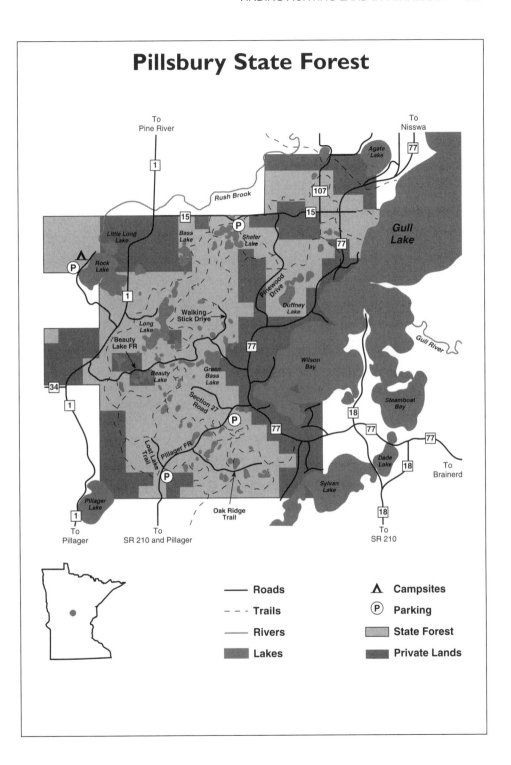

To Pine River

To Nisswa

Agate Lake

Rush Brook

Gull Lake

Little Long Lake

Bass Lake

Shafer Lake

Rock Lake

Walking Stick Drive

Pinewood Drive

Duffney Lake

Long Lake

Beauty Lake FR

Beauty Lake

Green Bass Lake

Section 27 Road

Wilson Bay

Gull River

Steamboat Bay

Lost Lake Trail

Pillager FR

Dade Lake

To Brainerd

Pillager Lake

Oak Ridge Trail

Sylvan Lake

To Pillager

To SR 210 and Pillager

To SR 210

Roads

Trails

Rivers

Lakes

▲ Campsites

ⓟ Parking

State Forest

Private Lands

Pine Island State Forest

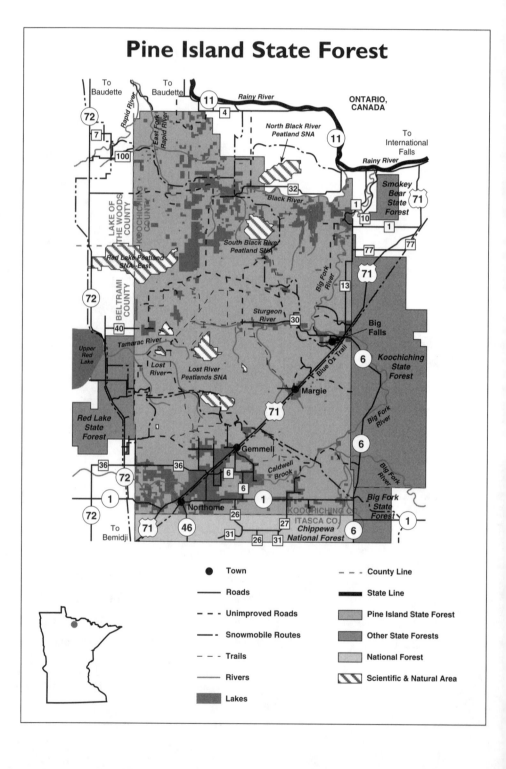

Richard J. Dorer Memorial Hardwood State Forest

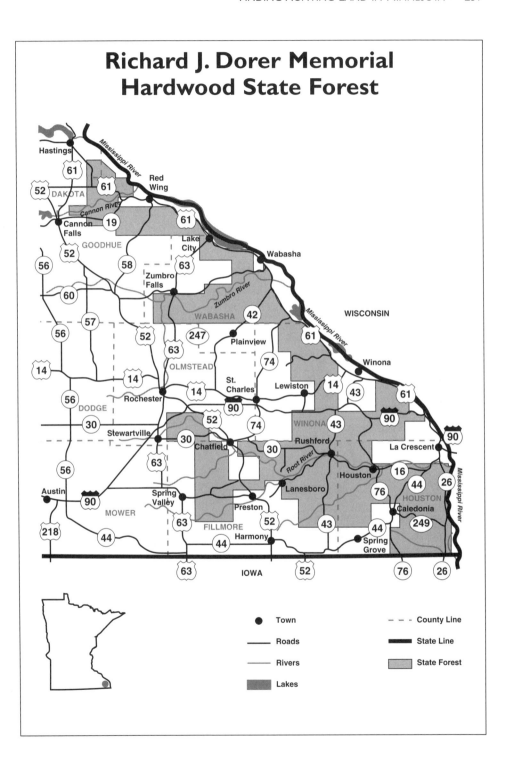

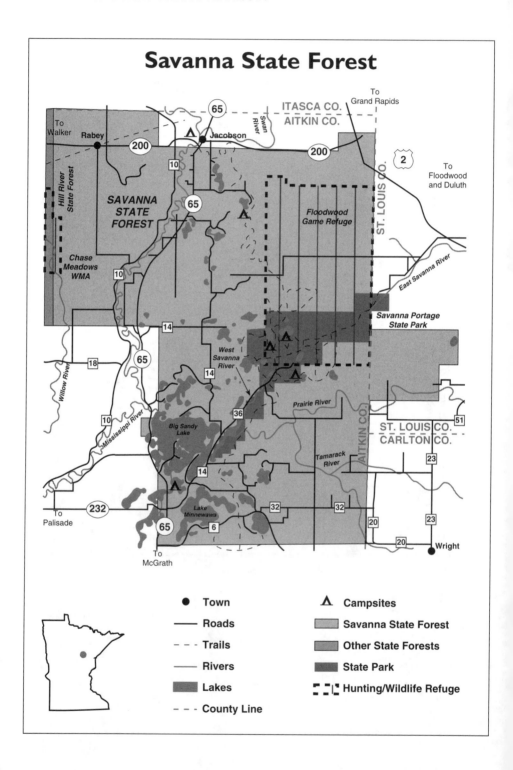

Savanna State Forest

NATIONAL FORESTS

Minnesota is home to two national forests: Chippewa National Forest located in north central Minnesota, and Superior National Forest in northeastern Minnesota.

Chippewa National Forest

Of the 156 national forests in the U.S., Chippewa National Forest was the first established in the eastern states. The forest boundary encompasses about 1.6 million acres of which 665,000 acres are managed by the U.S.D.A. Forest Service. Aspen, birch, pine, balsam fir, and maple trees blanket the rolling uplands of this forest. There is abundant water, with over 700 lakes, 920 miles of rivers and streams, and 150,000 acres of wetlands.

In addition to the large Chippewa National Forest map, which shows boundaries, forest roads, and other pertinent information, 12 detailed hunter walking trail maps are available to the upland hunter. These trails are closed to motorized traffic, and the maps are available from various ranger stations, which also have information about road closures that vary from year to year.

Chippewa National Forest has some of the best upland bird hunting for ruffed grouse, woodcock, and sharp-tailed grouse in the state. Waterfowl hunting is excellent as well.

Chippewa National Forest Supervisor's Office
Route 3, Box 244
Cass Lake, MN 56633
218-335-8600
Email: chippew/r9_chippewa@fs.fed.us
Website: www.fs.fed.us/chippewa/index.htm

Blackduck Ranger District
HC 3, Box 95
Blackduck, MN 56630
218-835-4291

Deer River Ranger District
P.O. box 308
Deer River, MN 56636
218-246-2123

Marcell Ranger District
HC 1, Box 15
Marcell, MN 56657
218-832-3161

Walker Ranger District
HCR 73, Box 15
Walker, MN 56484
218-547-1044

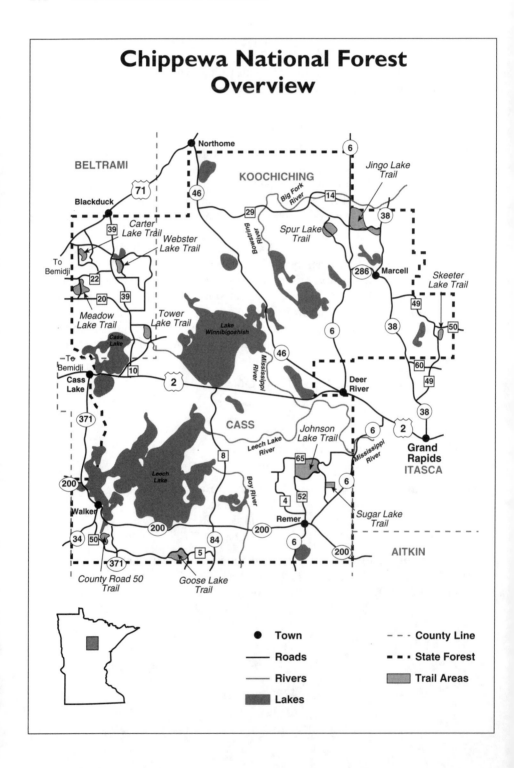

Chippewa National Forest Overview

Chippewa National Forest Carter Lake Trail

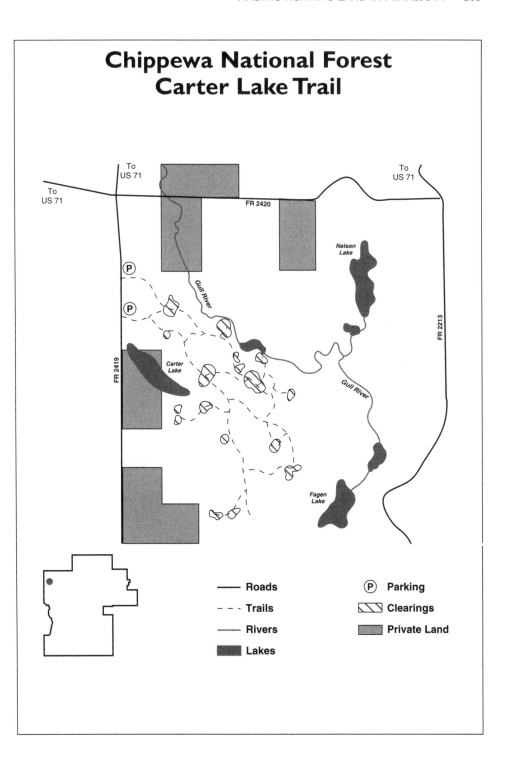

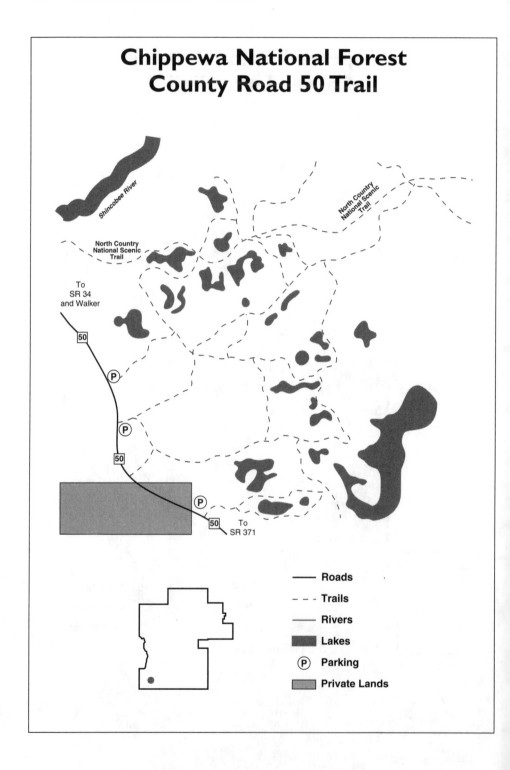

Chippewa National Forest
County Road 50 Trail

Chippewa National Forest
Goose Lake Trail

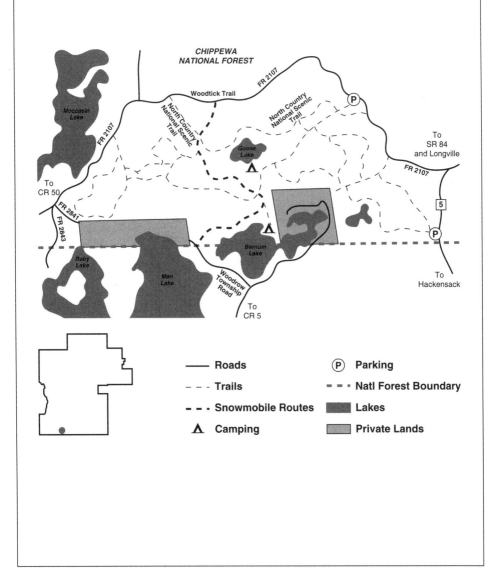

- —— Roads
- - - - Trails
- **- - - Snowmobile Routes**
- **Λ Camping**
- Ⓟ Parking
- **- - - Natl Forest Boundary**
- Lakes
- Private Lands

Chippewa National Forest
Jingo Lake Trail

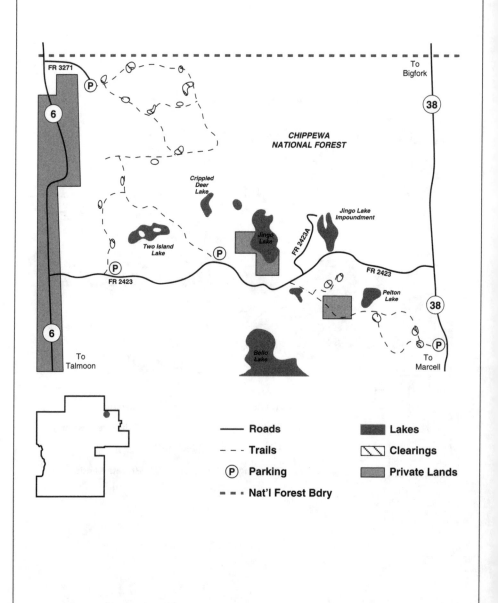

Chippewa National Forest
Johnson Lake Trail

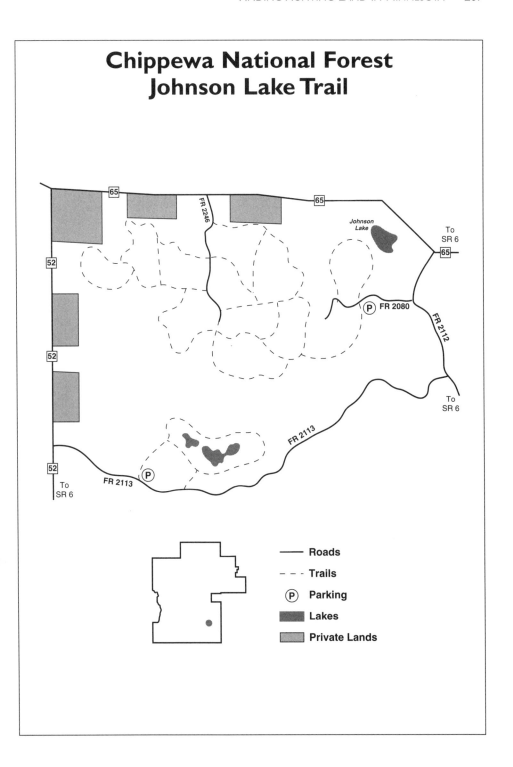

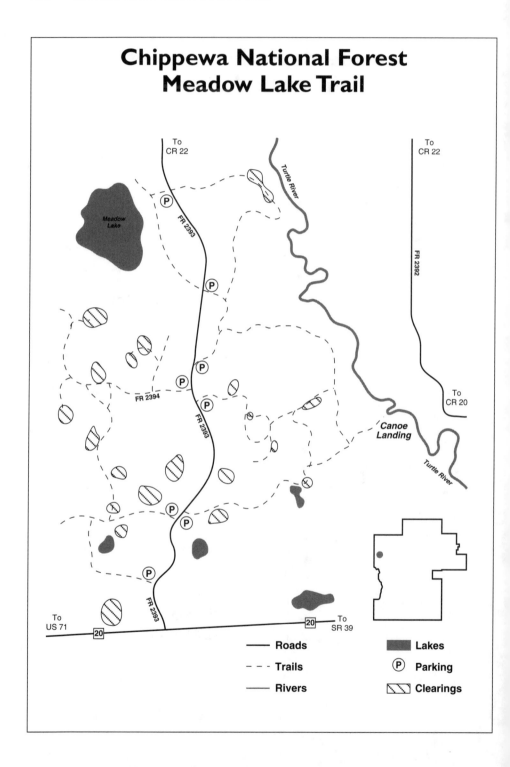

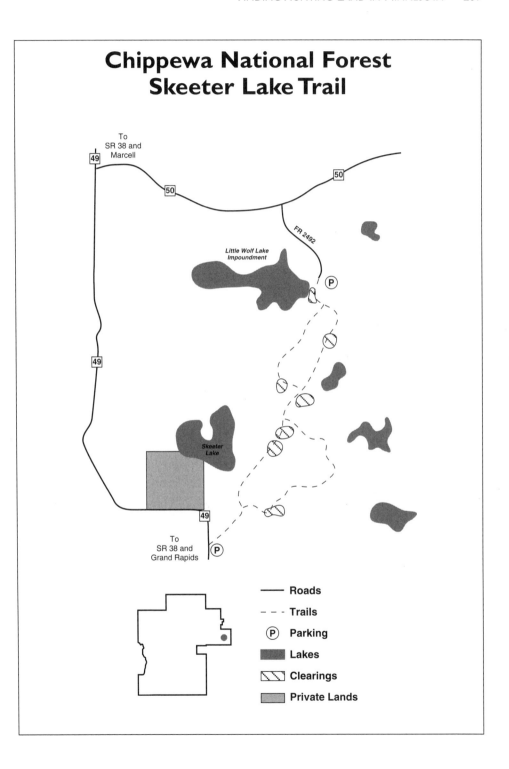

Chippewa National Forest
Skeeter Lake Trail

To
SR 38 and
Marcell

49

50

50

FR 2492

Little Wolf Lake
Impoundment

P

49

Skeeter
Lake

49

To
SR 38 and
Grand Rapids

P

——— Roads

- - - Trails

P   Parking

Lakes

Clearings

Private Lands

Chippewa National Forest
Spur Lake Trail

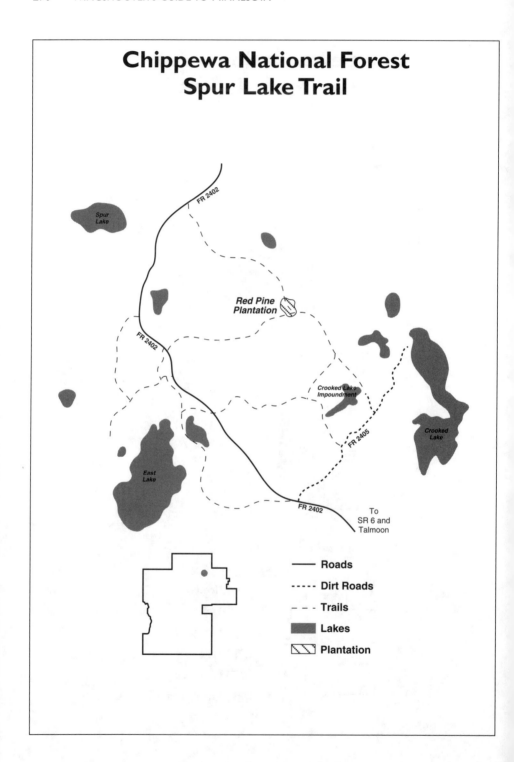

Chippewa National Forest
Sugar Lake Trail

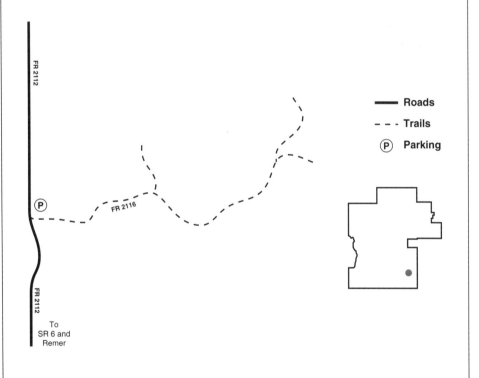

Roads
Trails
Ⓟ Parking

FR 2112

Ⓟ

FR 2116

FR 2112

To
SR 6 and
Remer

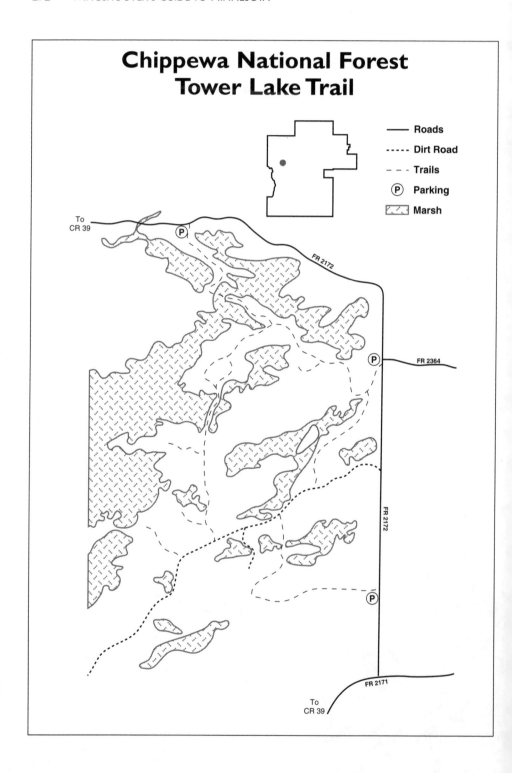

Chippewa National Forest
Tower Lake Trail

Roads
Dirt Road
Trails
Parking
Marsh

To
CR 39

FR 2172

FR 2364

FR 2172

FR 2171

To
CR 39

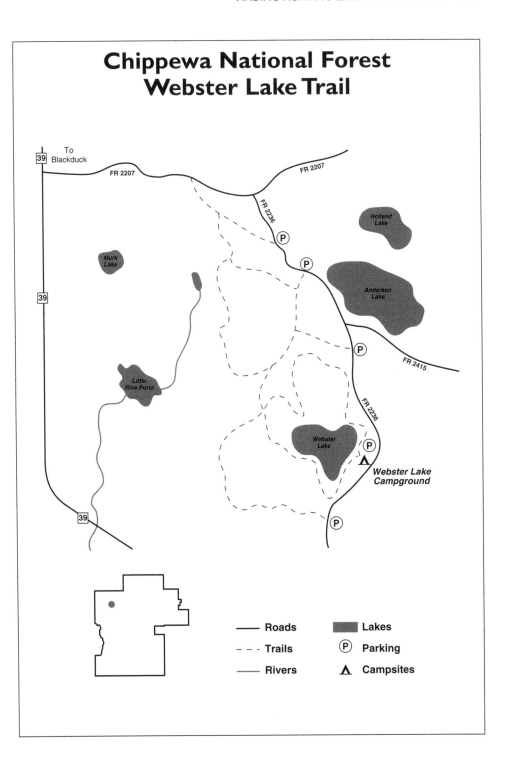

Superior National Forest

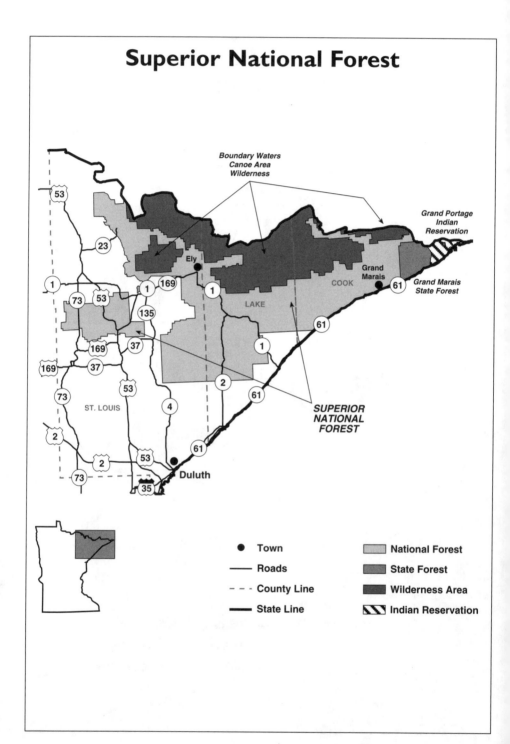

Boundary Waters Canoe Area Wilderness

Grand Portage Indian Reservation

Ely

Grand Marais

COOK

Grand Marais State Forest

LAKE

SUPERIOR NATIONAL FOREST

ST. LOUIS

Duluth

●	Town		National Forest
—	Roads		State Forest
- - -	County Line		Wilderness Area
—	State Line		Indian Reservation

Superior National Forest

Located in northeastern Minnesota, Superior National Forest spans 150 miles along the U.S.-Canada border. Within this 3-million-acre forest are rich and varied resources, including the Boundary Waters Canoe Area Wilderness. Over 445,000 acres, or 695 square miles, of the forest is surface water. In addition, more than 1,300 miles of coldwater streams and 950 miles of warmwater streams flow within Superior's boundaries. The northern forest community thrives with pine, fir, and spruce trees, and is home to numerous wildlife species.

The upland bird hunter should be aware that much of Superior National Forest is relatively undisturbed land. Upland birds, such as ruffed grouse and woodcock, may be few since they need disturbed forest areas to increase population densities. The best areas to find upland birds are along streams, pockets of young aspen and alder, and swamp edges.

Superior's website has an interesting interactive map of the forest that can be downloaded and printed. If you choose to hunt here, purchase the large forest map and get local hunting information from the closest ranger station or the Minnesota Department of Natural Resources area wildlife office.

Superior National Forest Supervisor's Office
8901 Grand Avenue Place
Duluth, MN 55808-1102
218-626-4300
Email: sbear@uslink.net
Website: www.gis.umn.edu/snf/

Gunflint Ranger District
P.O. Box 308
Grand Marais, MN 55604
218-387-1750 (winter)
218-387-2451 (summer)

Kawishiwi Ranger District
118 South 4th Avenue
Ely, MN 55731
218-365-7600

LaCroix Ranger District
P.O. Box 1085
Cook, MN 55723
218-666-5251

Laurentian Ranger District
318 Forest Road
Aurora, MN 55705
218-229-3371

Tofte Ranger District
P.O. Box 2157
Tofte, MN 55615
218-663-7981

Minnesota Federal Wetland Management Districts

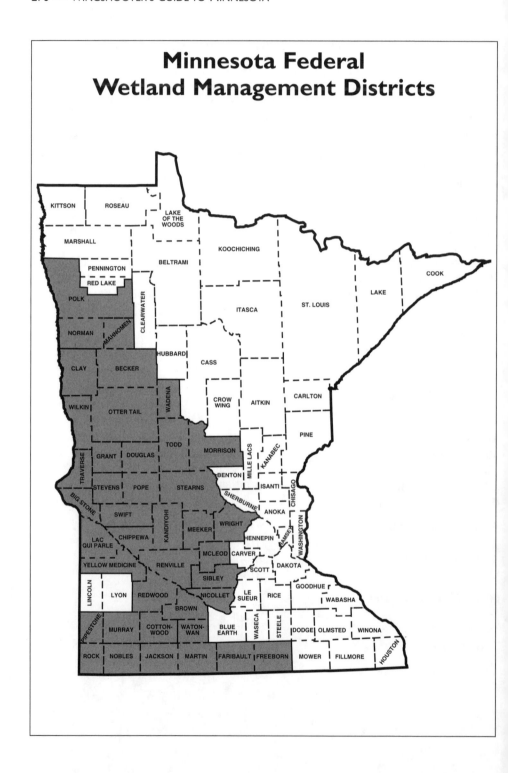

FEDERAL WETLAND MANAGEMENT DISTRICTS (WMDS) AND WATERFOWL PRODUCTION AREAS (WPAS)

Minnesota has five federal Wetland Management Districts managing 808 Waterfowl Production Areas covering close to 170,000 acres. Though these areas are managed for waterfowl, the fringe areas can hold a lot of upland birds, especially pheasant. These Waterfowl Production Areas are found mostly in western, west central, and southern Minnesota. The best maps for finding WPAs are the PRIM maps. For up-to-date information pertaining to these areas, contact the appropriate district listed below. When hunting upland birds in WPAs, only *nontoxic shot* can be used.

Detroit Lakes Wetland Management District
26624 North Tower Road
Detroit Lakes, MN 56501-7959
218-847-4431   Fax: 218-847-4156
E-mail: rick_julian@mail.fws.gov

WATERFOWL PRODUCTION AREAS: 157 units totaling 11,326 acres
COUNTIES IN DISTRICT: Becker, Clay, Mahnomen, Norman, and Polk

Fergus Falls Wetland Management District
Route 1, Box 76
Fergus Falls, MN 56537
218-739-2291   Fax: 218-739-9534
1-800-266-4972
E-mail: kevin_brennan@mail.fws.gov

WATERFOWL PRODUCTION AREAS: 219 units totaling 42,209 acres
COUNTIES IN DISTRICT: Otter Tail, Grant, Douglas, Wilkins, and Wadena

Litchfield Wetland Management District
971 East Frontage Road
Litchfield, MN 55355
320-693-2849   Fax: 320-693-2326
E-mail: tom_bell@mail.fws.gov

WATERFOWL PRODUCTION AREAS: 135 units totaling 30,000 acres
COUNTIES IN DISTRICT: Kandiyohi, McLeod, Meeker, Morrison, Nicollet, Renville, Sibley, Stearns, Todd, and Wright

Detroit Lakes
Wetland Management District

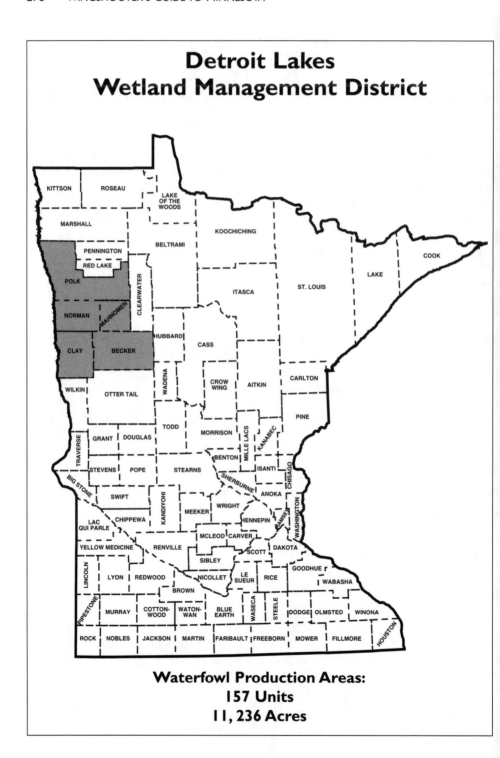

Waterfowl Production Areas:
157 Units
11,236 Acres

Fergus Falls
Wetland Management District

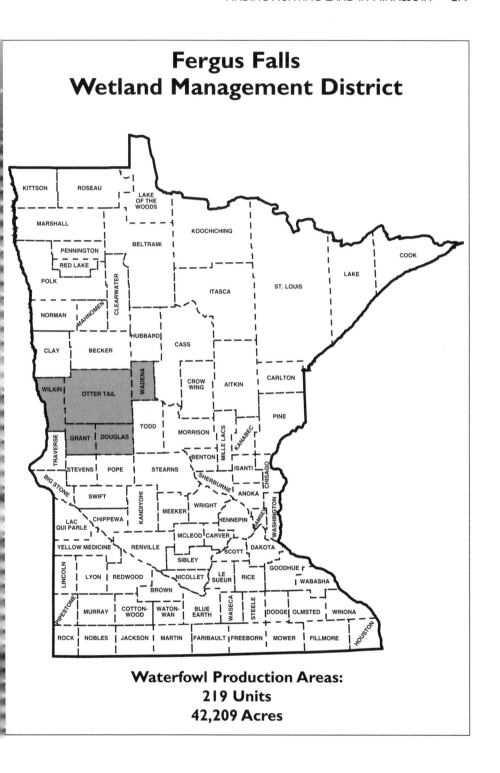

Waterfowl Production Areas:
219 Units
42,209 Acres

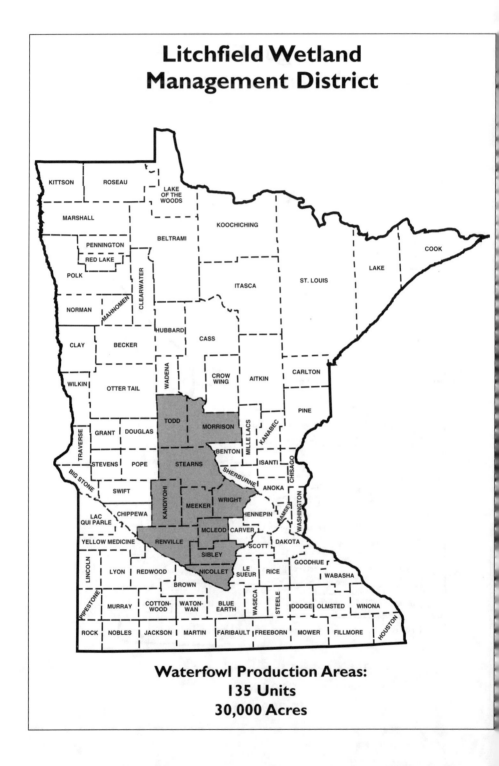

Litchfield Wetland Management District

**Waterfowl Production Areas:
135 Units
30,000 Acres**

Morris Wetland Management District

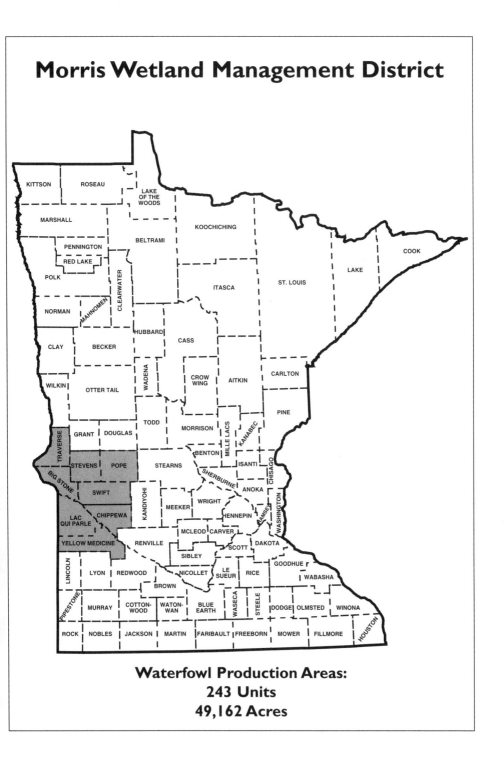

Waterfowl Production Areas:
243 Units
49,162 Acres

Windom Wetland Management District

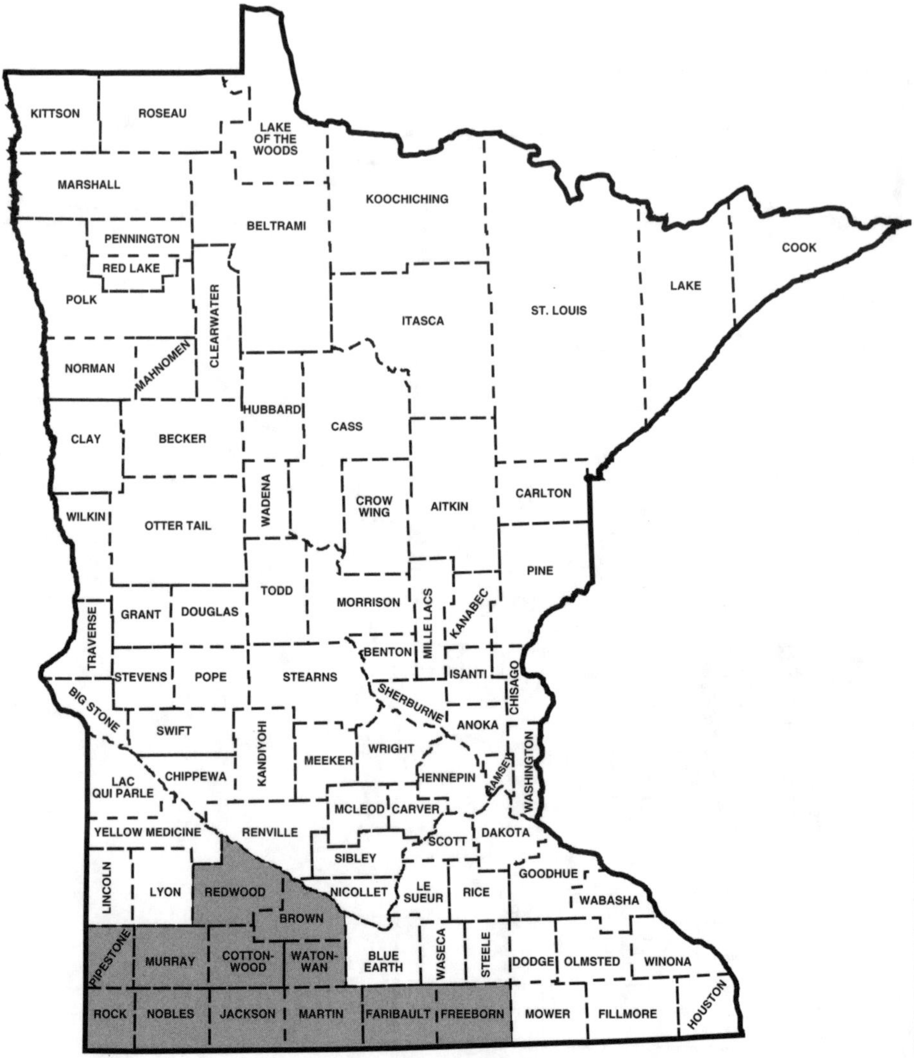

KITTSON
ROSEAU
LAKE OF THE WOODS
MARSHALL
KOOCHICHING
PENNINGTON
BELTRAMI
RED LAKE
POLK
CLEARWATER
ITASCA
ST. LOUIS
LAKE
COOK
NORMAN
MAHNOMEN
HUBBARD
CASS
CLAY
BECKER
WADENA
CROW WING
AITKIN
CARLTON
WILKIN
OTTER TAIL
PINE
TODD
MORRISON
MILLE LACS
KANABEC
TRAVERSE
GRANT
DOUGLAS
BENTON
BIG STONE
STEVENS
POPE
STEARNS
ISANTI
CHISAGO
SHERBURNE
ANOKA
SWIFT
KANDIYOHI
MEEKER
WRIGHT
HENNEPIN
RAMSEY
WASHINGTON
LAC QUI PARLE
CHIPPEWA
MCLEOD
CARVER
YELLOW MEDICINE
RENVILLE
SCOTT
DAKOTA
LINCOLN
SIBLEY
GOODHUE
LYON
REDWOOD
NICOLLET
LE SUEUR
RICE
WABASHA
BROWN
PIPESTONE
MURRAY
COTTON-WOOD
WATON-WAN
BLUE EARTH
WASECA
STEELE
DODGE
OLMSTED
WINONA
ROCK
NOBLES
JACKSON
MARTIN
FARIBAULT
FREEBORN
MOWER
FILLMORE
HOUSTON

Waterfowl Production Areas:
54 Units
10,650 Acres

Morris Wetland Management District
Route 1, Box 877
320-589-1001   Fax: 320- 589-2624
1-800-248-5868
E-mail: steve_delahanty@mail.fws.gov

WATERFOWL PRODUCTION AREAS: 243 units totaling 49,162 acres
COUNTIES IN DISTRICT: Big Stone, Lac Qui Parle, Pope, Stevens, Swift,
                      Traverse, Yellow Medicine, and Chippewa

Windom Wetland Management District
Route 1, Box 273A
Windom, MN 56101-9663
507-831-2220   Fax: 507- 831-5524
1-800-577-2875
E-mail: steve_kallin@mail.fws.gov

WATERFOWL PRODUCTION AREAS: 54 units totaling 10,650 acres
COUNTIES IN DISTRICT: Cottonwood, Jackson, Faribault, Freeborn, Martin, Murray,
                      Nobles, Pipestone, Watonwan, Brown, Redwood, and Rock

Sources for Waterfowl Production Area (WPA) Maps
Ask for: Public Recreation Information Maps (PRIM)
DNR Information Center
500 Lafayette Road
St. Paul, MN 55155-4040
651-296-6157   Fax: 651- 297-3618
1-888-646-6367
Website: www.dnr.state.mn.us

NATIONAL WILDLIFE REFUGES (NWR)

Minnesota has six National Wildlife Refuges (NWR), covering approximately 150,000 acres, that afford waterfowl and/or upland bird hunting opportunities. The U. S. Fish and Wildlife Service administers these refuges from its Region 3 Headquarters at Fort Snelling, Minnesota, and from offices located at each refuge. As the rules and regulations vary somewhat from refuge to refuge, it is advised that you contact the refuges at the addresses and/or telephone numbers included with each refuge's capsule description for up-to-date information and maps.

Great Lakes/Big River Region
U. S. Fish and Wildlife Service
1 Federal Drive
BHW Federal Building
Fort Snelling, MN 55111
612-713-5360
Website: www.fws.gov/r3pao/maps/minn.htm

Tamarac National Wildlife Refuge

The Tamarac National Wildlife Refuge is located where tallgrass prairie, northern hardwood, and coniferous forests meet. This transitional area is rich in Native American and early pioneer settler history. Much of the refuge remains in nearly pristine condition. At the top of a watershed, the refuge's numerous lakes, rivers, and marshes are free from invasion by exotic species and pollution. Stands of upland hardwoods, aspen, birch, and lowland conifer, as well as bogs and remnant grasslands, are managed to meet the needs of native wildlife species.

Ruffed grouse, woodcock, snipe, ducks, rails, and geese are all found on the refuge's 42,724 acres. *Nontoxic shot* is required on the refuge. For further information contact:

Tamarac National Wildlife Refuge
35704 County Hwy 26
Rochert, MN 56578-9638
218-847-2641   Fax: 218-847-9141
E-mail: jay_m_johnson@mail.fws.gov

Tamarac National Wildlife Refuge

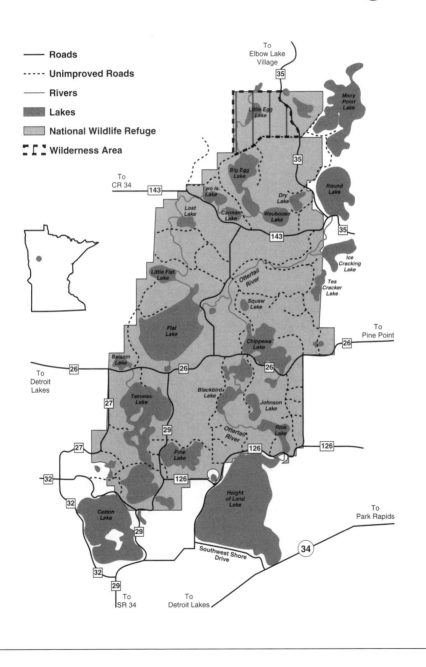

— Roads
---- Unimproved Roads
— Rivers
▨ Lakes
▨ National Wildlife Refuge
▮ ▮ ▮ Wilderness Area

To Elbow Lake Village

35

Many Point Lake

Little Egg Lake

35

To CR 34

143

Big Egg Lake

Two Is. Lake

Dry Lake

Round Lake

Lost Lake

Carman Lake

Wauboose Lake

143

35

Little Flat Lake

Ottertail River

Ice Cracking Lake

Tea Cracker Lake

Squaw Lake

Flat Lake

Chippewa Lake

To Pine Point

26

Balsam Lake

To Detroit Lakes

26

26

26

27

Tamarac Lake

Blackbird Lake

Johnson Lake

29

Ottertail River

Rice Lake

27

Pine Lake

126

126

32

126

Height of Land Lake

To Park Rapids

32

Cotton Lake

29

Southwest Shore Drive

34

32

29

To SR 34

To Detroit Lakes

Rice Lake National Wildlife Refuge

It is estimated that more than 100,000 ducks, including 75,000 ring-necked ducks, migrate through the refuge during autumn. The 18,281-acre refuge is located in the transition zone between the coniferous forests of northern Minnesota and the hardwood forests of the southern part of the state. A mixture of cedar swamps, tamarack bogs, forested uplands, scattered grasslands, and small lakes harbor countless plants and animals. As the name implies, Rice Lake produces large quantities of wild rice, which is utilized by waterfowl. Here one may hunt ruffed grouse, spruce grouse, sharp-tailed grouse, woodcock, and snipe. There is no waterfowl hunting on this refuge. For additional information and map contact:

> Rice Lake National Wildlife Refuge
> Route 2, Box 67
> McGregor, MN 55760
> 218-768-2402   Fax: 218-768-3040
> E-mail: eugene_patten@mail.fws.gov

A nice sharptail harvest.

Rice Lake National Wildlife Refuge

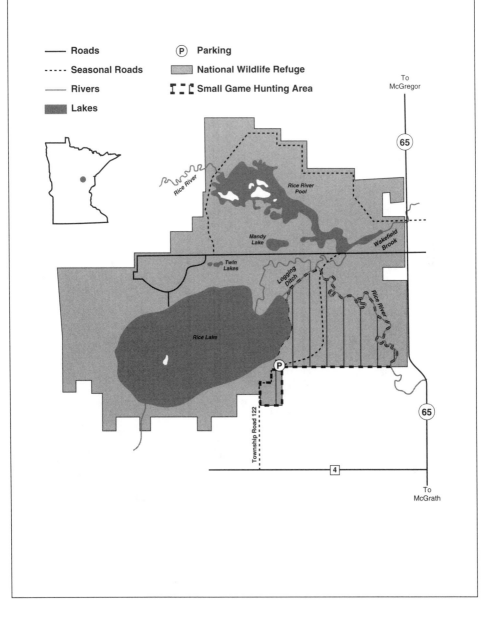

Sherburne National Wildlife Refuge

This refuge is a mosaic of prairie, wetland, oak savanna, and woodland set in a transition zone between forest and prairie. Set aside in 1965 to preserve this vanishing heritage, the refuge encompasses nearly 31,000 gently rolling acres. Huntable species include ruffed grouse, pheasant, woodcock, snipe, rail, and waterfowl. *Nontoxic shot* is required. For a refuge map and further information contact:

Sherburne National Wildlife Refuge
17076 – 293rd Avenue
Zimmerman, MN 55398
612-389-3323   Fax: 612-389-3493
E-mail: charles_blair@mail.fws.gov

Jump shooting on ponds isn't always this productive, but it certainly can be.

Sherburne National Wildlife Refuge

To Princeton

23 11 22 5 80

3 3

Santiago 80

86 3

48 42

St. Francis River

23 82

11 9

Blue Hill Trail

Manohmen Trail

9

Rice Lake

5

Wildlife Drive

47 1

11 Orrock

4 4

4

75 5 15 1

St. Francis River

To Zimmerman

● Town

— Roads

- - - - Unimproved Roads

— Rivers

Lakes

National Wildlife Refuge

To US 10, Big Lake, and Monticello

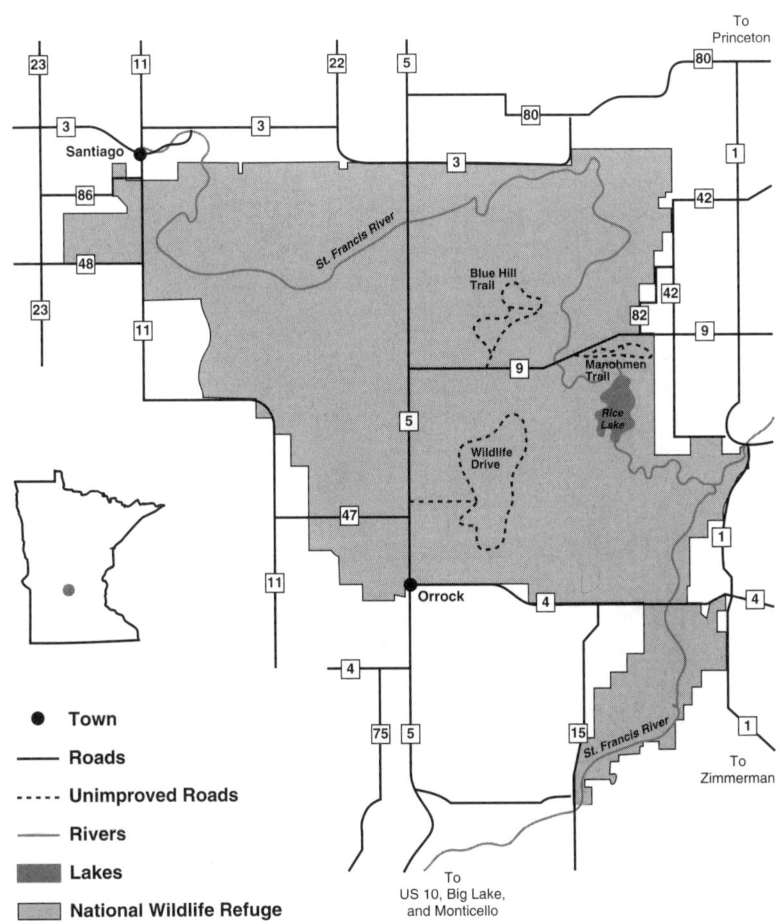

Big Stone National Wildlife Refuge

This 11,521-acre refuge is located along the Minnesota River near the South Dakota border. The reservoir and surrounding land offer a variety of habitat, including native prairie, floodplain, forest, wetland, and granite rock outcrops. In addition to hiking trails, the refuge has four miles of roads. Hunted species include pheasants and Hungarian partridge. *Nontoxic shot* use is mandated. For additional information and refuge map contact:

> Big Stone National Wildlife Refuge
> RR 1, Box 25
> Odessa, MN 56276
> 320-273-2191   Fax: 320-273-2231
> E-mail: ron_cole@mail.fws.gov

Pheasants have more to be wary of than hunters and predators.

Big Stone National Wildlife Refuge

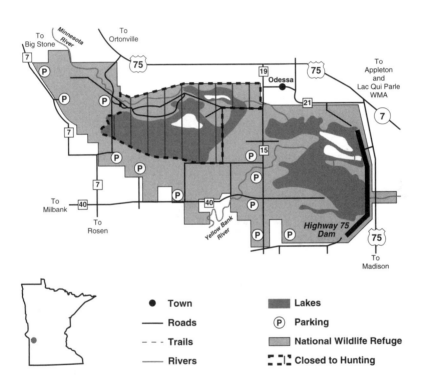

Minnesota Valley National Wildlife Refuge

One of the few urban national wildlife refuges in the country is located in the Twin Cities (Minneapolis and St. Paul). The Minnesota Valley National Wildlife Refuge stretches 34 miles along the Minnesota River from Jordan to Bloomington. Established in 1976, the refuge is a "work in progress." Units are being added to it on a fairly regular basis. Currently at 9500 acres, it is expected to reach a final size of 14,000 acres. The refuge has eight management units encompassing habitat ranging from bottomland hardwood forest to a rare calcareous fen community. Huntable species include wild turkey and waterfowl. *Nontoxic shot* is required. For further information on which management units are open to hunting and a refuge map contact:

> **Minnesota Valley National Wildlife Refuge**
> 3815 East 80th Street
> Bloomington, MN 55425
> 612-854-5900   Fax: 612-725-3279
> E-mail: richard_d_schultz@mail.fws.gov

*Without a dog, you might not be able to put this
wounded duck in your game bag.*

Minnesota Valley
National Wildlife Refuge

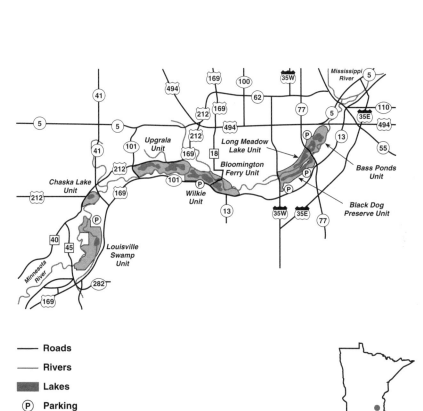

- Roads
- Rivers
- Lakes
- (P) Parking
- National Wildlife Refuge

Upper Mississippi National Wildlife and Fish Refuge

The Upper Mississippi National Wildlife and Fish Refuge extends 261 miles along the Mississippi River from the Chippewa River in Wisconsin to Rock Island, Illinois, encompassing 194,000 acres in parts of Minnesota, Wisconsin, Iowa, and Illinois. It is divided into four management districts, with the Minnesota portions being in the Winona and La Crosse Districts.

The Winona District consists of 32,000 acres of Mississippi River bottomland from River Mile 763.5 at the mouth of the Chippewa River above Nelson, Wisconsin, to Lock and Dam 6 at River Mile 714.3 near Trempealeau, Wisconsin. This area covers part of Pool 4 and all of Pools 5, 5a, and 6, and includes land and water in both Minnesota and Wisconsin.

The La Crosse District extends from Lock and Dam 6 to the top of Pool 9 and includes Pools 7 and 8. Hunting is prohibited at Upper Halfway Creek Marsh and Lake Onalaska in Pool 7, and at Goose Island and the Wisconsin Islands in Pool 8.

Habitat includes wooded river bottomland (mostly silver maple, ash, elm, cottonwood, and willow), backwater marshes (cattail, bulrush, and other emergent and submergent plants), deep open water areas above each dam, and numerous sloughs and channels. Ruffed grouse, woodcock, and wild turkey are the huntable species. *Nontoxic shot* is required for huntable species other than wild turkey. Lead shot is permissible for wild turkey hunting. For specific regulations as well as the refuge map contact:

Upper Mississippi River National Wildlife and Fish Refuge
Winona District
51 East 4th Street, Room 101
Winona, MN 55987
507-452-4232   Fax: 507- 452-0851
E-mail: jim_fisher@mail.fws.gov

La Crosse District
555 Lester Avenue
Onalaska, WI 54650
608-783-8403
E-mail: mary_stefanski@mail.fws.gov

Upper Mississippi River
National Wildlife Refuge, Pool 4

Pepin

35

25

Lake
Pepin

To
Lake City, MN

61

25

WISCONSIN

35

Truedale
Lake

Big
Lake

MINNESOTA

Mississippi River

60 Wabasha

- ● Town
- — Roads
- ----- Unimproved Roads
- — Rivers
- ▬ Dam/Lock
- ▮ Lakes/Water Bodies
- ⌐ ⌐ Restricted Hunting Area
- ▮ National Wildlife Refuge

61

24

24

61

Zumbro River

To
Kellogg, MN

Lock
and Dam
Number 4

37

35

To
Buffalo, WI

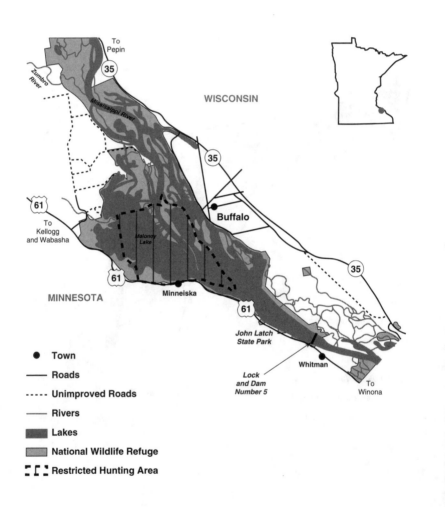

Upper Mississippi River National Wildlife Refuge, Pool 5

To Pepin

35

Zumbro River

Mississippi River

WISCONSIN

35

61

To Kellogg and Wabasha

Maloney Lake

Buffalo

61

35

MINNESOTA

Minneiska

61

John Latch State Park

Whitman

Lock and Dam Number 5

To Winona

● Town

—— Roads

- - - - Unimproved Roads

—— Rivers

▓ Lakes

☐ National Wildlife Refuge

⌐ ⌐ ⌐ Restricted Hunting Area

Upper Mississippi River National Wildlife Refuge, Pool 5A

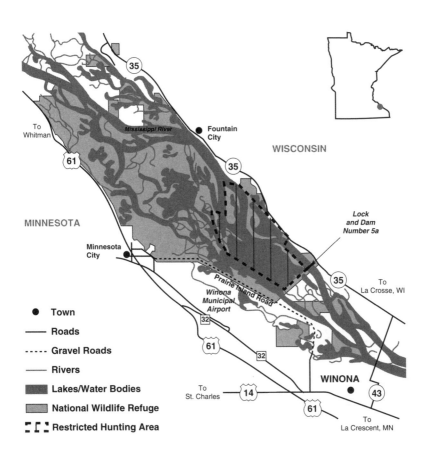

Town

Roads

Gravel Roads

Rivers

Lakes/Water Bodies

National Wildlife Refuge

Restricted Hunting Area

Upper Mississippi River
National Wildlife Refuge, Pool 6

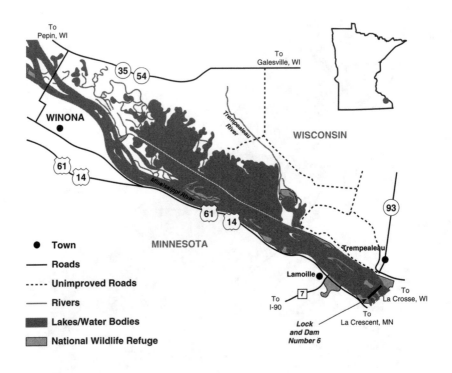

Upper Mississippi River
National Wildlife Refuge, Pool 7

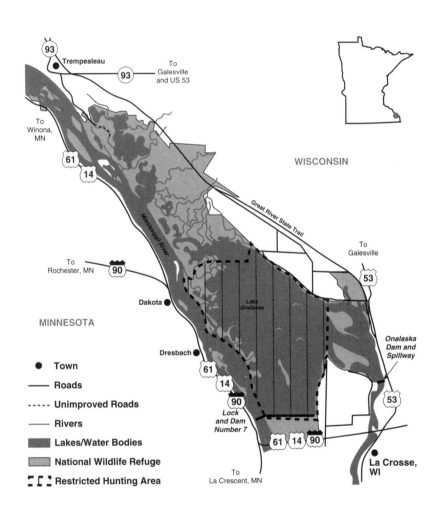

MINNESOTA

WISCONSIN

Trempealeau

To Galesville and US 53

To Winona, MN

To Rochester, MN

Dakota

Lake Onalaska

Dresbach

To Galesville

Onalaska Dam and Spillway

Lock and Dam Number 7

La Crosse, WI

To La Crescent, MN

Great River State Trail

Mississippi River

- ● Town
- — Roads
- ---- Unimproved Roads
- — Rivers
- ▨ Lakes/Water Bodies
- ▨ National Wildlife Refuge
- ▊ ▊ ▊ Restricted Hunting Area

Upper Mississippi River National Wildlife Refuge, Pool 8

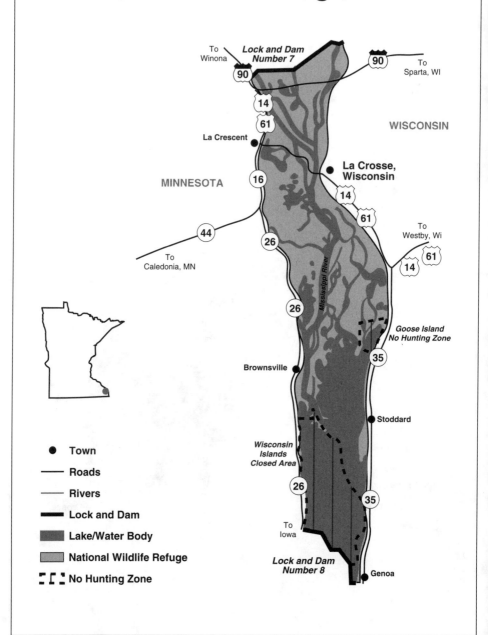

To Winona

Lock and Dam Number 7

90

90

To Sparta, WI

14

61

La Crescent

WISCONSIN

La Crosse, Wisconsin

MINNESOTA

16

14

61

44

26

To Westby, Wi

61

14

To Caledonia, MN

Mississippi River

26

Goose Island No Hunting Zone

35

Brownsville

Stoddard

Wisconsin Islands Closed Area

26

35

To Iowa

Lock and Dam Number 8

Genoa

● Town

— Roads

— Rivers

▬ Lock and Dam

Lake/Water Body

National Wildlife Refuge

No Hunting Zone

OTHER HUNTING LAND OPPORTUNITIES

State Game Refuges

State game refuges are normally closed to the hunting of animals and birds. Exceptions are listed in the Minnesota Hunting and Trapping Regulations Handbook distributed each year prior to the opening of the hunting season. Even though a refuge may be open, it could contain privately owned land on which the landowner may prohibit hunting.

Goose or Waterfowl Refuges

State goose refuges are closed to goose or waterfowl hunting (as posted) except when specifically open during special seasons (these are listed in the Minnesota Hunting and Trapping Regulations Handbook and the Waterfowl Hunting Regulations Supplement).

State Scientific and Natural Areas (SNA)

State Scientific and Natural Areas (SNAs) are closed by law to hunting unless they are listed as exceptions in the Minnesota Hunting and Trapping Regulations handbook. Vegetation is not to be damaged on SNAs.

State Parks

State parks are refuges by law and therefore closed to upland bird and waterfowl hunting.

A good choice of cover when hunting ducks is to stand on the edge of cover that surrounds a pond.

Walking up to a dog on point is still one of the best parts of a hunting expedition.

Appendix I
Traveling with Dog and Gun

Regulations for transporting dogs and firearms on a plane vary from airline to airline. Listed below are some basic guidelines, but it is in your best interest to check into an airline's specific policies at the time you make your flight reservations.

Insurance is available for both dogs and firearms. Check with your airline for costs and policy limits.

Dogs

1. Your dog(s) will have to be checked as baggage. Most airlines charge an extra fee per dog (usually around $50).
2. You will need an approved travel kennel for each dog accompanying you. Kennels are available at most pet supply houses and at some airports. It is best to acclimate your dog(s) to the travel kennel two to three weeks prior to the trip. Your dog(s) must be able to stand up, turn around, and lie in a comfortable position. There must be absorbent material in the bottom of the kennel (a towel or newspaper is acceptable). Two empty dishes for food and water must be accessible from outside the kennel. Also, don't forget to label your dog's kennel with your name, address, phone number, and final destination. It is necessary to attach certification that the dog has been fed and watered within four hours of the departure time. Label the kennel with signs stating "Live Animal" and "This Side Up" with letters at least one inch high.
3. You will need a certificate of health from your veterinarian, including proof of rabies vaccination. Tranquilizers are not recommended because high altitude can cause dangerous side effects. If you must sedate your dog, be sure to discuss it with your veterinarian first.
4. Federal regulations exist regarding safe temperatures for the transport of your dog. Animals will not be accepted if the temperature is below 10°F at any point in transit. If the temperature at your destination is below 45°F, a certificate of acclimation stating that your dog is used to low temperatures will be necessary. This is available from your vet. Temperatures above 85°F can be dangerous for animals in transit. Many airlines will not accept dogs if the temperature at any transit point is more than 85°F. Temperatures in Minnesota in the fall can vary widely. It is a good idea to check with the reservation desk regarding current temperatures and make your reservations accordingly. If you run into difficulty transporting your dog, remember these regulations are for your dog's safety.

Guns and Ammunition

1. Firearms and ammunition must be checked as baggage and declared by the passenger. You will be required to fill out a declaration form stating that you are aware

of the federal penalties for traveling with a loaded firearm and that your gun is unloaded.

2. Guns must be packed, unloaded, in a hard-sided crushproof container with a lock specifically designed for firearm air transport. If you do not already have a case, they are usually available at the airport. Call your airline for details about dimensions. If using an airline firearm container, allow enough extra time to pack it properly at the airport. If your gun does not arrive on the baggage carousel, you may be required to claim it at a special counter in the baggage claim area.

3. Ammunition must be left in the manufacturer's original packaging and securely packed in a wood or metal container separate from the firearm. Most cities in Minnesota have sporting goods stores that carry a large variety of ammunition. It might be easier to purchase ammunition at your destination rather than traveling with it. If you use a rare or special type of ammunition, you can preship it through a service like UPS. In fact, you might consider preshipping your firearm(s) the same way.

Appendix II
Conditioning of Hunting Dogs

Ideally, hunting dogs should be in top physical shape before taking them afield. Realistically, many of us ignore the conditioning of our dogs until the last minute before a trip.

Start with a visit to the veterinarian to update all shots and vaccines. Lyme disease is a fact of life in Minnesota, and your dog should be vaccinated against this disease. Your veterinarian can give you insight as to your dog's proper weight and whether pounds have to be shed or added prior to the hunting season.

When exercising or conditioning your dog, try to simulate the cover and terrain that you will be hunting. In Minnesota, this usually means dense, young woody cover with considerable deadfalls thrown in for good measure. Dense hazel brush and raspberry canes are a fact of life in the grouse woods. If hunting waterfowl, then water exercise and conditioning should be done.

Proper diet cannot be ignored. Several weeks prior to the hunting season, I switch my dogs to a high performance dog food, containing a higher percentage of fat and protein. Sometimes I supplement this dog food (moistened with water) with a tablespoon or two of vegetable oil. In the field, I strive to feed the dogs within an

A good retriever will go the distance with the right treatment.

hour after the conclusion of hunting. I do not feed my dogs regular dog food during the course of the hunting day. However, I make boiled white rice mixed with corn syrup and water (a handful or two per dog) available to the dogs as a noon "power" treat. This is easily digested, not disruptive to the dog, and provides an energy boost.

During the course of the hunting day, I make sure water is available to the dogs. Many areas of Minnesota have plenty of water at hand, such as small streams, puddles, and ponds. If you're not sure that water will be available, take along a water bottle for the dog.

If you travel with two or more dogs and hunt them one at a time, the dog or dogs left behind can create quite a racket with incessant barking. Upon your return, you may find that these dogs are rather lethargic when hunting. One dog training expert recommends that the dogs left behind wear bark collars—not because of the noise but to conserve the glucose (an energy source) that incessant barking can deplete.

After the hunt, remember to visually and physically check your dog for ticks, cuts, abrasions, foreign objects, etc. Provide comfortable quarters for your canine hunting companions.

If you're hunting ruffed grouse and/or woodcock in Minnesota's forested areas, it is advisable to use some sort of location device, because the density of the woods and understory can make visual contact with your dog virtually impossible. Bells, beeper collars, and beeper/stimulation collars will work. I personally use a beeper or beeper/stimulation collar, because I sometimes tend to daydream while in the woods. Under such circumstances, a dog with a bell, on point, would be hard to find.

A dog equipment checklist is available in "Appendix V."

Appendix III
Hunter Conditioning
and Clothing

Hunting for ruffed grouse and/or woodcock in most of Minnesota's forested areas is not as physically challenging as, for instance, the slopes of the Carolinas or Tennessee. The exceptions are the far southeast (Mississippi bluff country) and the northeast (bordering Lake Superior) portions of the state. But hunting in Minnesota is still more physically challenging than your normal "8 to 5" day.

First, shed those extra and unneeded pounds. If necessary, consult with an expert on your proper training and conditioning regimen. During the course of your walking/running exercise regimen, try to cover the same type of terrain that you'll be hunting—relatively flat and dense woods and understory. As you progress in your conditioning program, wear the boots and basic clothing that you'll be using on your hunting trip. Later, add a vest with shells and personal items, as well as a shotgun (if politically incorrect to carry a shotgun while exercising, consider a piece of metal or plastic pipe filled with the correct weight of lead decoy strapping). If you find yourself short of energy because of your metabolic needs, consider a trail mix or energy bar supplement. Most hunting forays will be one to two hours in duration with a break in between as you drive to a new cover.

The foundation of your clothing needs is footwear. To assure proper fit when purchasing hunting boots, take a pair of wool socks and a pair of moisture-wicking polypropylene socks to wear when buying new boots. Your boots should be moisture proof, and the soles should be compatible for the terrain you'll be hunting.

Briarproof pants and/or chaps are recommended for dense understory. From the waist up, use the layered approach since there can be quite a temperature swing during the course of your Minnesota hunting trip. The state of Minnesota requires some blaze orange outerwear be worn from the waist up (including headgear). If you will be hunting in dense, wooded areas, don't shortchange yourself or your hunting companions by not wearing plenty of blaze orange clothing. It's better to be seen and safe than to be shot!

Lightweight rainwear will come in handy if you hit a "wet spell" while bird hunting. Baseball-style hats tend to stay on your head longer than other hat styles. There will be a lot of brush to push out of the way, so gloves can make you more comfortable. If you plan to hunt waterfowl from a boat or canoe, you must have an approved personal flotation device (PFD)—this is required by law in Minnesota.

For personal items, you may want to include a compass, a small knife, matches, a whistle, a hemostat, water, and a power/snack bar.

A hunter clothing and equipment checklist is available in "Appendix V."

Appendix IV
The Hunting Rig

Next to the selection of a hunting dog or a gun, nothing brings out stronger feelings and personal choices as much as the selection of the hunting rig. The following comments are directed mostly to those individuals hunting ruffed grouse or woodcock in Minnesota's forests.

First and foremost, your hunting rig should be in good mechanical shape and current as to its maintenance schedule. Basic equipment should include jumper cables, folding shovel, towing or snatch strap, come-a-long, 1×1×¾" plywood squares (to support jack bases on soft ground), cell phone and local towing/service station phone numbers, 12-volt air compressor, tire gauge, maps of local area, and basic tool kit.

Many good hunting areas are accessible to 2WD vehicles. If you want to get farther into the "deep" woods and away from casual hunters, then your choice will be a 4WD rig. High centering your vehicle most often happens when driving on a two-track road that crosses soft, low boggy areas. Study your topographical maps and check recent weather before venturing too far into the unknown.

If you are towing a dog trailer, you should be aware that there are tight quarters deep in the woods. Be sure to have a spare trailer tire and make sure that wheel bearings and fittings are in good shape and properly lubricated.

A vehicle gear checklist is available in "Appendix V."

Appendix V
Equipment Checklists

Clothing

___ Polypropylene underwear
___ Wool socks
___ Polypropylene inner socks
___ Long sleeve canvas/chamois shirts
___ Briarproof pants
___ Hunting boots
___ Billed hat (blaze orange)
___ Camp clothing and shoes

___ Shooting gloves
___ Shooting glasses
___ Ear protectors
___ Hunting vest/coat (blaze orange)
___ Down vest/coat
___ Raingear
___ Hip boots/waders (waterfowling)
___ Handkerchief

Dog Equipment

___ Dog food
___ Water/food bowl
___ Hemostat (quill removal)
___ Dog first aid kit
___ Dog lead(s)
___ Bark collar
___ Beeper charger/extra batteries
___ Rice/corn syrup power boost mix

___ Water carrier (5 gallon)
___ *Field Guide to Dog First Aid*
___ Skunk Off (odor remover)
___ Dog health records (copies)
___ Dog tie-out stake and chain
___ Beeper collar/transmitter
___ Dog snacks
___ Dog whistle

Hunter's Equipment

___ Compass
___ Shells
___ Swiss Army knife
___ Flashlight
___ Power (energy) bars
___ Small camera
___ Maps
___ Choke tubes and wrench
___ Binoculars
___ Bird calls
___ Ice chest(s)
___ Bird knife with gut hook
___ GPS receiver
___ Knee length hose
___ (for bird mounting)

___ Shotgun
___ Nontoxic shells
___ Lip balm
___ Water bottle(s)
___ Trail mix
___ Gun cleaning kit
___ Hunting license
___ Thermos
___ Decoys
___ Cell phone
___ Topographical maps
___ Game shears
___ *Wingshooter's Guide to Minnesota*
___ Camouflage parka, hat, gloves,
___ face mask for waterfowl hunting

Vehicle Equipment

___ Folding shovel

___ Two strap

___ Tire guage

___ Jumper cables

___ Local phone numbers

___ Plastic trash bags

___ Air compressor

___ Come-along

___ Spare tire for trailer

___ Basic tool kit

___ 1×1×¾ plywood squares

Dog First Aid Equipment

___ Vet wrap (various widths)

___ Waterproof tape

___ Buffered aspirin

___ Nolvasan® solution for ears

___ Wound-kote® spray would dressing

___ Electrolyte powder

___ Hemostats

___ Hydrocortisone cream

___ Muzzle (wire or leather)

___ Gauze

___ Tweezers

___ Scissors

___ Opticlear® (eyewash)

___ Wound powder

___ Ophthalmic ointment

___ Cotton balls

___ Benadryl® (insect bites)

Appendix VI
Preserving Game Birds for Mounting

by John and Laurel Berger, Berger's Taxidermy

Exploding into the sky with a cackle and brilliant color, the rooster pheasant flushed and I momentarily lost my mind. Regaining my composure, I pulled the trigger and with the crack of my shotgun, the bird fell. That pheasant was a memory well worth preserving, and it now glides across our living room wall in a graceful, open-winged mount.

When deciding if you should mount a game bird, there are a few things to consider. The bird should be mature and have good plumage—we recommend saving birds that have been shot late in the season, ideally after the first of November. However, this doesn't apply to all game birds. Look for pinfeathers on the head and neck, and check the beak, feet, tail, and wings for shot damage. Since most taxidermists use the bird's skull, a bird that has been head-shot may be too damaged or disfigured to be mountable. All of these factors will affect the quality of a finished mount.

If a downed bird is wounded and in good enough condition to mount, do not ring the neck because it will cause skin damage and hemorrhaging. We feel the best method is to grasp the bird from the back just behind wings and then, with your thumb on one side of the rib cage and your fingers on the other, squeeze firmly. This will kill the bird in a humane and timely manner without causing damage to the feathers.

Keep the birds that you plan to have mounted separate from the others in your bag. Carrying them from the field by the feet saves them from damage and allows some cooling. We do not recommend carrying the bird in your game vest because feathers may become damaged, broken, or bloodstained.

After you've chosen the best bird or birds to mount, stop any bleeding by placing tissue or a cotton ball in the wounds. Wipe off any blood that may have run onto the feathers with a dabbing motion. Try not to push the blood down into the feathers. Also, place a cotton ball in the mouth to catch any body fluids that may potentially leak out onto the feathers.

Although some washing may be necessary before mounting, a taxidermist prefers that the bird be blood and dirt free upon delivery. Gently smooth the feathers into place, tuck the head to the chest, and wrap in clean paper towels. Place the bird head first into a plastic bag and store in a cool, protected place until the bird can be frozen.

Another popular method for preserving a bird is using a nylon stocking or cheesecloth. After caring for the bird, place the bird, with its head tucked, chest first into the nylon or cheesecloth. If you choose this method, remember that the only way to get the bird back out is to cut a hole in front of the chest and head and then push it through. If you pull it out by the feet, there will be feather damage.

Once the bird is securely in the nylon or cheesecloth, put the bird in a plastic bag to prevent dehydration or freezer burn. It is best to freeze the bird as soon as possible, and it can be stored in the freezer until you are able to get it to a taxidermist. Make sure that the bag is labeled with the type of bird, date harvested, as well as your name and license number. Taxidermists are required to have this information while the bird is in their possession.

When possible, take two birds to the taxidermist for determining which bird has the best plumage and is in the best shape for mounting.

With just a little care, you can preserve the memory of your hunt through the art of taxidermy. Bird mounts are easy to care for and will provide you with years of enjoyment.

Tip: To clean a mounted bird, use a cottonball dampened with rubbing alcohol. Start from the head using a sweeping motion in the direction of the feathers and work down the bird. Dust is lifted onto the cottonball, and the alcohol will evaporate. Make sure to change the cottonball regularly because they become soiled quickly.

A multiple harvest of beautiful ducks.

Appendix VII
Field Preparation of Game Birds for the Table

The two most important tools for field preparation of birds for the table are game shears and a knife with a gut hook.

Early in the season, when temperatures are in the 70- to 90-degree range, I draw my birds immediately or shortly after I leave the field. You can draw your birds by several methods. I make a cut with my shears at the end of the breast, making a small entry hole into the body cavity. I then take my gut hook, insert it into the cavity, and pull out the intestines and other body parts. The other method I use is to take my shears and cut up the center of the bird's back, splitting the bird in two. Then I use my gut hook and knife to clean out the intestines and other male parts. To help cool the birds (if I have drawn the birds in the field away from my vehicle), I place damp grass or leaves into the body cavity.

I like to place birds in a cooler while driving a vehicle. When back at camp, I finish the process by plucking or skinning the bird, trimming off unneeded parts (check the state's game bird transport laws before this step), wash, wrap in plastic, then place in a ziplock bag (remove air by submerging bag into water-filled container up to the level of of the zipper), and place in freezer. Remember, it is easier to mark a bag with the contents and date prior to placing game in the bag.

If you want, you could hang your birds prior to the packing steps outlined in the previous paragraph. Or you could "age" your birds by leaving them in the refrigerator for a few days after thawing them out.

Appendix VIII
Game Bird Recipes

Mickey Johnson

When I want to relax, the activities that come to mind are hunting, flyfishing, photography, and, nearest and dearest to my stomach, cooking. I learned the joy of preparing food for others from my mother, who taught me to try any kind of food at least once.

As for cooking wild game, it seems to me that many people are trying to kill game twice, once in the field and once in the kitchen. As with any meat, game should be handled properly, although wild game is less likely to be contaminated than its domestic counterpart. Many types of game meat are far better when seared properly and served medium to medium rare rather than well done. Too often, those who claim they do not like wild game have either had it served overcooked and dry or, in the case of fowl, swimming in cream of mushroom soup.

With the help and tolerance of a very dear friend, Gayle Grossman, I find that I want to experiment more when it comes to cooking wild game. While trying to keep recipes simple, I also like to have enough variables that anyone can enjoy and prepare wild game to their liking.

Grouse (or Pheasant) with Linguini and Pesto Sauce

This recipe came to me while driving home from Montana with Roland Kehr. I wanted to combine color, texture, and a different flavor, and the long drive across North Dakota offered plenty of opportunity to use my imagination.

2 ruffed grouse, breasted out
1 each, green, yellow, and red pepper
1 shallot or small sweet onion
2 cups mushrooms (baby portobello or morels are excellent options)
1 cup pesto sauce (if you purchase this, DiGiorno makes a good one)
2 tbsp Paul Prudhomme cajun blackening seasoning (or his poultry seasoning)
4 tbsp olive oil
1 package (12 oz.) fettucine

1. Start by bringing water to a boil and adding pasta. Cook to desired texture. Drain and combine with pesto sauce.
2. Prepare vegetables. Slice peppers and shallot (or onion) into long, thin strips. Slice mushrooms.
3. While pasta is cooking, combine olive oil and seasoning.

A spruce grouse keeps a watchful eye on his surroundings.

4. Cut meat into strips approximately 2 inches long and ¼ inch wide. Marinate in olive oil/seasoning mixture while heating a frying pan to medium high.
4. Sear the meat for about 5 minutes and remove from pan.
5. Using the same frying pan, sauté the vegetables for about 5 to 7 minutes. You may need to add an extra tablespoon of olive oil. When done, add meat.
6. Serve meat mixture over pasta and garnish with freshly grated Parmesan cheese. Accompany with garlic bread and a tart, crisp white wine.

Cajun Game

The following recipe, from Gayle Grossman, is easy to prepare and a sure-fire hit. It can be prepared as an appetizer or as a main dish. It's an especially good recipe if you have been looking for something new and different to do with sharp-tailed grouse. I have even enjoyed cooking this with sage grouse as an afternoon snack out on Montana's open buttes. When traveling or hunting in the West, I like to have my portable stove and a few spices along so that I can cook something up on the spot. Under clear blue skies on a cool autumn day, it's a real treat to have a hot meal out in the middle of nowhere.

As an appetizer:
1 stick of butter, margarine, or ⅓ cup olive oil
1 tbsp Paul Prudhomme's cajun blackening seasoning (can use up to 2 tbsp)
1 pheasant, breasted out (or other fowl), thinly sliced

1. Preheat a skillet to medium high until it is almost smoking.
2. Melt the butter and add seasoning.
3. Add the butter mixture to the meat and stir to coat.
4. Add meat mixture to skillet and stir occasionally for 3 to 4 minutes.
5. Serve on a warm tray and have toothpicks available.

As a main dish:
Green onions, diced
Zest of 1 orange
Juice from the orange and 1 cup cold chicken broth mixed with 1 tbsp of cornstarch
Optional: Shot of Grand Marnier

5. Remove the cooked meat mixture from the pan and add green onions and orange zest.
6. Add juice and broth mixture to pan and bring to bubbling, stirring with a fork or wire wisk constantly.
7. Add Grand Marnier, if desired.
8. Add meat mixture to sauce and serve over brown or wild rice.

Pheasant Stuffing or Casserole

While traveling in New England during the holidays, I tasted a bread stuffing that I thought was truly out of the ordinary. When I returned home, I wanted to duplicate the recipe and expand it to include pheasant as well as making it a casserole that could be served as a main dish.

2 cups finely diced, cooked pheasant breast	4 eggs
1 cup finely diced ham	1 cup chicken or pheasant stock
1 cup diced, smoked sausage	1 tsp salt
2 cups wild rice, cooked	½ tsp ground pepper (preferably fresh)
½ cup butter	1 tsp crumbled sage
6 cups plain croutons	¼ tsp thyme
2 onions, diced	¼ tsp marjoram
2 stalks celery, diced	¼ tsp mace

1. In a large skillet, melt the butter and add the vegetables. Cook over low heat for about 10 minutes.
2. Add the pheasant, ham, and sausage to the vegetables and cook a few minutes more, stirring occasionally.
3. Combine the wild rice and croutons in a large mixing bowl and then add the meat/vegetable mixture.
4. In another bowl, beat the eggs and add the seasonings and stock. Pour over the ingredients in large mixing bowl and stir until mixed.
5. At this stage, you can either stuff a turkey and bake it or place the mixture in a buttered baking dish, cover it, and bake at 325 degrees for an hour.

Pheasant or Game Stock

8 cups water	1 tbsp salt
1 onion	2 tsp cracked black pepper
2 carrots	2 bay leaves
2 stalks celery	1 tbsp five-spice powder, optional

1. While bringing water to a boil over medium high heat, roughly chop the vegetables (these are for flavor only and will be strained out later). When water is boiling, add vegetables and spices and simmer for about 20 minutes.
2. Add leftover bones and legs from poultry or game birds. A combination of birds works fine. Bring back to a boil for several minutes and then cover and remove from heat. Let it sit for an hour and then strain it.
3. This makes more than you will need for most recipes. Freeze in whatever size you find most useful—cup, pint, quart, etc. It's also a good idea to freeze some of the stock in an ice cube tray and then remove the frozen cubes to another container (recloseable freezer bag, plastic freezer container, etc.). These are handy to use for gravy, sauces, or soups.

Goose Jerky

One day at work a friend brought in some freshly made jerky. Most of us were surprised when he told us it was made from Canada goose. The more I thought about this, I came to the conclusion that goose could be prepared like beef or venison due to its dark meat.

7 lbs goose breast	1 tbsp saltpeter
1 lb salt	¾ tsp onion powder
¾ cup brown sugar	1 tbsp black pepper (try cayenne for zing)

1. Cut the goose breast into ½-inch strips.
2. Mix the other ingredients well, and then rub into the strips.
3. Place strips in a nonmetallic container and put in the refrigerator overnight.
4. After curing, each piece of meat should be rinsed with cold water, making sure you get all the salt residue off.
5. Pat dry with a paper towel and then set aside to dry. Make sure the pieces are not touching. It takes about 2 hours for the strips to dry.
6. To finish in the oven, place a grate near the top of the oven, then pierce each strip with a toothpick and hang from the grate. Cook for 1 to 1½ hours at 200 degrees.
7. If you have a smoker, smoke the jerky for 2½ hours or longer, depending on how dry you like it.
8. Store in an airtight container in the refrigerator or freezer.

Don't hesitate to experiment with other seasonings for the dry rub. There are also some excellent products on the market that can make the process simpler or with different flavors that you might want to try. Check your supermarket or meat market for these products.

Goose Stroganoff, Chubby Style

After deciding that goose could be treated like red meat, I came up with this recipe using one of Gayle Grossman's recipes as a basis. Give it a gander.

3 cups goose meat	4 crushed garlic cloves
1 tsp butter	1 onion, sliced
1 tbsp olive oil	1 green bell pepper, sliced in strips
1 pkg Knorr (or other brand) dried soup mix	2 cups mushrooms, thinly sliced
1 cup sour cream	2 tsp paprika

1. Prepare the vegetables and set aside. Mix dried soup with the amount of milk called for on package.
2. Cut the goose meat into thin strips approximately 2 inches long, ¼ inch thick, and ½ inch wide. Salt and pepper the meat to your taste and set aside.
3. Heat a large skillet to medium high and then add the butter and olive oil. Add the onions, peppers, and crushed garlic and sauté for a few minutes.

This southwestern farm field has certainly attracted a few snow geese.

4. Add the goose meat, turning and cooking as you would for stir fry for 6 to 8 minutes.
5. Add the mushrooms and continue cooking for 2 more minutes, stirring constantly.
6. Remove the mixture to a bowl and return the skillet to the burner, then add the soup mixture. Cook until it becomes thickened and then reduce to a simmer.
7. Add the meat mixture to the soup mixture and combine well.
8. Add sour cream and paprika and heat for 5 more minutes.
9. Serve over your choice of wide egg noodles, wild rice, or baby red potatoes.

For lower fat, use reduced or no fat sour cream. You can also put plain yogurt in a strainer lined with a paper towel and placed over a bowl. Let this sit overnight or longer while the water separates from the solids. This can be used as a substitute for sour cream.

Grilled Peking Duck (in the Blind)

I love to grill year-round because no matter what I cook, it adds extra flavor. I prefer a charcoal grill, but a gas grill works as well for any of my recipes. While hunting ducks with my friend, Vern Imgrund, I was thinking about some new way to prepare duck. I came up with this recipe by combining my love of grilling with the flavors of mandarin duck or duck a la orange. This has a wonderful flavor and works equally well with a plucked or skinned duck.

It was on this same hunting trip that I thought I had killed my first albino grouse. However, it was really a chicken, and I have never figured out how it came to be in the middle of the North Woods all by itself. Maybe surviving up there had made it strong, because it was one of the toughest birds I've ever cooked. Even my chasing it down and falling on it didn't do a thing to tenderize it. Years later, I learned that boiling it would have been the best method for cooking it.

1 or 2 ducks, skinned or plucked
1 cup orange marmalade
½ cup teriyaki sauce

1. If you are using a charcoal grill, put a split piece of white oak, hickory, apple, or other fruitwood on the bottom and to one side of the grill, placing the coals on the other side. This creates two heat zones as well as a smoked flavor to your food.
2. Split the duck in half along the backbone and rub with cooking oil (peanut oil works best) and then salt and pepper to taste.
3. When the coals are ready, place the duck on the hottest side of the grill and sear 4 minutes on each side.
4. Move the duck to the other side of the grill and baste with the marmalade/teriyaki mixture. Cover and cook for 15 minutes and baste again. Do this again after 10 minutes.
5. Move the duck back to the hotter side of the grill and cook 2 minutes more on each side. They should be done at this point.
6. If you have any remaining basting sauce, heat and serve over the duck.

Garlic Pheasant

This recipe combines two of my favorite flavors: garlic and Oriental spices. Pheasant and Oriental seasonings are just a natural combination, since ringnecks originally came from the Orient, and they were probably preferred to chicken at one time. This beautiful bird is not only a challenge and privilege to hunt, it makes excellent table fare.

2 pheasants
1 orange, both juice and zest
1 cup cilantro, shredded

¼ tsp red pepper flakes
1 tsp curry powder
¼ cup peanut oil

A nice shot for a rooster pheasant.

12 garlic cloves, chopped   ⅓ cup soy sauce
1 tbsp Szechuan peppercorns (crushed)

Note: If you can't find Szechuan peppercorns, use black pepper, fresh if possible. Also grapeseed oil substitutes nicely for peanut oil.

1. Cut pheasant into bite-sized pieces.
2. Prepare the cilantro and garlic and then combine with the rest of the ingredients, mixing well. Add the meat, then cover the bowl, place in the refrigerator, and marinate for a minimum of 4 hours or overnight, which is even better.
3. Cook meat over high heat for 10 minutes in a skillet or wok.
4. Serve as a main dish (with rice if you like) or as an appetizer served with toothpicks.

Goose Meat Loaf

After one of my goose hunting trips, I heard some other hunters complaining about what they were going to do with all the geese they had bagged. They were tired of simply roasting or frying it and wanted some new ways of cooking it. My idea of treating goose meat as you would red meat opens up a lot of possibilities. I know I don't plan to stop hunting geese, and there are plenty of ways to cook a cow! Some of my favorite new goose cooking methods are meatballs and meat loaf. Hot or cold, they are both delicious and make wonderful sandwiches.

1½ lbs ground goose
½ lb ground pork
2 cups unseasoned bread crumbs
1½ tsp salt
1 tsp fresh cracked black pepper
¼ ground nutmeg
2 cloves of garlic, crushed

1 onion, finely diced
1 green pepper, diced
¼ cup celery, diced
1 tbsp Worcestershire sauce
4 strips of bacon
2 eggs, beaten

1. Preheat oven to 350 degrees.
2. In large bowl, beat eggs and add the salt, pepper, nutmeg, and Worcestershire sauce.
3. Add meat and mix thoroughly, then add garlic, onion, celery, and green pepper.
4. Form the meat into the shape of a loaf of bread and place in roasting pan. Place bacon strips over top.
5. Bake for an hour and 15 minutes.
6. Alternative: shape into meatballs and bake on a cookie sheet for 45 minutes at 350 degrees.

A bearnaise sauce poured over either the meat loaf or meatballs makes a wonderful addition. Knorr makes a good dry mix, but there are others available. Add 3 to 4 tablespoons of tomato paste to the sauce for a slightly different flavor.

Appendix IX
Recommended Product
Sources

Ainley
1945 Washington Street
Dubuque, IA 52001
319-583-7615
Dog boxes and trailers

Ballistic Products, Inc.
20015 75th Avenue North, Box 293
Corcoran, MN 55340
888-273-5623
www.ballisticproducts.com
Reloading supplies and shotshells

Cabela's
One Cabela Drive
Sidney, NE 69160-9555
800-237-4444
www.cabelas.com
*Clothing, dog equipment, waterfowl
gear, and hunting rig gear*

Herter's
P.O. Box 1819
Burnsville, MN 55337-0499
800-654-3825
www.herters.com
*Clothing, dog equipment, hunting rig
equipment, and waterfowl gear*

Kevin's
3350 Capital Circle Northeast
Tallahassee, FL 32308
800-953-8467
www.kevinsguns.com
Clothing

Lion Country Supply
P.O. Box 480
Port Matilda, PA 16870
800-662-5202
www.LCSUPPLY.com
Clothing and dog equipment

Crow River Fabricating, Inc.
229 County Road 5 Southwest
Cokato, MN 55321
800-230-4023
Dog boxes and dog trailers

Dunn's Supply Store, Inc.
P.O. Box 509
Grand Junction, TN 38039-0509
800-353-8621
www.dunnscatalog.com
*Clothing, waterfowl gear, and dog
equipment*

Drs. Foster & Smith, Inc.
2253 Air Park Road, P.O. Box 100
Rhinelander, WI 54501-0100
800-826-7206
www.drsfostersmith.com
Dog equipment and dog care products

L.L. Bean
Freeport, ME 04033-0001
800-221-4221
www.llbean.com
*Clothing, waterfowl gear, and dog
equipment*

Lovett's Electronics
840 East Pinckley Street
Brazil, IN 47834
800-446-1093
Dog equipment

Nite Lite Company, Inc.
P.O. Box 8300
Little Rock, AR 72222-8300
800-648-5483
Clothing and dog equipment

Pointing Dog Journal
c/o Wildwood Press
P.O. Box 509
Traverse City, MI 49685-9968
800-447-7367
Magazine

Scott's Dog Supply
9252 Crawfordsville Road
Indianapolis, IN 46234
800-966-3647
www.scottsdog.com
Dog equipment

Quilomene
3042 Kincaid Road
Billings, MT 59101
800-585-8804
www.quilomene.com
Clothing

Redhead/Bass Pro Shops
2500 East Kearney
Springfield, MO 65898-0123
800-227-7776
www.basspro.com
*Clothing, waterfowl gear, hunting rig
gear, and dog equipment*

Retriever Journal
c/o Wildwood Press
P.O. Box 509
Traverse City, MI 49685-9968
800-447-7367
Magazine

Grouse Tales
c/o Ken Szabo
17130 Chatfield
Cleveland, OH 44111
Bimonthly grouse newsletter

Shooting Sportsman
P.O. Box 37048
Boone, IA 50037-2048
www.shootingsportsman.com
Magazine

Stafford's
715 Smith Avenue
P.O. Box 2055
Thomasville, GA 31799-2055
800-826-0948
www.stafford-catalog.com
Clothing

Timothy's (Division of Nite Lite)
P.O. Box 8300
Little Rock, AR 72222-8300
800-762-7049
Clothing and dog equipment

Appendix X
Minnesota Information Sources
Map Sources

Minnesota Department of Transportation (MnDOT)
Map and Manual Sales
Room G-9, Mail Stop 260
Transportation Building
St. Paul, MN 555155
651-296-2216
www.dot.state.mn.us
State highway maps, county highway maps

24-Hour Road Condition Information
651-405-6030
1-800-542-0220
www.dot.state.mn.us

Minnesota Department of Tourism Travel Information Center
500 Metro Square
121 Seventh Place
St. Paul, MN 55101-2146
Tel: 651-296-5029 (Twin cities area)
1-800-657-3700 (U. S. or Canada)
www.exploreminnesota.com
Maps, accommodations, events, and general travel information

Minnesota Department of Natural Resources (DNR)
DNR Information Center
500 Lafayette Road
St. Paul, MN 55155-4040
Tel: 651-297-6157
1-888-MINNDNR (1-888-646-6367)
Fax: 651-297-3618
www.dnr.state.mn.us
PRIM (Public Recreation Information Map) information, outdoor maps and brochures order form, Minnesota wildlife lands map, etc.

U. S. Fish and Wildlife Service
P. O. Box 25486
Denver Federal Center
Denver, CO 80225
Tel: 303-236-8155
www.fws.gov
National Wildlife Refuge maps and information

"Cybermap" Sources

DeLorme
Two DeLorme Drive
P. O. Box 298
Yarmouth, ME 04096
Product Information: 207-846-7058
Sales: 1-800-452-5931
www.delorme.com
State atlases and gazetteers, computer mapping products, GPS mapping products, Cybermaps™, and computer generated topographical maps. Topo map integration with various GPS systems.

Maptech, Inc.
1 Riverside Drive
Andover, MA 01810-1122
Tel: 978-933-3000
Fax: 978-933-3040
www.maptech.com
Computer generated topographical maps for numerous states, including Minnesota. Topo map integration with various GPS systems.

Mapquest
www.mapquest.com
Free computer generated travel map, city maps, and more.

Maps On Us
www.MapsOnUs.switchboard.com
Free map, route, and yellow page server.

Lowrance Electronics, Inc.
1200 Skelly Dr.
Tulsa, OK 74128-2486
1-800-324-1356
www.lowrance.com
Handheld GPS products with MapCreate™ CD-ROM.

Garmin International, Inc.
1200 E. 151st Street
Olathe, KS 66062
Tel: 913-397-8200
Fax: 913-397-8282
www.garmin.com
Handheld GPS mapping products accessing Map-Source™ CD-ROM.

Magellan Corporation
471 El Camino Real
Santa Clara, CA 95050-4300
Tel: 408-615-5100
Fax: 408-615-5200
www.magellangps.com
Handheld GPS products with Map Send™ and Data Send™ CD-Roms.

Minnesota Department of Natural Resources Regional Wildlife Offices

Region I: Northwest Regional Wildlife Headquarters
2115 Birchmont Beach Road Northeast
Bemidji, MN 56601
218-755-3955; Fax 218-755-4024

Region II: Northeast Regional Wildlife Headquarters
1201 East Highway 2
Grand Rapids, MN 55744
218-327-4413; Fax 218-327-4263

Region III: Central Regional Wildlife Headquarters
1601 Minnesota Drive
Brainerd, MN 56401
218-828-2615; Fax 218-828-2439

Region IV: Southwest Regional Wildlife Headquarters
Box 756, Highway 15 South
New Ulm, MN 56073
507-359-6030; Fax 507-359-6018

Region V: Southeast Regional Wildlife Headquarters
2300 Silver Creek Road Northeast
Rochester, MN 55903
507-285-7435; Fax 507-285-7144

Region VI: Metro Regional Wildlife Headquarters
1200 Warner Road
St. Paul, MN 55106
651-772-7942; Fax 651-772-7977

Appendix XI
Organizations

An organization's true value cannot be judged only by its current impact but how it will affect the future as well. Following is a list of organizations that have made a major contribution to wildlife as a whole, not just a particular species. Also included is an organization seeking to provide sporting opportunites for those who are physically challenged.

The future of hunting as well as the wildlife available for all to enjoy will be guided by these groups, among others. These organizations need your support in order to continue their efforts. If you are concerned about what is being done to protect and enhance wildlife and hunting, then it is important to participate in these groups.

Teaching youth the importance of firearm safety, hunting etiquette, knowledge of the environment, and respect for wildlife and the landowners who grant hunting privileges is a key component for ensuring the future of hunting.

While monetary support is essential for these organizations, it is even more important that members participate in their activities. Remember that if you leave all the decision-making to others, you can't complain about hunting and wildlife conditions.

The Ruffed Grouse Society

This organization was formed on October 24, 1961, to address concerns for the well being of ruffed grouse and other forest wildlife. Headquartered in Pennsylvania, the society's main purpose is to increase ruffed grouse, woodcock, and other forest wildlife through state-of-the-art habitat management techniques and improvement projects.

Grants from the society have helped create programs to educate private landowners about implementing tested wildlife management practices on their property. Of special interest is the Project Coverts program, which is being implemented in a growing number of states under the guidance of state-based conservation agencies cooperating with the Ruffed Grouse Society. This program teaches forest habitat management techniques to a core group of landowners, who, in turn, provide habitat development information to their neighbors on a one-to-one basis.

This group also provides funds to public land managers to augment their program budgets so that necessary forest habitat alterations can be done. Federal, state, and county lands have all benefited from this program, with many thousands of acres of new or revitalized forest habitat being affected. In Minnesota, 70 habitat areas have been established through the efforts of this group.

The society has also sponsored youth programs, workshops for landowners and managers, and provided professional consultants for development of management plans beneficial to wildlife.

The Ruffed Grouse Society
451 McCormick Road
Coraopolis, PA 15108
412-262-4044
888-564-6747

Pheasants Forever

Formed in 1982, Pheasants Forever was formed to address the continuing decline in ring-necked pheasant populations. This is a nonprofit organization dedicated to the enhancement and protection of pheasants and other wildlife that share the same habitat. Implementation of these goals includes habitat improvement, public awareness, education, and participating in the land management policies that benefit both private landowners and wildlife alike.

Pheasants Forever has a unique, grassroots approach to fundraising and project development in which members can see the direct results of their contributions. Virtually 100 percent of the funds raised by chapters, excluding membership fees, remain with local chapters for habitat projects in their area. With the help of resource professionals, chapters establish habitat restoration programs customized to meet the needs of pheasants and other wildlife in their area.

Now comprised of 550 chapters and 81,000 members, Pheasants Forever is having an impact on work projects, legislation, and education concerning the needs and rights of both hunters and wildlife.

Pheasants Forever, Inc.
1783 Buerkle Circle
St. Paul, MN 55110
612-773-2000   Fax: 612-773-5500
Email: pf@pheasantsforever.org
Website: www.pheasantsforever.org

Ducks Unlimited

The origin of this organization was the result of Joseph Palmer Knapp's conviction that something was needed to halt the decline of waterfowl during the 1930s. Its first name was More Game Birds in America Foundation, and eventually, it was incorporated as Ducks Unlimited on January 29, 1937.

This was the first organization to dedicate its efforts to wetland conservation in North America. It initially concentrated its efforts on the prairies of Canada, where 70 percent of North America's waterfowl reproduce. In 1974, Ducks Unlimited turned its attention to the south, establishing projects in Mexico to secure habitat for wintering waterfowl. And in 1984, it started projects within the United States to provide both wintering habitat and stopover sites along migration corridors.

In recent years, DU has been instrumental in developing the North American Waterfowl Management Plan, an international agreement between the governments of the United States, Canada, and Mexico. It has also formed conservation partnerships with agricultural communities in order to help preserve the 74 percent of remaining wetland in the U.S. that is privately owned. Minnesota alone has 45,228 members and a total of 1,458,017 project areas addressing waterfowl needs within the state.

Ducks Unlimited
One Waterfowl Way
Memphis, TN 38120-2351
901-758-3826   Fax: 1-800-45-DUCKS

National Wild Turkey Federation

This group was first established in 1973 in Fredericksburg, Virginia, and moved to Edgefield, South Carolina, later that same year. Its goals are to aid the reestablishment of wild turkeys in North America through habitat projects and hunter education programs. It is a grassroots organization with 180,000 members and over 101 chapters in the United States, Canada, and Mexico.

Currently, the Federation's major program, "Project 2000," is designed to restore wild turkey to as much of its original range as possible. Cooperating with state and federal agencies, it is providing both funding and habitat project work that means the future of wild turkeys is brighter than ever.

National Wild Turkey Federation
P.O. Box 530
Edgefield, SC 29824
803-637-3106 or 800-THE-NWTF

Minnesota Sharp-tailed Grouse Society

This Society's goal is to bring the sharp-tailed grouse population back to the level found in the state prior to the 1940s. With volunteers working to create and protect existing sharptail habitat, the organization is increasing sharptail range through working with state agencies and by acquiring more territory for these native birds.

The key to good habitat is a complex blend of grassland mixed with a mosaic of brush and open woodland. In Minnesota, creation of this type of cover depends on the disturbance of forest areas or the addition of brush and trees to more open areas. This is usually found in large grassy or herbacious areas that are the result of fire, logging, mining, abandoned farm clearings, or natural large open bogs.

Minnesota Sharp-tailed Grouse Society	or	MSGS Metro Office
P.O. Box 3338		P.O. Box 16074
Duluth, MN 55803		St. Paul, MN 55116-0074

Geese Unlimited

This conservation organization is dedicated to returning the Canada goose to its wild origins rather than the urban beggar and nuisance it has become in some areas. Through their research, it has been discovered that goslings imprint and return to the place where they learned to fly rather than where they were born. This has lead to the translocation of some 40,000 goslings from the Twin Cities to 10,000 square miles of pristine forest habitat in northern Minnesota.

Its goals for the future are to be involved in the process of creating and changing state and federal regulations, develop and implement educational programs, promote quality hunting and hunter ethics, fund food plots, develop and fund research program to better understand geese, and work with state and federal agencies to improve goose habitat.

Geese Unlimited, Inc.
111 Northwest Fifth Street
P.O. Box 647
Grand Rapids, MN 55744
218-327-0774 or 888-326-3564

Capable Partners

This nonprofit organization, based in the Twin Cities, has brought together sports enthusiasts who volunteer their time and talent to provide hunting, fishing, and related opportunities for those who are physically challenged.

Goals include: outreach to assist new and existing members to participate and realize their potential; education about and promotion of issues concerning disability; create accessible outdoor opportunities through growth of participants, locations, and events; increase the number of members who have the experience and skills to plan and lead events.

Values of the organization include friendship and fraternity, family participation and support, independence through doing, education and awareness, building self esteem and a sense of accomplishment.

Capable Partners
P.O. Box 28543
St. Paul, MN 55128
651-542-8156   Fax: 612-542-8156

Appendix XII
Guides, Outfitters, and Lodges

Minnesota has few upland bird guides, and there is no listing available as there are in some states. Waterfowl guide numbers are slightly better. In certain areas of the state, such as around Lac Qui Parle, there are many options to be found. Following is a list of services by region and what game is available. These are not personal choices —they are simply a listing of what is available. It is always a good idea to ask for references and then find out how other hunters rate the service.

REGION 1

Viking Valley Hunt Club
Route 1, Box 198
Ashby, MN 56309
218-747-2121
Woodcock and Geese

Sunset Lodge
P.O. Box 42
Oak Island, MN 56741
800-634-1863
Ducks and Grouse

Wheeler's Point Resort
Route 1, Box 190
Baudette, MN 56623
800-542-2435
Online: www.fishandgame.com/wheelers
Ducks and Grouse

Riverview Resort
Route 1, Box 152
Baudette, MN 56623
800-343-6909
Online: www.fishandgame.com/riverview
Geese and Ducks

Zippel Bay Resort
HC 2, Box 51
Williams, MN 56686
800-222-2537 or 218-783-6235
Waterfowl and Grouse

Northern Flight Outfitting
Route 2, Box 229
Parkers Prairie, MN 56361
218-338-5013
Waterfowl

Lock and Load Hunting Club
RR1, Box 44
Middle River, MN 56737
218-222-3714
Specializes in goose hunting
Accommodations on premises

REGION 2

Bunt's Bed and Breakfast Inns
Lake Kabetogama
12497 Burma Road
Ray, MN 56669
218-875-2691 or 888-741-1020
Grouse

Gunflint Lodge
750 Gunflint Trail
Grand Marais, MN 55604
218-388-2294 or 800-328-3325
Grouse

Roaring Stoney Lodge
7299 Hill Road
Virginia, MN 55792
218-365-2115 summer
218-741-0174 winter
Grouse

Cedar Hill
Box 482
Northome, MN 56661
218-897-5659
Grouse

Clear Creek Outdoors
2550 Highway 23
Wrenshall, MN 55797
218-384-3670
Grouse and Woodcock

Lakewood's Retrievers
3455 Zimmerman Road
Duluth, MN 55804
218-729-8229
Grouse and Woodcock

Sawmill Inn
2301 Pokegama Avenue South
Grand Rapids, MN 55744
218-326-8501 or 800-804-8006
Grouse and Woodcock

Leech Lake Guide Coalition
HCR 84, Box 1207
Walker, MN 56484
218-547-3212
Woodcock and Waterfowl

Roaring Winds and Wings
28728 Underwood Road
Grand Rapids, MN 55744
218-326-5638
Grouse and Woodcock

REGION 3

Little Moran Hunting Club
Rural Route 1, Pleasant Valley Road
Staples, MN 56479
218-894-3852 or Fax 218-894-2660
Grouse and Woodcock

MGK Guide Service
320-294-5802   Tom
612-758-5046   Bill
218-686-0463   Doug
Grouse, Woodcock, Pheasant,
and Waterfowl

Larson's Guide Sesrvice
P.O. Box 131
Minnetonka Beach, MN 55361
612-471-8385
Ruffed and Sharp-tailed Grouse

Kluge Guide Service
Route 1, Box 186
Clearwater, MN 55320
612-558-2741
Waterfowl

Mille Lacs Hunting Lodge
8673 340th Street
Onamia, MN 56359
320-532-3384 or Fax 320-532-4504
Grouse and Woodcock

American Heritage Hunting Club
Route 2, Box 131
Eagle Bend, MN 56446
218-738-5143
Waterfowl

REGION 4

Charlie's Hunting Club
Rural Route 1, Box 173
Danvers, MN 56231
320-567-2276
Geese

Cottonwood Creek Hunting Preserve
Route 1, P.O. Box 92
Danvers, MN 56231
320-567-2383 or 320-793-6604
Geese

Carol's Outback
Route 2, Box
Dawson, MN 56232
320-752-4274
Geese

Lac qui Parle Hunting Camp
Route 5, Box 68
Montevideo, MN 56265
320-269-9769 or 320-269-7034
Geese

Take A Gander Guide Service
Hutchinson, MN 55350
320-275-2545
Geese

Crow River Outdoors, Inc.
903 Highway 15
Hutchinson, MN 55350
320-587-0464
Geese

Ideal Hunting
Dawson, MN 56232
320-752-4730 or 320-752-4238
Geese

REGIONS 5 AND 6

Oakleaf Adventures
Rochester, MN
507-931-3572 or 507-931-2234
Geese

Wub's Outdoors Inc.
9464 Hamlet Avenue South
Cottage Grove, MN 55016
651-459-6766
Geese

H & Q Goose Hunts
Rochester, MN
507-288-8450
Geese

Westline Guide Service
4364 Cimarron Court Northwest
Rochester, MN 55901
507-282-8375 or 877-77GOOSE
Geese

NorthFlight Guide Service
2329 58th Street Northwest
Rochester, MN 55901
507-287-6944 or 800-860-6907
Geese

Final Approach
Rochester, MN
507-288-5733, 507-367-2374 or
  507-364-5379

Northwest Guide Service
Rochester, MN
507-282-3715
Geese

Hilltop Goose Hunts
Rochester, MN
507-282-0017 or 507-288-9257
Geese

Premier Flight
801 12th Avenue Northeast
Rochester, MN 55902
507-252-5957 or 888-354-4484
Geese

Recommended Reading

American Game Birds of Field and Forest. Frank C. Edminster. New York: Castle Books, 1954.

Autumn Passages: A Ducks Unlimited Treasury of Waterfowling Classics. Ducks Unlimited and Willow Creek Press, 1995.

Best Way to Train Your Gun Dog: The Delmar Smith Method. Bill Tarrant. New York: David McKay Company, Inc., 1977.

Ducks, Geese & Swans of North America. Frank C. Bellrose. Harrisburg, PA: Stackpole Books, 1976.

• *A Field Guide to Dog First Aid.* Randy Acker, DVM. Gallatin Gateway, MT: Wilderness Adventures Press, 1994.

Fool Hen. William L. Robinson. Madison, WI: The University of Wisconsin Press, 1980.

Gamebirds of North America. Leonard Lee Rue, III. New York: Harper & Row, 1973.

Game Management. Aldo Leopold. Madison, WI: University of Wisconsin Press, 1933.

Grouse Hunter's Guide. Dennis Walrod. Harrisburg, PA: Stackpole Books, 1985.

Grouse and Quails of North America. Paul A. Johnsgard. Lincoln, NE: University of Nebraska Press, 1973.

Grouse & Woodcock: A Gunner's Guide. Don L. Johnson. Iola, WI: Krause Publications, 1995.

Grouse of North America. Tom Huggler. Minocqua, WI: Willow Creek Press, 1990.

Grouse of the North Shore. Gordon Gullion. Oshkosh, WI: Willow Creek Press, 1984.

Hey Pup, Fetch It Up: The Complete Retriever Training Book. Bill Tarrant. Mechanicsburg, PA: Stackpole Books, 1979.

How to Hunt Birds with Gun Dogs. Bill Tarrant. Mechanicsburg, PA: Stackpole Books, 1994.

A Hunter's Road. Jim Fergus. New York: Henry Holt and Co., 1992.

Hunting the Sun. Ted Nelson Lundrigan. Traverse City, MI: Countrysport Press, 1997.

Hunting Upland Birds. Charles F. Waterman. New York: Winchester Press, 1972.

Hunting Upland Gamebirds. Steve Smith. Harrisburg, PA: Stackpole Books, 1987.

Life Histories of North American Gallinaceous Birds. Arthur Cleveland Bent. New York: Dover Publishing, Inc., 1963.

• *Meditations on Hunting.* José Ortega y Gasset. Gallatin Gateway, MT: Wilderness Adventures Press, 1995.

Migratory Shore and Upland Game Bird Management. Thomas Tacha and Clait Braun. Lawrence, KS: Allen Press, 1994.

Minnesota Atlas & Gazetteer. DeLorme Mapping. Freeport, ME: DeLorme Mapping, 1997.

More and Better Pheasant Hunting. Steve Smith. New York: Winchester Press, 1986.

North American Game Birds of Upland and Shoreline. Paul A. Johnsgard. Lincoln, NE: University of Nebraska Press, 1975.

• *Pheasants of the Mind.* Datus C. Proper. Gallatin Gateway, MT: Wilderness Adventures Press, 1994.

Ruffed Grouse. Sally Atwater and Judith Schnell. Harrisburg, PA: Stackpole Books, 1989.

A Sand Country Almanac. Aldo Leopold. New York: Oxford University Press, 1949.

Timberdoodle Tales. Tom F. Waters. St. Paul, MN: Riparian Press, 1993.

• *Training the Versatile Retriever to Hunt Upland Birds.* Bill Tarrant. Gallatin Gateway, MT: Wilderness Adventures Press, 1996.

Waterfowl: An Identification Guide to the Ducks, Geese and Swans of the World. Houghton Mifflin Co.

• *Waterfowling Horizons: Shooting Ducks and Geese in the 21st Century.* Christopher S. and Jason A. Smith. Gallatin Gateway, MT: Wilderness Adventures Press, 1997.

Woodcock Shooting. Steve Smith. Harrisburg, PA: Stackpole Books, 1988.

The World of the Ruffed Grouse. Leonard Lee Rue, III. Philadelphia, PA: J. B. Lippincott Company, 1973.

• Available from Wilderness Adventures Press

Index

A

Ada   105–106
Agassiz National Wildlife Refuge   87
Aitkin County   148, 237
Albert Lea   202–203
Alexandria   115–117
American wigeon   68
Anoka County   212, 239, 242
ATV   25

B

Baudette   87, 95, 97, 241, 244, 332
Bear Lake   202
Becker County   110, 236, 277
Beeper collar   38, 309
Beltrami County   102, 235, 241
Beltrami Island State Forest   228, 248
Bemidji   102–104, 106, 109, 241, 244, 327
Benson   172–173, 238
Benton County   158
Berger, John and Laurel   311
Big Stone County   172
Big Stone National Wildlife Refuge   290–291
Bismuth   13, 33, 62, 71, 77, 81
Black duck   66
Blue Earth County   189, 241
Blue Earth River   189–190
Blue goose   78
Bluebill
    See lesser scaup and greater scaup
Blue-winged teal   67, 69, 95, 102, 137, 148, 152, 155, 206, 232
Border waters   2
Boundary Waters Canoe Area Wilderness   119, 127, 130, 274
Bowstring Lake   137
Brainerd   141, 148–151, 241, 245, 327
Brainerd International Raceway   148
Brainerd Lakes   141, 148, 151
Brant   78
Broadbill, see also greater scaup   75
Bronko Nagurski Football Museum   124
Brown County   182
Browns Valley   115

Bufflehead   73–74
Bullsby Lake   199

C

Caledonia   204–205, 246
Canada goose   11, 79, 81–82, 84, 148, 155, 158, 160, 162, 182, 318, 330
    Special permit   1
    September Goose Hunt   11
    December Goose Hunt   11
Canvasback   74, 76
Capable Partners   331
Carlos Avery Wildlife Management Area   212, 213, 217, 227, 242
Carlton County   133, 237, 241
Carter Lake Trail (Chippewa National Forest)   263
Carver County   209, 239, 242
Cass County   107, 137, 148, 237
Chippewa County   172
Chippewa National Forest   137–138, 262–273
Chippewa River   173, 177, 294
Chisago County   162, 238, 241
Chubb Lake   199
Clay County   110, 236, 277
Clearwater County   102, 235, 241
Clothing   7, 25, 71, 307, 309, 323–324
Common snipe
    See snipe, common
Common timber rattlesnake   193
Conservation Reserve Program (CRP)   29–32, 42, 95, 98, 100, 102, 105, 107, 110, 112, 115, 124, 127, 130, 133, 137, 148, 152, 155, 158, 160, 162, 172, 174, 177, 179, 182, 184, 186, 189, 199, 202, 204, 206, 209, 212
Cook County   130
Cottonwood County   186, 238, 242
County Road 50 Trail (Chippewa National Forest)   264
Croft Mine Historical Park   141
Crookston   100–101, 106, 241
Crow Wing County   148, 237
Crow Wing River   148

D

Dabblers
  See Ducks
Dakota County   209, 239, 242
Dakota Indians   141, 202
Dancing grounds (sharp-tailed grouse)   53
December goose hunt (Canada goose)   11
Department of Natural Resources (DNR)
  2, 8–11, 13–15, 18, 32, 37, 42–44, 54,
  59–60, 70, 81, 87, 97, 99, 101, 104,
  106, 110–111, 114, 117, 126, 129,
  132, 136, 139, 151, 154–155, 157,
  161, 164, 167, 173, 178, 181, 185, 188,
  201, 203, 208–209, 211, 225–226,
  233, 240–241, 243, 274, 278, 325, 327
  Area Forestry Offices   225
  Area Wildlife Offices   241
  License Bureau   1–2, 9, 11, 14–15, 60
Department of Tourism   243, 325
Des Moines River   186
Detroit Lakes   110–111, 241, 244
Detroit Lakes Wetland Management
  District   277, 279
Divers
  See ducks
Diving ducks
  See ducks
Division of Forestry   243
Dodge County   199, 242
Dog First Aid   309–310
Dogs, Conditioning of Hunting   305
Douglas County   115, 241
Drum, drumming (ruffed grouse)   21–23,
  23, 47, 151
Ducks   65–77
  Dabblers   65–71
    American wigeon   68
    Black duck   66
    Blue-winged teal   67, 69, 95, 102,
      137, 148, 152, 155, 206, 232
    Gadwall   69
    Green-winged teal   68
    Mallard   65–66, 69, 80, 85, 98, 107,
      160, 174, 209
    Northern pintail   67
    Northern shoveler   69
    Wood duck   66, 100, 107
  Divers   72–77
    Bufflehead   73–74

    Canvasback   74, 76
    Goldeneye   74–75
    Greater scaup   75
    Hooded merganser   75
    Lesser scaup   72–73, 75
    Redhead   72, 77
    Ring-necked duck   72
    Ruddy duck   76
Ducks Unlimited   329–330
Duluth   37, 119, 132–136, 157, 274, 330, 333

E

Eastern wild turkey
  See turkey
Elk River   160–161
Ely   127–129, 241, 274
Equipment Checklists   309

F

Fairmont   186–188
Falconry season   12
Fall wild turkey hunt   16
Faribault County   189, 241
Federal duck stamp   3, 9
Federal Migratory Bird Hunting and
  Conservation Stamp   3, 9
Federal Migratory Waterfowl Stamp   3, 9
Fergus Falls   112–114, 236, 241, 277
Fergus Falls Wetland Management District
  277, 280
Fillmore County   204, 242
Flotation device   307
Fool hen
  See spruce grouse
Foothills State Forest   249
Forest Lake   212–213, 227, 239, 242
Fort Snelling   219, 284
Freeborn County   202

G

Gadwall   69
Game refuges   243, 301
Geese   78–85
  Blue goose   78
  Canada goose   11, 79, 81–82, 84, 148,
    155, 158, 160, 162, 182, 318, 330
  Special permit   1
  September Goose Hunt   11
  December Goose Hunt   11

Lesser snow goose 78
Ross' goose 78
White-fronted goose 78
Geese Unlimited 330–331
George Washington State Forest 250
Goldeneye 74–75
Goodhue County 199, 242
Goose Lake Trail (Chippewa National Forest) 265
Goose Lake 137
Goose or Waterfowl Refuges 301
Gores Pool Wildlife Management Area 209
Grand Marais 119, 130–132, 241, 245, 274, 332
Grand Mound 124
Grand Rapids 119, 137–139, 241, 327, 331, 333
Grant County 115, 241
Gray (Hungarian) partridge 4, 7, 19, 40–45, 88, 95, 98, 100, 142, 152, 158, 160, 167–168, 172, 174, 177, 179, 182, 184, 186, 189–190, 193–194, 199–200, 202, 204, 207, 232, 290
  Description 41–45
  Distribution 40, 88, 142, 168, 194
Great Hinckley Fire 155
Great Plains 133
Greater scaup 75
Green-winged teal 68
Grindstone River 155
Grossman, Gayle 314, 316, 318
Grouse
  See ruffed grouse, sharp-tailed grouse, and spruce grouse
Gunflint Trail 119, 130, 332

H
Hallock 98–99
Harvest Information Program (HIP)
  See also Migratory Bird Harvest Information Program 5, 63, 309
Hastings 209–211, 239
Hennepin County 212, 239, 242
Hill River State Forest 251
Hinckley 155–157, 241, 245
  Great Hinckley Fire 155
Hooded merganser 75
Houston County 204, 242

Hub Cities
Ada 105–106
Albert Lea 202–203
Alexandria 115–117
Baudette 87, 95, 97, 241, 244, 332
Bemidji 102–104, 106, 109, 241, 244, 327
Benson 172–173, 238
Brainerd 141, 148–151, 241, 245, 327
Caledonia 204–205, 246
Crookston 100–101, 106, 241
Detroit Lakes 110–111, 241, 244, 277, 279
Duluth 37, 119, 132–136, 157, 274, 330, 33
Elk River 160–161
Ely 127–129, 241, 274
Fairmont 186–188
Fergus Falls 112–114, 236, 241, 277, 280
Forest Lake 212–213, 227, 239, 242
Grand Marais 119, 130–132, 241, 245, 274, 332
Grand Rapids 119, 137–139, 241, 327, 331, 333
Hallock 98–99
Hinckley 155–157, 241, 245
Hutchinson 179, 181, 334
International Falls 119, 124–126, 129, 241
Little Falls 59, 152–154, 241
Mankato 189, 191, 241
Minneapolis 173, 176, 178, 181, 183, 185, 201, 203, 208, 211, 213–215, 219–220
Montevideo 177–178, 230, 334
Mora 157, 162–164
Owatonna 199–201, 203, 242
Park Rapids 107–109, 241, 244
Redwood Falls 181–183, 241
Rochester 79, 205–208, 242, 327, 334
St. Cloud 59, 117, 154, 158–159, 161, 241, 246
St. Paul 1–2, 9, 14–15, 60, 81, 173, 176, 178, 181, 183, 185, 193, 201, 203, 208, 211, 213, 219–220, 222–223, 225–226, 242–243, 278, 325, 327, 329–331
Willmar 174, 176, 178, 242
Worthington 184–185

Hubbard County   107
Hungarian partridge
  See gray partridge
Hunter Conditioning   307
Hunter walking trails   25, 264–275
Huntersville State Forest   252
Hunting rig   308, 323–324
Hutchinson   179, 181, 334
Hutchinson Brothers   179

I
Information Sources   242, 325, 327
International Falls   119, 124–126, 129,
  241
Iowa, state of   32, 186, 294
Isanti County   162, 238, 241
Itasca County   124, 137
Itasca State Park   107

J
Jacksnipe
  See snipe, common
Jackson County   186, 238, 242
Jingo Lake Trail (Chippewa National
  Forest)   266
Johnson Lake Trail (Chippewa National
  Forest)   267

K
Kabetogama State Forest   253
KaKaBikans   152
Kanabec County   155, 237, 241
Kandiyohi County   174, 242
Kensington Runestone   115
Kittson County   98, 233–234, 241
Koochiching County   124
Koochiching State Forest   254

L
La Crosse District   294
Lac Qui Parle County   177, 241
Lac Qui Parle Lake   230
Lac Qui Parle Wildlife Management Area
  14, 167, 177, 230, 241–242
Lake Agassiz   87
Lake Bemidji   102
Lake County   127, 130, 237, 241
Lake Geneva   202
Lake of the Woods   95–97, 241

Lake of the Woods County   87, 95, 233
Lake Okabena   184–185
Lake Superior   119, 130, 132–134
Lakes
  Bear   202
  Bemidji   102
  Bowstring   15, 137, 244
  Brainerd Lakes   141, 148, 151
  Bullsby   199
  Carter   263
  Chubb   199
  Geneva   202
  Goose   137
  Lac Qui Parle   230
  Lake of the Woods   95–97, 241
  Leech   107, 333
  Marsh   61, 191, 227, 230, 294
  Meadow   236, 268
  Mud   32, 35, 61–62, 137, 236
  Okabena   184–185
  Rice   286–287
  Spur   29, 270
  Squaw   137
  Sugar   87, 105, 271, 318
  Superior   60, 119, 130, 132–134,
    136–137, 191, 261, 274
  Talcot   184–185, 232, 238
  Tower   245, 272, 277
  Webster   273
Lamprey Pass Wildlife Management Area
  212
Land O'Lakes State Forest   255
Le Sueur County   189, 241
Lea, Lt. Albert Miller   202
Leech Lake   107, 333
Lek   53
Lesser scaup   72–73, 75
Lesser snow goose   78
Licenses   1–3, 5, 7, 9, 11, 14–16, 59–60,
    309, 312
  Fees   1, 87, 329
  Requirements   1, 7, 9, 14–15, 36, 52
  Small game   1, 3–5, 7, 9, 14–15, 60
Lincoln County   182
Lindbergh, Charles A.   152
Litchfield Wetland Management District
  277, 281
Little Falls   59, 152–154, 241
Loads   33, 39, 62, 82–84, 332–333

Lyme disease 27, 305
Lyon County 182

M

Mahnomen County 105, 235–236, 241
Mallard 65–66, 69, 80, 85, 98, 107, 160,
174, 209
Mankato 189, 191, 241
Maps
Department of Natural Resources
(DNR) Regions Map 240
Region 1 86
Bird distributions 88–93
Region 2 118
Bird distributions 120–123
Region 3 140
Bird distributions 142–147
Region 4 166
Bird distributions 168–171
Regions 5 and 6 192
Bird distributions 194–198
National Forests 262–263
Chippewa National Forest Trails
263–274
Superior National Forest 274
National Wildlife Refuges (NWR) 285,
287, 289, 291, 293, 295–300
State Forests, selected 248–260
Wetland Management Districts (WMD)
276, 279–283
Wildlife Management Areas (WMA)
227–232
Marsh Lake 230
Marsh snipe
See snipe, common
Marshall County 98, 233–234, 241
Martin County 186, 238, 242
Massasauga snake 193
Mayo Clinic 206
Mayo, William W. 206
McLeod County 179
Meadow Lake Trail (Chippewa National
Forest) 268
Meeker County 174, 242
Merganser, hooded 75
Mesabi Iron Range 119, 133, 137
Mickelson Wildlife Management Area 12
Migratory Bird Harvest Information
Program (HIP) 5, 63, 309

Migratory Waterfowl Stamps 1, 9
Mille Lacs County 155, 237, 241
Mille Lacs Indian Museum 141
Mille Lacs Wildlife Management Area
155, 229, 241
Mineral Springs Park 199
Minneapolis 173, 176, 178, 181, 183, 185,
201, 203, 208, 211, 213–215, 219–220
Minnesota Central Railway 199
Minnesota Department of Tourism 243,
325
Minnesota Department of Transportation
(MnDOT) 325
Minnesota Migratory Waterfowl Stamp
3, 9
Minnesota River 167, 177, 182, 189–190,
290, 292
Minnesota Sharp-tailed Grouse Society
54, 330
Minnesota Small Game License 9
Minnesota Valley National Wildlife Refuge
292–293
Minnesota Waterfowl Hunting Regulations
Supplement 9
Mississippi bluff country 307
Mississippi River 107, 152, 158, 167,
193, 199, 204, 206, 209–210, 219, 221,
294–300
Montevideo 177–178, 230, 334
Mora 157, 162–164
Morris Wetland Management District
278, 282
Morrison County 152, 241
Motel Cost Key xii
Mower County 202
Mud Lake 137
Murray County 184, 241

N

National Forests 119, 225, 261–275
Chippewa National Forest 137–138,
262–273
Superior National Forest 130, 133,
263, 274–275
National Wild Turkey Federation 330
National Wildlife Refuges (NWR) 87, 107,
110, 209, 225, 284–300, 326
Agassiz 87
Big Stone 290–291

National Wildlife Refuges (NWR) *continued*
  Minnesota Valley 292–293
  Rice Lake 286–287
  Sherburne 288–289
  Tamarac 107, 110, 284–285
  Upper Mississippi River 209,
    293–300
Nemadji State Forest 256
Nicollet County 189, 241
Nobles County 184, 241
Nonmotorized trails 25
Nontoxic loads, shells, and shot 7, 13,
  62–63, 71, 77, 83, 277, 284, 288, 290,
  292, 294, 309
Norman County 105, 235–236, 241
North American Waterfowl Management
  Plan 329
North Shore 119, 131, 133–134
Northern pintail 67
Northern shoveler 69

O
Ojibway Indians 141
Olmsted County 206
Onamia 141, 229, 237, 241, 333
Ontario 38, 48
Otter Tail County 112
Otter Tail River 112
Owatonna 199–201, 203, 242

P
Park Rapids 107–109, 241, 244
Parkers Prairie 112, 332
Partridge
  See gray (Hungarian) partridge
Pennington County 100
Pheasant (ring-necked) 1, 3–4, 19,
  28–33, 38, 42–43, 51, 63, 89, 110,
  112, 115, 143, 148, 152, 155, 158, 160,
  162, 167, 169, 172, 174, 177, 179, 182,
  184, 186–187, 189–190, 193, 195,
  199–200, 202, 204, 206–207, 209,
  212, 277, 288, 311, 316–317,
  320–321, 329, 333
  Dscription 29–33
  Distribution 28, 89, 143, 169, 195
Pheasant Stamps 1
Pheasants Forever 29, 209, 329
Pillsbury State Forest 257

Pine County 155, 237, 241
Pine Island State Forest 258
Pipestone County 184, 241
Pochard 72
Polk County 100
Pope County 115, 241
Prairie grouse
  See sharp-tailed grouse
Preserving Game Birds 311
Project 2000 330
Project Coverts 328
Public Recreation Information Maps
  (PRIM) 25, 155, 158, 204, 224–225,
  243, 277–278, 325
Puddle ducks, see ducks

R
Rail, sora 63
Rail, Virginia 4, 63
Rainy River 95–96, 124–125
Ramsey County 212, 239, 242
Rattlesnake, timber 193
Recipes 27, 314–315, 317–321
Red Lake County 100
Red Lake River 100
Red Lake Wildlife Management Area
  87, 97, 228, 241
Red River 87
Red Wing 210, 221
Redhead 72, 77
Redwood County 182
Redwood Falls 181–183, 241
Regional maps
  See maps
Regulations, hunting 1–18, 98, 167, 225,
  233, 243, 284, 294, 301, 303, 331
Rennville County 179
Rice County 199, 242
Rice Lake 286–287
Rice Lake National Wildlife Refuge
  286–287
Richard J. Dorer Memorial Hardwood
  State Forest 209, 246, 259
Ringbill
  See ring-necked duck
Ring-billed duck
  See ring-necked duck
Ringneck
  See pheasant

Ring-necked duck   72
Ring-necked pheasant
   See pheasant
Rivers
   Blue Earth   189–190
   Chippewa   173, 177, 294
   Crow Wing   148
   Des Moines   186
   Elk   160–161
   Grindstone   155
   Minnesota   167, 177, 182, 189–190,
      290, 292
   Mississippi   107, 152, 158, 167, 193,
      199, 204, 206, 209–210, 219, 221,
      294–300
   Otter Tail   112
   Rainy   95–96, 124–125
   Red Lake   100
   Red   87
Rochester   79, 205–208, 242, 327, 334
Rock County   184, 241
Roseau County   87, 95, 233
Roseau River Wildlife Management Area
   95
Ross' goose   78
Ruddy duck   76
Ruffed grouse   19–27, 30, 38–39, 47, 49,
      51, 87, 90, 95, 98, 100, 102, 105, 107,
      110, 112, 115, 120, 124–125, 127,
      130–131, 133, 137, 144, 148–149,
      151–152, 155–156, 158, 160, 162,
      165, 174, 179, 196, 200, 204, 207,
      209, 212, 228–229, 231, 243, 261,
      274, 284, 286, 288, 294, 306–308,
      314, 328–329
   Description   21–27
   Distribution   20, 90, 120, 144, 196
Ruffed Grouse Society   137, 328–329
Runestone Museum   115

S
Saint Peter and Winona Railway   199
Salmonella   71
Savanna State Forest   260
Sawbill
   See merganser, hooded
Scaup
   Greater   75
   Lesser   72–73, 75

Scientific and Natural Areas (SNA)   225,
      301
Scott County   209, 239, 242
Sears and Roebuck Company   182
Sears, Richard   182
September goose hunt (Canada goose
      only)   11
Sharp-tailed grouse   4–6, 19, 21, 30,
      50–55, 91, 100, 121, 124, 137, 145,
      148, 155, 261, 286, 316, 330, 333
   Description   51–55
   Distribution   50, 91, 121, 145
Sherburne County   160, 238, 241
Sherburne National Wildlife Refuge
      288–289
Shooting preserves   9
Sibley County   179
Sibley, Henry Hastings   209
Singing ground (woodcock)   35–36
Skeeter Lake   269
Skeeter Lake Trail (Chippewa National
      Forest)   269
Small game hunting licenses   1
Snipe, common   4–5, 8, 12, 14, 19, 36, 61
      –62, 95, 284, 286, 288
Snow goose, lesser   78
Sora rail   63
South Dakota   177, 290
Special Canada goose permits   1
Specklebelly   78
Spring wild turkey hunt   16
Spruce grouse   4, 19, 21, 46–49, 87, 92,
      95, 98, 122, 124, 127, 130, 133, 137,
      228, 286, 315
   Description   47–49
   Distribution   46, 92, 122
Spruce hen
   See spruce grouse
Spur Lake   270
Spur Lake Trail (Chippewa National
      Forest)   270
Squaw Lake   137
St. Cloud   59, 117, 154, 158–159, 161, 241,
      246
St. Louis County   127, 133, 237, 241
St. Paul   10–2, 9, 14–15, 60, 81, 173, 176,
      178, 181, 183, 185, 193, 201, 203, 208,
      211, 213, 219–220, 222–223, 225–226,
      242–243, 278, 325, 327, 329–331

State Duck Stamp   3, 9
State Forests   225, 243–260
   Beltrami Island   228, 248
   Foothills   249
   George Washington   250
   Hill River   251
   Huntersville   252
   Kabetogama   253
   Koochiching   254
   Land O'Lakes   255
   Nemadji   256
   Pillsbury   257
   Pine Island   258
   Richard J. Dorer Memorial Hardwood
      209, 246, 259
   Savanna   260
State Forest Area Offices   244–246
State Forests Distribution and Amount of
   Ownership   246–247
State Game Refuges   301
Stearns County   158
Steel shot   13, 33, 71, 77, 82, 84
Steele County   199, 242
Stevens County   115, 241
Sugar Lake   271
Sugar Lake Trail (Chippewa National
   Forest)   271
Superior National Forest   130, 133, 262,
   275
Swift County   172
Szabo, Ken   324

T

T steel shot   33, 84
Talcot Lake   184–185, 232, 238
Talcot Lake Wildlife Management Area
   184, 232, 241
Tamarac National Wildlife Refuge   107,
   110, 284–285
Thief Lake Wildlife Management Area
   54, 87, 98–99, 241
Todd County   152, 241
Tower Lake   272
Tower Lake Trail (Chippewa National
   Forest)   272
Traveling   1, 303–304, 316–317
Traverse County   115, 241
Tungsten-iron   13, 33, 62, 71, 77, 81–82
Tungsten-polymer   13, 33, 62, 71, 77, 81

Turkey, eastern wild   1–2, 14–16, 18–19,
   56–60, 93, 105, 112, 115, 146, 152,
   155, 158, 160, 162, 170, 172, 174, 177,
   179, 182, 184–186, 190, 197, 200,
   202, 204, 206–207, 209, 212, 231,
   243, 292, 294, 317, 330
   Description   57–60
   Distribution   56, 93, 146, 170, 197
   Reintroduction   160, 207
   Fall hunt   16
   Spring hunt   16

U

U.S. Fish and Wildlife Service   18, 81, 284,
   325
University of Minnesota   219, 229
Upland bird descriptions   19–63
   Gray (Hungarian) partridge   41–45
      Distribution   40, 88, 142, 168, 194
   Pheasant (ring-necked)   29–33
      Distribution   28, 89, 143, 169, 195
   Ruffed grouse   21–27
      Distribution   20, 90, 120, 144, 196
   Sharp-tailed grouse   51–55
      Distribution   50, 91, 121, 145
   Snipe   61–62
   Sora rail   63
   Spruce grouse   47–49
      Distribution   46, 92, 122
   Turkey, Eastern wild   57–60
      Distribution   56, 93, 146, 170, 197
   Virginia rail   63
   Woodcock   35–39
      Distribution   34, 94, 123, 147, 171,
         198
Upper Mississippi National Wildlife and
   Fish Refuge   209, 293–300

V

Vikings   115
Virginia rail   4, 63
Voyageurs National Park   119, 124

W

Wabasha County   206
Wadena County   112
Waseca County   189, 241
Washington County   212, 239, 242
Waterfowl Hunting Regulations   9, 14, 301

Waterfowl Migration & Hunting Report   13
Waterfowl Production Areas (WPA)   33, 277–283
Watonwan County   186, 238, 242
Webster Lake   273
Webster Lake Trail (Chippewa National Forest)   273
Wetland Management Districts (WMD)   274, 276–283
  Detroit Lakes   277, 279
  Fergus Falls   277, 280
  Litchfield   277, 281
  Morris   278, 282
  Windom   278, 283
Weyerhaeuser, Charles   152
White-fronted goose   78
Whitewater Wildlife Management Area   206, 231, 242
Wich a wan   160
Wigeon
  See American wigeon
Wildlife Management Area(s) (WMA)   11, 14, 19, 54, 81, 87, 95, 97–99, 155, 157, 167, 177, 184–185, 206, 209, 213, 217, 226–239, 241–242
  Description of   226–239
  Carlos Avery   212–213, 217, 227, 239, 242
  Gores Pool   209, 239
  Lac Qui Parle   11, 14, 167, 172, 177–178, 230, 238, 241–242, 278, 332, 334
  Lamprey Pass   212, 239

Mickelson   212
Mille Lacs   141, 155, 157, 229, 237, 241, 333
Red Lake   87, 97, 100, 228, 235, 241, 244
Roseau River   87, 95, 233, 241
Talcot Lake   184–185, 232, 238, 241
Thief Lake   54, 87, 98–99, 233, 241
Whitewater   206, 231, 242
Wilken County   112
Willmar   174, 176, 178, 242
Windom Wetland Management District   278, 283
Winona County   206
Winona District   294
Wood duck   66, 100, 107
Woodcock   4–5, 8, 12, 19, 27, 34–39, 61–62, 87, 94–95, 98, 100, 102, 105, 107, 110, 112, 123–124, 127, 130, 133, 137, 147–149, 152, 155, 158, 160, 162, 171, 174, 193, 198–200, 204, 206–207, 209, 212, 228, 243, 261, 274, 284, 286, 288, 294, 306–308, 328, 332–333
  Description   35–39
  Distribution   34, 94, 123, 147, 171, 198
Worthington   184–185
Wright County   160, 238, 241

Y

Yellow Medicine County   177, 241
Youth Waterfowl Hunt   14

WILDERNESS ADVENTURES GUIDE SERIES

If you would like to order additional copies of this book or our other Wilderness Adventures Press guidebooks, please fill out the order form below or call **1-800-925-3339** or **fax 800-390-7558.** Visit our website for a listing of over 2000 sporting books—the largest online: **www.wildadv.com**

Mail to: Wilderness Adventures Press, P.O. Box 627,
Gallatin Gateway, MT 59730

☐ **Please send me your quarterly catalog on hunting and fishing books.**

Ship to:
Name _____
Address _____
City _____State_____ Zip_____
Home Phone_____Work Phone_____

Payment: ☐ Check ☐ Visa ☐ Mastercard ☐ Discover ☐ American Express

Card Number _____Expiration Date_____
Signature_____

Qty	Title of Book and Author	Price	Total
	Wingshooter's Guide to Montana	$26.00	
	Wingshooter's Guide to South Dakota	$26.95	
	Wingshooter's Guide to North Dakota	$26.95	
	Wingshooter's Guide to Arizona	$26.95	
	Wingshooter's Guide to Idaho	$26.95	
	Wingshooter's Guide to Iowa	$26.95	
	Wingshooter's Guide to Kansas	$26.95	
	Flyfisher's Guide to Colorado	$26.95	
	Flyfisher's Guide to Idaho	$26.95	
	Flyfisher's Guide to Montana	$26.95	
	Flyfisher's Guide to Northern California	$26.95	
	Flyfisher's Guide to Wyoming	$26.95	
	Flyfisher's Guide to Oregon	$26.95	
	Flyfisher's Guide to Washington	$26.95	
	Flyfisher's Guide to Northern New England	$26.95	
Total Order + shipping & handling			

Shipping and handling: $4.00 for first book,
$2.50 per additional book, up to $11.50 maximum